Countering Rabbinic Judaism

Countering Rabbinic Judaism

A Messianic Perspective

by Louis Ruggiero

For further studies and apologetics-related material,
the author's website can be found at
www.kingmessiahproject.com

Unless otherwise specified, all Scriptures are taken from the King James Version of the Bible. All Hebrew and Greek word studies are provided by *Strong's Exhaustive Concordance of the Bible* by James Strong.

COUNTERING RABBINIC JUDAISM
© 2005 by Louis Ruggiero

Printed in the United States of America

ISBN 1-933641-03-7

In loving memory of Barbara Dufresne

Table of Contents

A Special Dedication

God has placed many good people in my path to assist me with this book. However, because of the tremendous amount of time and effort involved, none of this would have been possible without the love and support of my darling wife. I am blessed to have her in my life. It is to her, this very special person, to whom this book is dedicated.

Another Dedication

When things become difficult, good friends rise to the occasion with prayer and encouragement. I would like to especially thank my pastor and good friend Leroy "Skip" Hellmig, as well as Rev. Randall S. Mumper and Ellen Mumper. They are proof that the battle belongs to the LORD. He placed them in my life at just the right time.

Contributors to This Book

I would like to extend a very special thanks to Benzion Melechson and Ezra Aharon, two friends who took the time and effort to contribute toward some of the critical material in this book.

Introduction

For almost two thousand years, many believers in Jesus the Messiah have dedicated their lives to spread God's wonderful news to mankind. Since there are multitudes of people who strongly oppose change, these brave men and women have risked bodily harm with many in order to reach the few who would listen. The hazards are great for those who dedicate themselves to teach the Gospel to others. However, the spiritual rewards are even greater.

Through the shed blood of Jesus, God's only begotten Son, everyone is offered everlasting life. Upon one's confession that He is Lord and Savior, and that God raised Him from the dead, Romans 10:9 teaches that eternal life is secured.

Regarding the Gospel message, there are two types of difficulties confronting today's believers. The first is the threat of physical violence. The second is the doctrinal challenges made by those with opposing viewpoints, particularly the well educated. This book is written to respond to their theological arguments while, at the same time, placing those who oppose Jesus on the defensive.

Defenders of rabbinic Judaism, sometimes called "counter–missionaries," provide some of the most sophisticated arguments against the Gospel message. Since they haphazardly use the scriptures to support their incorrect positions, believers in Jesus need to be aware that there is an appropriate biblical response to every challenge they make.

While stating what they believe, Judaism's defenders inappropriately isolate certain passages and verses, cite one-half of a verse, or take various passages out of context in order to justify their flawed beliefs. Many of them mean well, and this is the way they are taught. However by doing this, they are unaware that they are attacking the very fabric of God's Word. It should also be made clear that most defenders of Judaism are extremely zealous in their faith. Though this may be true, they can lead believers in Jesus who are willing to listen to them into spiritual confusion because they are not prepared to respond to their arguments.

For Christians and messianic Jews alike, it has become increasingly necessary to meet these doctrinal challenges using the Bible as their sole means of defense. Ephesians 6:12–13 states:

> For we wrestle not against flesh and blood, but against principalities, against powers, against the rulers of the darkness of this world, against spiritual wickedness in high places. Wherefore take unto you the whole armour of God, that ye may be able to withstand in the evil day, and having done all, to stand.

First Peter 3:15–16 tells us,

> But sanctify the Lord God in your hearts: and be ready always to give an answer to every man that asketh you a reason of the hope that is in you with meekness and fear: Having a good conscience; that, whereas they speak evil of you, as of evildoers, they may be ashamed that falsely accuse your good conversation in Christ.

We must always remember to show the love of Christ when dialoguing with those who disagree. However, it is an absolute necessity to defend the faith. If one's faith cannot be defended, it is not worth defending!

Finally, every believer in Jesus can make a difference. Because the battle belongs to the LORD, we are not in this alone. He is in control! According to Romans 8:31, ". . . If God be for us, who can be against us?" To those special men and women all over the world with a heavenly calling to share and defend the Gospel message, it is to you whom this book is dedicated. God bless you all!

Part One

Jesus of Nazareth:
The Fulfillment of Bible Prophecy

Chapter One

The Seventy Weeks of Daniel

I. Introduction

Throughout the centuries and up until this present moment, people who reject the Bible continuously attack its credibility. In spite of this, the Hebrew scriptures remain infallible. In John 5:39 Jesus tells us, "Search the scriptures; for in them ye think ye have eternal life: and they are they which testify of me."

Jesus' words are certainly true, because Moses and the prophets described Him in great detail. And it was with pinpoint accuracy, flawless precision, and in absolute defiance to the unbeliever, that God revealed through Daniel the exact month and year that Jesus the Messiah would make His entrance into the world. This prophecy found in Daniel 9:24–27 records the words of the angel Gabriel who tells the prophet:

> Seventy weeks are determined upon thy people and upon thy holy city, to finish the transgression, and to make an end of sins, and to make reconciliation for iniquity, and to bring in everlasting righteousness, and to seal up the vision and prophecy, and to anoint the most Holy. Know therefore and understand, that from the going forth of the commandment to restore and to build Jerusalem unto the Messiah the Prince shall be seven weeks, and threescore and two weeks: the street shall be built again, and the wall, even in troublous times. And after

threescore and two weeks shall Messiah be cut off, but not for himself: and the people of the prince that shall come shall destroy the city and the sanctuary; and the end thereof shall be with a flood, and unto the end of the war desolations are determined. And he shall confirm the covenant with many for one week: and in the midst of the week he shall cause the sacrifice and the oblation to cease, and for the overspreading of abominations he shall make it desolate, even until the consummation, and that determined shall be poured upon the desolate.

In 607/606 B.C., King Nebuchadnezzar conquered Jerusalem and began taking its people captive into Babylon. In this passage, Gabriel appears to Daniel toward the end of their captivity. Daniel 9:2 states, "In the first year of his [Darius, the son of Ahasuerus'] reign I Daniel understood by books the number of the years, whereof the word of the LORD came to Jeremiah the prophet, that he would accomplish seventy years in the desolations of Jerusalem."

According to this verse, Daniel was fully aware of the prophecy written in Jeremiah 25:11 that reads, "And this whole land shall be a desolation, and an astonishment; and these nations shall serve the king of Babylon seventy years."

The prophet was also aware that, after the seventy-year expiration, the children of Israel would be allowed to return. Jeremiah 29:10 adds, "For thus saith the LORD, That after seventy years be accomplished at Babylon I will visit you, and perform my good word toward you, in causing you to return to this place."

In the beginning of Daniel 9, Daniel prayed. He confessed his own sins as well as the sins of the people that resulted in their punishment. He admitted that they had done wickedly and committed iniquity and rebellion against God. Just as importantly, he was concerned whether his people had truly repented for their sins. We can find evidence of this in verse 13 when he said, "As it is written in the law of Moses, all this evil is come upon us: yet made we not our prayer before the LORD our God, that we might turn from our iniquities, and understand thy truth."

Daniel was concerned about his people's repentance for a reason. In

Leviticus 26 the LORD told Moses that, should the children of Israel fail to repent and be reformed during their punishment, He would push the punishment to the next level and punish them seven times more for their hardness of heart. In the case of the Babylonian captivity, this could result in an additional 490 years on top of the 70 years that were about to expire. The applicable passages from Leviticus 26 follow:

> And I will set my face against you, and ye shall be slain before your enemies: they that hate you shall reign over you; and ye shall flee when none pursueth you. And if ye will not yet for all this hearken unto me, then I will punish you seven times more for your sins. . . . And your strength shall be spent in vain: for your land shall not yield her increase, neither shall the trees of the land yield their fruits. And if ye walk contrary unto me, and will not hearken unto me; I will bring seven times more plagues upon you according to your sins. . . . And if ye will not be reformed by me by these things, but will walk contrary unto me; Then will I also walk contrary unto you, and will punish you yet seven times for your sins.
> —Leviticus 26:17–18,20–21,23–24

After nearly seventy years of captivity, seven times the punishment was more than Daniel could bear. So he repented on behalf of his people and reminded God of what He said in Leviticus 26:40–43, which was:

> If they shall confess their iniquity, and the iniquity of their fathers, with their trespass which they trespassed against me, and that also they have walked contrary unto me; And that I also have walked contrary unto them, and have brought them into the land of their enemies; if then their uncircumcised hearts be humbled, and they then accept of the punishment of their iniquity: Then will I remember my covenant with Jacob, and also my covenant with Isaac, and also my covenant with Abraham will I remember; and I will remember the land. The land also shall be left of them, and shall enjoy her sabbaths, while she lieth desolate without them: and they shall accept of the punishment of their iniquity:

because, even because they despised my judgments, and because their soul abhorred my statutes.

Even though Daniel pled to the LORD for mercy and forgiveness, God's response through the angel contained both good and bad news as follows: Because of Israel's failure to repent, their punishment would continue in accordance with Leviticus 26. In other words, for an additional seventy weeks of years, or seventy sevens, there would be nonfulfillment of any of God's promises provided in Daniel 9:24. As a result, Israel would have to wait an additional seventy weeks of years for the fulfillment of the entire prophecy.

According to Daniel 9:25, the angel also informed Daniel when the 490-year countdown would begin. It would commence with the eventual word, or decree, to restore and build Jerusalem. Furthermore, it would be 69 weeks of years [69 x 7], or 483 years, from the time the word is given to rebuild Jerusalem to the time the Messiah would begin fulfilling the promises in Daniel 9:24. And according to Daniel 9:26, the Messiah would be cut off or killed at the end of this 69–week or 483–year period.

II. Seven Weeks Plus Sixty-two Weeks: Why the Breakdown?

Many people wonder why the sixty-nine weeks in Daniel 9:25 are broken down into increments of seven–week and sixty-two–week periods. In order to answer this question, it is important to realize that one of the reasons for Israel's captivity was their failure to keep the Sabbath rest of the land as commanded in Leviticus 25. This is explained in 2 Chronicles 36:20–21 as follows:

And them that had escaped from the sword carried he away to Babylon; where they were servants to him and his sons until the reign of the kingdom of Persia: To fulfil the word of the LORD by the mouth of Jeremiah, until the land had enjoyed her sabbaths: for as long as she lay desolate she kept sabbath, to fulfil threescore and ten years.

It is significant to note that in the case of the Sabbath rest of the land, God used cycles of seven years or weeks of years when counting time. The 70-week or 490-year prophecy that would begin with the word to restore and build Jerusalem was a continuation of seven-year cycles that included the land's rest. God never intended to terminate these cycles after Israel's return to the land and was stressing that they should continue until the Messiah's advent and the fulfillment of the promises in Daniel 9:24.

In the Torah, Leviticus 25 describes God's demands when Israel is brought into the land. Leviticus 25:1–2 begins, "And the LORD spake unto Moses in mount Sinai, saying, Speak unto the children of Israel, and say unto them, When ye come into the land which I give you, then shall the land keep a sabbath unto the LORD."

The Bible explains in Leviticus 25:3–4 that there would be six years of sowing and reaping and, on the seventh year, the land should remain inactive and rest. It reads as follows, "Six years thou shalt sow thy field, and six years thou shalt prune thy vineyard, and gather in the fruit thereof; But in the seventh year shall be a sabbath of rest unto the land, a sabbath for the LORD: thou shalt neither sow thy field, nor prune thy vineyard."

Then Leviticus 25:8–10 teaches that after seven sabbaths of years, or forty-nine years, on the tenth day of the seventh month (which coincides with the Day of Atonement or Yom Kippur, see Leviticus 16:29), the trumpet would sound proclaiming liberty to all the land's inhabitants. This fiftieth year, beginning on Yom Kippur, is called the year of Jubilee:

> And thou shalt number seven sabbaths of years unto thee, seven times seven years; and the space of the seven sabbaths of years shall be unto thee forty and nine years. Then shalt thou cause the trumpet of the jubile to sound on the tenth day of the seventh month, in the day of atonement shall ye make the trumpet sound throughout all your land. And ye shall hallow the fiftieth year, and proclaim liberty throughout all the land unto all the inhabitants thereof: it shall be a jubile unto you; and ye shall return every man unto his possession, and ye shall return every man unto his family.

This proclamation, which began on the fiftieth year on Yom Kippur, had a major significance. On that day, the high priest provided atonement for all Israel's sins by the animal sacrifices that were made. We can see in Leviticus 16:30, "For on that day shall the priest make an atonement for you, to cleanse you, that ye may be clean from all your sins before the LORD."

During the year of Jubilee, two things took place. First, all debts between everyone were declared null and void. Secondly, the nation became completely restored to God as the result of the sacrifices on Yom Kippur. Leviticus 25:11 states that, "A jubile shall that fiftieth year be unto you: ye shall not sow, neither reap that which groweth of itself in it, nor gather the grapes in it of thy vine undressed."

The combination of both the Day of Atonement and the Year of Jubilee foreshadows the future reign of the Messiah. This is because by Him mankind will be reconciled to the Holy God of Israel and there will be absolute liberty in the land through His everlasting peace.

Daniel 9:25–26 tells us that, at the end of the first 7 weeks or 49 years, Israel would celebrate the Jubilee. This would then provide the foundation for the next 62 weeks or 434 years. The first Jubilee after Israel's return and every Jubilee to follow would mark Israel's preparation for their coming Messiah.

III. The Persian Kings

Even though the people's captivity into Babylon actually began in 607/606 B.C., Nebuchadnezzar's destruction of Jerusalem was not concluded until the summer of 586 B.C. when the temple was destroyed.[1] Then in 539 B.C., the Babylonian Empire fell to the Persian king Cyrus the Great. The Persian Empire lasted until approximately 332 B.C. [some sources claim 330 B.C.] when it was defeated by the Greek general Alexander the Great at the battle of Guagemala River.[2] In this year, the Greek Empire took control of the Persian Empire and dominated most of the civilized world.

According to recorded history, the Persian Empire ruled over Israel for a total of 207 years, from 539 B.C. to 332 B.C. It began with Cyrus the Great and ended with Alexander the Great's victory over King Darius III. These facts are important because the Persian kings played critical roles with respect to Bible prophecy, especially regarding the seventy weeks of Daniel. It was one of these kings, Artaxerxes I, who provided the word to restore and rebuild Jerusalem (Dan. 9:25).

History provides **all** dates of the reigns of the Persian kings mentioned in the Bible. When viewing the history of these kings, it is important to be aware that, just like the titles Caesar and Tsar, Artaxerxes is a title given to a Persian king. It is not a name at all!

Throughout the duration of the Persian Empire, there were several kings who were known as Artaxerxes, including Smerdis who was an imposter to the throne. Additionally, the king who provided the decree to restore and rebuild Jerusalem was also called Artaxerxes. Some historical materials refer to him as either Artaxerxes I or Artaxerxes Longimanus. He was the son of Xerxes, who was called Ahasuerus in the Bible.

In recorded history, the chronological order of the Persian kings from Cyrus the Great to Darius III is supported and documented as follows:

* Cyrus the Great—559 B.C. to 530/529 B.C.[3]
* Cambyses II, also known as Ahasuerus—530/529 B.C. to 522/521 B.C.[4]
* Smerdis, also known as Artaxerxes—522 B.C.[5]
* Darius the Great—522 B.C. to 485 B.C.[6]
* Xerxes, also known as Ahasuerus—485 B.C. to 465 B.C.[7]
* Artaxerxes I [Longimanus]—465 B.C. to 425/424 B.C.[8]
* Darius II—423 B.C. to 404 B.C.[9]
* Artaxerxes II—404 B.C. to 359 B.C.[10]
* Artaxerxes III—359 B.C. to 338 B.C.[11]
* Darius III—338 B.C. to 332/330 B.C.[12]

The Persian Kings in Secular and Biblical History

The Hebrew scriptures identify all six kings from Cyrus the Great to Artaxerxes I. The events described in the Old Testament end with the book of Nehemiah and the reign of Artaxerxes I. The historical and biblical significance of these kings are as follows:

The First King: *Cyrus the Great.* He became king of Persia in 559 B.C. In 553 B.C., a date firmly established in the Babylonian historical records *Annals of Nabonid,*[13] he revolted against Media, and in 550 B.C. he conquered the entire Median kingdom. Then in 546 B.C., he conquered the kingdom of Lydia.[14] In the following year, he took the whole of Asia Minor.[15] While large parts of the Babylonian territories were conquered, he did not defeat the Babylonian Empire and establish world dominance until 539 B.C. Cyrus ruled over Israel from 539 B.C. to 530/529 B.C. and, during the first year of that reign, he issued the decree to allow the Jews to return home and rebuild the temple:[16]

> Now in the first year of Cyrus king of Persia, that the word of the LORD by the mouth of Jeremiah might be fulfilled, the LORD stirred up the spirit of Cyrus king of Persia, that he made a proclamation throughout all his kingdom, and put it also in writing, saying, Thus saith Cyrus king of Persia, The LORD God of heaven hath given me all the kingdoms of the earth; and he hath charged me to build him an house at Jerusalem, which is in Judah. Who is there among you of all his people? his God be with him, and let him go up to Jerusalem, which is in Judah, and build the house of the LORD God of Israel, (he is the God,) which is in Jerusalem.
>
> —Ezra 1:1–3

The Second King: *Cambyses II, also known as Ahasuerus.* He reigned from 530/529 B.C. to 522 B.C. He was King Cyrus' son and successor. Like his father, he continued in world dominance. After conquering Egypt in 526 B.C., he was made Pharoah.[17] He was assassinated in 522 B.C. while traveling back from Egypt with his army.[18] In the Bible, he is the Ahasuerus mentioned in Ezra 4:6.

The Third King: *Smerdis, also known as Artaxerxes . . . an imposter to the throne.* He is the Artaxerxes mentioned in Ezra 4:7,24. The Bible tells us that after he became aware that the Jews were building the walls of Jerusalem without any authorization while they were building the temple, he provided a declaration ceasing **all** building until he gave a further decree. He was killed by the future King Darius before providing that proclamation. Ezra 4:21 confirms his order which was: "Give ye now commandment to cause these men to cease, and that this city be not builded, until another commandment shall be given from me."

The Fourth King: *Darius the Great.* A remote cousin of Cambyses II, he ruled from 522 B.C. to 485 B.C. He built the great cities of Susa and Persepolis, as well as a tremendous road system throughout his empire. He tried to expand his empire westward and invaded Greece. In 499 B.C. some of the Ionian Greek cities in the Grecian settlements along the Turkish coast rebelled against him, and in 494 B.C. he stopped the uprising.[19] Having set out to conquer the remainder of Greece, his troops were defeated at the battle of Marathon in 490 B.C.[20] The Persian wars began with this battle and lasted a total of forty-two years into the reigns of both his son and grandson. The Bible tells us that King Darius, in the second year of his reign, reversed Smerdis' decree and allowed the temple to finally be completed. It was during his reign, in 516 B.C., that the temple was finished.[21] "Then ceased the work of the house of God which is at Jerusalem. So it ceased unto the second year of the reign of Darius king of Persia" (Ezra 4:24).

> *Author's note:* According to Ezra 6:15, the temple was completed "in the sixth year of the reign of Darius the king." Since history records that Darius began his reign in 522 B.C. the temple must have been completed in 516 B.C. And since Jeremiah 52:12–13 reveals that Israel's temple was destroyed in the nineteenth year of Nebuchadnezzar king of Babylon, which would have been 586 B.C., 586 B.C. minus 516 B.C. equals seventy years. This confirms the accuracy of Israel's seventy-year captivity foretold by Jeremiah the prophet in Jeremiah 25:11–12 and Jeremiah 29:10 on the basis of the destruction of the first temple and the completion of the second temple.

The Fifth King: *Xerxes, also known as Ahasuerus.* He reigned from 485 B.C. to 465 B.C. He became the Persian king after the death of King Darius in 485 B.C. In 480 B.C., he took two hundred thousand men and a thousand ships and moved by land and sea through Thracia in eastern Greece. He eventually defeated the Greeks at the battle of Thermopylae.[22] In 479 B.C. he took Athens, but while he was burning the temples of the Acropolis, the Athenians quashed his fleet of ships at the battle of Salamis.[23] Then in the same year, his army was defeated at the battle of Plataea.[24]

The prophet Daniel specifically foretold that the fourth Persian king, who was Xerxes, would succeed in inciting a lasting hatred between the Persians and the Greeks. Daniel 11:2 states: "And now will I shew thee the truth. Behold, there shall stand up yet three kings in Persia; and the fourth shall be far richer than they all: and by his strength through his riches he shall stir up all against the realm of Grecia."

In 465 B.C., Xerxes was assassinated by one of his sons. In the Bible, he is known as Ahasuerus in the Book of Esther: "Now it came to pass in the days of Ahasuerus, (this is Ahasuerus which reigned, from India even unto Ethiopia, over an hundred and seven and twenty provinces:) That in those days, when the king Ahasuerus sat on the throne of his kingdom, which was in Shushan the palace" (Est. 1:1–2).

The Sixth King: *Artaxerxes I, Longimanus.* He ruled from 465 B.C. to 425/424 B.C. and was Xerxes' son. His empire was one of peace and tranquility. Under his rulership, there was little or no expansion. In 449 B.C. he ended the Persian wars that were started by Darius the Great.[25] History records that his elder brother murdered him in 425/424 B.C. in a power struggle for the throne.[26] According to the Bible, he was the king who provided the word to restore and rebuild Jerusalem. Artaxerxes I reigned during the days of Nehemiah, as shown in the Book of Nehemiah: "Moreover from the time that I [Nehemiah] was appointed to be their governor in the land of Judah, from the twentieth year even unto the two and thirtieth year of Artaxerxes the king, that is, twelve years, I and my brethren have not eaten the bread of the governor" (Neh. 5:14).

Alexander the Great
The Greeks never forgot what happened to their cities and temples at the hands of the Persian Empire during Xerxes' reign in 479 B.C. It would be 147 years later, in 332 B.C., when Alexander the Great and his army took

vengeance on the Persian Empire by defeating Darius III at the historic battle of Guagemala River. Daniel 11:3–4 foretells:

And a mighty king shall stand up, that shall rule with great dominion, and do according to his will. And when he shall stand up, his kingdom shall be broken, and shall be divided toward the four winds of heaven; and not to his posterity, nor according to his dominion which he ruled: for his kingdom shall be plucked up, even for others beside those.

This passage prophesies the fate of the Greek Empire. At the height of Alexander's power, he died. After his death, his empire was divided into four smaller kingdoms in fulfillment of Daniel 11:4.[27]

Cyrus, Darius and Artaxerxes

According to the Scriptures, three Persian kings provided decrees in support of rebuilding the temple and Jerusalem. Ezra 6:14 identifies them in order of their reign as Cyrus, Darius, and Artaxerxes:

And the elders of the Jews builded, and they prospered through the prophesying of Haggai the prophet and Zechariah the son of Iddo. And they builded, and finished it, according to the commandment of the God of Israel, and according to the commandment of Cyrus, and Darius, and Artaxerxes king of Persia.

As we have seen in Ezra 1:1–3, it was King Cyrus who decreed the temple be rebuilt during the first year of his reign. Prophesied almost two hundred years prior to Cyrus, Isaiah 44:28 foretold, "That saith of Cyrus, He is my shepherd, and shall perform all my pleasure: even saying to Jerusalem, Thou shalt be built; and to the temple, Thy foundation shall be laid."

Cyrus provided his edict in approximately 538 B.C. Though he certainly acknowledged that Jerusalem would be rebuilt, the Bible tells us that he only gave the order to rebuild the temple, not the city.

Ezra 4:7,21 points out that, in spite of Cyrus' approval for Israel to build the temple, Artaxerxes (Smerdis) stopped the work because the Jews were taking it upon themselves to rebuild the walls and gates of Jerusalem without any authorization. Eventually, it would be King Darius who allowed the temple, the house of God, to be finished. Much like Cyrus' decree, Darius' order dealt only with the temple, not the city. Ezra 6:7–12 records his decree as follows:

> Let the work of this house of God alone; let the governor of the Jews and the elders of the Jews build this house of God in his place. Moreover I make a decree what ye shall do to the elders of these Jews for the building of this house of God: that of the king's goods, even of the tribute beyond the river, forthwith expenses be given unto these men, that they be not hindered. And that which they have need of, both young bullocks, and rams, and lambs, for the burnt offerings of the God of heaven, wheat, salt, wine, and oil, according to the appointment of the priests which are at Jerusalem, let it be given them day by day without fail: That they may offer sacrifices of sweet savours unto the God of heaven, and pray for the life of the king, and of his sons. Also I have made a decree, that whosoever shall alter this word, let timber be pulled down from his house, and being set up, let him be hanged thereon; and let his house be made a dunghill for this. And the God that hath caused his name to dwell there destroy all kings and people, that shall put to their hand to alter and to destroy this house of God which is at Jerusalem. I Darius have made a decree; let it be done with speed.

Though both Cyrus and Darius issued commandments to rebuild the temple, it was King Artaxerxes I (Longimanus), a successor of King Darius, who provided the word to rebuild Jerusalem. Artaxerxes I began his reign in 465 B.C. Up until this moment in time and according to the information provided in Nehemiah 1:3–4 and Nehemiah 2:3, the gates and walls of the city had not yet been rebuilt:

- **Nehemiah 1:3–4:** "And they said unto me [Nehemiah], The remnant that are left of the captivity there in the province are in great affliction and reproach: the wall of Jerusalem also is broken down, and the gates thereof are burned with fire. And it came to pass, when I heard these words, that I sat down and wept, and mourned certain days, and fasted, and prayed before the God of heaven.

✦ **Nehemiah 2:3:** "And said unto the king, Let the king live for ever: why should not my countenance be sad, when the city, the place of my fathers' sepulchres, lieth waste, and the gates thereof are consumed with fire?"

After considering Nehemiah's request, Artaxerxes gave the authorization to restore and rebuild Jerusalem in the month of Nisan, in the twentieth year of his reign. Nehemiah 2:1–8 provides evidence of the king's decree as follows:

> And it came to pass in the month Nisan, in the twentieth year of Artaxerxes the king, that wine was before him: and I [Nehemiah] took up the wine, and gave it unto the king. Now I had not been beforetime sad in his presence. Wherefore the king said unto me, Why is thy countenance sad, seeing thou art not sick? this is nothing else but sorrow of heart. Then I was very sore afraid, And said unto the king, Let the king live for ever: why should not my countenance be sad, when the city, the place of my fathers' sepulchres, lieth waste, and the gates thereof are consumed with fire? Then the king said unto me, For what dost thou make request? So I prayed to the God of heaven. And I said unto the king, If it please the king, and if thy servant have found favour in thy sight, that thou wouldest send me unto Judah, unto the city of my fathers' sepulchres, that I may build it. And the king said unto me, (the queen also sitting by him,) For how long shall thy journey be? and when wilt thou return? So it pleased the king to send me; and I set him a time. Moreover I said unto the king, If it please the king, let letters be given me to the governors beyond the river, that they may convey me over till I come into Judah; And a letter unto Asaph the keeper of the king's forest, that he may give me timber to make beams for the gates of the palace which appertained to the house, and for the wall of the city, and for the house that I shall enter into. And the king granted me, according to the good hand of my God upon me.

According to this passage, Nehemiah told the king that he was saddened by the fact that the city and gates of Jerusalem had not yet been built and remained in ruins. He requested that the king grant him permission to rebuild the city and its gates. According to verse 8, the king granted his request with an official letter to Asaph, the keeper of the king's forest, for materials needed to make beams for the gates and walls of the city.

It is logical to conclude that since history records that Artaxerxes began his reign as king in 465 B.C., and Nehemiah 2:1 reveals that his decree to rebuild Jerusalem was made in the month of Nisan in his twentieth year as king, the order must have been given in Nisan 445 B.C.

Referring back to Daniel 9:25, Gabriel indicated that "from the going forth of the commandment to restore and to build Jerusalem unto the Messiah the Prince shall be seven weeks, and threescore and two weeks," which is a total of 69 weeks of years, or 483 years. Therefore, since Artaxerxes provided the word to restore and rebuild Jerusalem in Nisan 445 B.C., it was at this moment in history when the countdown to the Messiah began.

IV. The Arithmetic

As history shows, Artaxerxes' command to restore and build Jerusalem was made in Nisan 445 B.C. and, according to Daniel 9:25, it would be 69 weeks or 483 years from the time this word was given to the advent of the Messiah. Before calculating the foretold month and year of the Messiah's coming, it is important to realize that God measures time on the basis of a 360-day per year calendar, *not* a 365.25–day per year calendar. Proof of this is found quite early in the Bible and is shown in Genesis 7:11 and Genesis 8:3–4. These verses provide the precise month and day the great flood began and ended.

In Genesis 7:11, during the days of Noah, the flood began "in the second month, the seventeenth day of the month." And according to Genesis 8:3–4, the waters subsided "in the seventh month, on the seventeenth day of the month." In the latter passage, important information is supplied that this precise five-month period is equivalent to a "hundred and fifty days." Since 150/5 = 30, God is on a thirty-day month or a 30 x 12 = 360 day per year calendar. The following verses provide the proof:

The Rain and Flood Began—"In the six hundredth year of Noah's life, in the second month, the seventeenth day of the month, the same day were all the fountains of the great deep broken up, and the windows of heaven were opened" (Gen. 7:11).

The Rain and Flood Were Abated—"And the waters returned from off the earth continually: and after the end of the hundred and fifty days the waters were abated. And the ark rested in the seventh month, on the seventeenth day of the month, upon the mountains of Ararat" (Gen. 8:3–4).

In the New Testament, we can find further evidence of a 30-day month or a 360-day per year calendar in Revelation 11:2–3, Revelation 12:6, and Revelation 13:5. Here we see that 1,260 days are equivalent to precisely 42 months; thus, a 30-day month or 360-day per year calendar. These describe the seventieth week of Daniel, which consists of two 42-month periods, a total of 84 months, or seven years . . . which is the seven-year Tribulation period foretold in Daniel 9:27:

* **Revelation 11:2–3:** "But the court which is without the temple leave out, and measure it not; for it is given unto the Gentiles: and the holy city shall they tread under foot forty and two months. And I will give power unto my two witnesses, and they shall prophesy a thousand two hundred and threescore days, clothed in sackcloth."
* **Revelation 12:6:** "And the woman fled into the wilderness, where she hath a place prepared of God, that they should feed her there a thousand two hundred and threescore days."
* **Revelation 13:5:** "And there was given unto him a mouth speaking great things and blasphemies; and power was given unto him to continue forty and two months."

Since the Bible teaches that God is on a 360-day per year calendar as opposed to a 365.25-day per year solar calendar, the 483 years or 69 prophetic weeks in Daniel 9:25 need to be converted into solar years. Therefore, it is necessary to multiply 483 years by 360 days, which is a total of 173,880 days. Then we need to convert the 173,880 days into solar years by dividing by 365.25, the number of days in a solar year.

173,880 divided by 365.25 = 476.057 solar years, or 476 solar years. Since Artaxerxes' order was given in 445 B.C., 445 B.C. + 476 solar years = A.D. 32 (remember, there is no year zero, so we must add one). And it was in Nissan A.D. 32 when Jesus came into Jerusalem riding on a donkey proclaiming to be Israel's King Messiah. Less than a week later, He was crucified or cut off in fulfillment of Daniel 9:26. Matthew 21:6–9 verifies that the messianic prophecy of Zechariah 9:9 was fulfilled by Jesus Himself:

+ **Zechariah 9:9:** "Rejoice greatly, O daughter of Zion; shout, O daughter of Jerusalem: behold, thy King cometh unto thee: he is just, and having salvation; lowly, and riding upon an ass, and upon a colt the foal of an ass."

+ **Matthew 21:6–9:** "And the disciples went, and did as Jesus commanded them, And brought the ass, and the colt, and put on them their clothes, and they set him thereon. And a very great multitude spread their garments in the way; others cut down branches from the trees, and strawed them in the way. And the multitudes that went before, and that followed, cried, saying, Hosanna to the Son of David: Blessed is he that cometh in the name of the Lord; Hosanna in the highest."

In his book *The Coming Prince*, written in 1895, Lord Robert Anderson wrote:

The Julian date of that 10th Nisan was Sunday the 6th April, A.D. 32. What then was the length of the period intervening between the issuing of the decree to rebuild Jerusalem and the public advent of 'Messiah the Prince,'—between the 14th March, B.C. 445, and the 6th April, A.D. 32? The interval contained exactly and to the very day 173,880 days, or seven times sixty-nine prophetic years of 360 days, the first sixty-nine weeks of Gabriel's prophecy.[28]

In summary, Artaxerxes provided the decree to rebuild Jerusalem in Nisan 445 B.C. Exactly sixty-nine prophetic weeks of years later, Jesus the Messiah came into Jerusalem in the month of Nisan in fulfillment of the Daniel 9:25–26 prophecy.

V. Jesus Provides Reconciliation for Iniquity in Heaven

Chapter six of the Book of Isaiah records the time when God commissioned Isaiah the prophet to speak to the children of Israel. At that moment, he was taken up into the heavens. Isaiah 6:6 tells us that there is an altar in Heaven. It states, "Then flew one of the seraphims unto me, having a live coal in his hand, which he had taken with the tongs from off the altar."

Remembering this, shortly after Jesus' resurrection, He appeared to Mary by the sepulchre. He advised her not to touch Him because He had not yet ascended to His Father. According to John 20:17, "Jesus saith unto her, Touch me not; for I am not yet ascended to my Father: but go to my brethren, and say unto them, I ascend unto my Father, and your Father; and to my God, and your God."

That very same evening, the first day of the week according to John 20:19, Jesus came to His disciples when they were gathered together. John 20:20 tells us that, ". . . he shewed unto them his hands and his side. Then were the disciples glad, when they saw the Lord."

According to John 20, it is unclear whether Jesus' disciples were permitted to touch Him when He first appeared to them after His death and resurrection. But Luke 24:36–43 decribes the same event in greater detail. It states as follows:

> And as they thus spake, Jesus himself stood in the midst of them, and saith unto them, Peace be unto you. But they were terrified and af-frighted, and supposed that they had seen a spirit. And he said unto them, Why are ye troubled? and why do thoughts arise in your hearts? Behold my hands and my feet, that it is I myself: handle me, and see; for a spirit hath not flesh and bones, as ye see me have. And when he had thus spoken, he shewed them his hands and his feet. And while they yet believed not for joy, and wondered, he said unto them, Have

ye here any meat? And they gave him a piece of a broiled fish, and of an honeycomb. And he took it, and did eat before them.

In this passage, specifically verse 39, it is clear that Jesus permitted the disciples to touch Him. But back at the tomb earlier that day, Mary was forbidden to touch Him. Why? The answer is clear: Jesus could not be defiled by the touch of human hands, by Mary, until He offered Himself up at the altar [in Heaven]. Jesus permitted the disciples to touch Him that very same evening because, after He left Mary and before He met the disciples, He ascended into Heaven and made "reconciliation for iniquity" in partial fulfillment of Daniel 9:24.

In summary, Jesus first appeared to Mary at the tomb where she was forbidden to touch Him. Shortly after, He ascended into Heaven. It was there where He provided reconciliation for iniquity. Then He returned to His disciples that very same evening. Since He had already offered Himself up as spotless and undefiled, His disciples were allowed to touch Him. This position is clearly supported in the Book of Hebrews. Hebrews 9:11–14 states:

> But Christ being come an high priest of good things to come, by a greater and more perfect tabernacle, not made with hands, that is to say, not of this building; Neither by the blood of goats and calves, but by his own blood he entered in once into the holy place, having obtained eternal redemption for us. For if the blood of bulls and of goats, and the ashes of an heifer sprinkling the unclean, sanctifieth to the purifying of the flesh: How much more shall the blood of Christ, who through the eternal Spirit offered himself without spot to God, purge your conscience from dead works to serve the living God?

VI. Countering Rabbinic Judaism's Argument

Even though Jesus fits perfectly into the 69 weeks of Daniel's prophecy, the rabbis maintain an entirely different view of Gabriel's message to the prophet. Many of them claim that the 70 weeks, or 490 years, represent the dates between the destruction of both the first and last temples. Since history reveals that Israel's last temple was destroyed in A.D. 70[29] this would mean that, according to Judaism, the first temple must have been destroyed in 421 B.C. (70 – 490 – 1 = 421 B.C.), not 586 B.C. As a result, the rabbis are missing 165 years (586 – 421) of recorded history. Regarding this matter, it is important to keep in mind that the entire secular world disagrees with rabbinic Judaism's own private dating system.

Most counter-missionaries, in an attempt to find another candidate for the sixty-nine weeks described in Daniel 9:25–26, try to place King Cyrus into the passage. Their theory is seriously flawed for a couple of reasons. First, Cyrus died in 530/529 B.C., which is approximately eighty-four years (529 – 445 years) prior to Artaxerxes' decree to rebuild Jerusalem. Daniel 9:25–26 specifically states that someone would be cut off, or killed, after the decree is made to rebuild Jerusalem, not before. This is one reason why the subject of this passage cannot be Cyrus.

A second reason is as follows. Daniel 9:26 states, "And after threescore and two weeks shall Messiah be cut off, but not for himself: and the people of the prince that shall come shall destroy the city and the sanctuary; and the end thereof shall be with a flood, and unto the end of the war desolations are determined." According to this verse and according to rabbinic Judaism, it would be 62 weeks of years, or 434 years, from the time that the anointed one, or Messiah, is killed until the destruction of the temple in A.D. 70. Since historical records indicate that Cyrus died in 530/529 B.C., there are 598 years (529 + 70 – 1) from the time that he died to the razing of the second temple. Remember, there is no year zero, so we must subtract one. Therefore, regarding Cyrus as the subject of Daniel 9:26, Judaism's position lacks all credibility by 164 years (598 – 434).

As a result of these inconsistencies, it is impossible to fit Cyrus into the prophetic calendar described in Daniel 9:25–26. Only Jesus makes perfect sense!

For Rabbinic Judaism, a Missing One-Week Covenant

As previously mentioned, Judaism generally teaches that the seventieth week of Daniel ended in A.D. 70 with the destruction of the last temple. Regarding this matter, it is important to pay close attention to the words written in Daniel 9:27 describing the seventieth week as follows: "And he shall confirm the covenant with many for one week: and in the midst of the week he shall cause the sacrifice and the oblation to cease."

It has already been determined that one week is equivalent to seven years. Therefore, in order to support their claim that the 490-year period ended with the destruction of the last temple, the rabbis are required to produce historical evidence of an agreement or covenant that took place within seven years of this time, between A.D. 63 and A.D. 70. Unfortunately for them, no such agreement or covenant exists. As a result, the only possible conclusion is as follows: the seventieth week of Daniel has not yet taken place in our history. But it will . . . in the future!

VII. The Seventieth Week of Daniel

As we have seen, the completion of the sixty-ninth week of Daniel occurred when Jesus rode into Jerusalem on a donkey. Approximately forty years later, the Romans entered the city and destroyed the temple, or sanctuary, in fulfillment of Daniel 9:26. It has now been almost two thousand years since Israel has had a temple. This long period of time was foretold in the Book of Hosea as follows: "For the children of Israel shall abide many days without a king, and without a prince, and without a sacrifice, and without an image, and without an ephod, and without teraphim" (Hos. 3:4).

Since Jesus' crucifixion and the destruction of the last temple, the prophetic calendar described in Daniel 9:25–26 has stopped! We have been living in a period called the "church age" where salvation is offered to both Jews and Gentiles.

The Bible teaches that when this church age is finished, God will once again turn toward His people. Luke 21:24 records what Jesus prophesied would occur shortly after His crucifixion as follows: "And they [the Jews] shall fall by the edge of the sword, and shall be led away captive into all nations: and Jerusalem shall be trodden down of the Gentiles, until the times of the Gentiles be fulfilled." Like Jesus foretold, since A.D. 70, the children of Israel have been dispersed throughout the world. And as He stated in Luke 21:24, this would continue until the times of the Gentiles are fulfilled.

Since 1948 and the rebirth of the nation of Israel, God continues to bring His people back into the promised land. The signs of the times point to one thing: the church age is almost finished, and the seventieth week of Daniel is about to begin.

The information contained within Daniel 9:27 tells us that the seventieth week has not yet begun. This is because Israel has not yet built its temple so that sacrifices can be reinstated. The verse foretells that a certain individual will cause these sacrifices to cease in the middle of the seventieth week and, until Israel builds its temple and enters into this seven-year agreement, there can be no fulfillment.

From A.D. 63 to this present day, there is no historical record of Israel entering into a seven-year covenant with anyone. Interestingly, Isaiah 28:15 describes their future agreement as "a covenant with death," and an agreement with Hell. It reads as follows: "Because ye have said, We have made a covenant with death, and with hell are we at agreement; when the overflowing scourge shall pass through, it shall not come unto us: for we have made lies our refuge, and under falsehood have we hid ourselves."

It seems that Isaiah 28:15 foretells the day Israel makes an agreement with death and hell, with someone who will prove to be their greatest enemy, the devil himself. And according to Daniel 9:27, it will be he who breaks this seven-year covenant and causes the sacrifices to stop.

Second Thessalonians 2:3–4 places the son of perdition, the incarnate devil himself, in the midst of Israel's future agreement. Revelation 13:4–8 cross-references Daniel 9:27, indicating that, in the middle of this seven-year covenant, the last forty-two months or three and one-half years will bring the greatest period of Tribulation in world history. The applicable passages follow:

- **2 Thessalonians 2:3–4:** "Let no man deceive you by any means: for that day shall not come, except there come a falling away first, and that man of sin be revealed, the son of perdition; Who opposeth and exalteth himself above all that is called God, or that is worshipped; so that he as God sitteth in the temple of God, shewing himself that he is God."
- **Revelation 13:4–8:** "And they worshipped the dragon which gave power

unto the beast: and they worshipped the beast, saying, Who is like unto the beast? who is able to make war with him? And there was given unto him a mouth speaking great things and blasphemies; and power was given unto him to continue forty and two months. And he opened his mouth in blasphemy against God, to blaspheme his name, and his tabernacle, and them that dwell in heaven. And it was given unto him to make war with the saints, and to overcome them: and power was given him over all kindreds, and tongues, and nations. And all that dwell upon the earth shall worship him, whose names are not written in the book of life of the Lamb slain from the foundation of the world."

Though all this will occur as prophesied, the scriptures provide some wonderful news for both the children of Israel and the entire world. God's everlasting covenant with Abraham, Isaac, and Jacob will prove to be far stronger than Israel's future agreement with the devil. Through the Messiah, the LORD God will intercede on behalf of His people. Isaiah 28:16–18 reveals that, through this precious cornerstone, Israel's future treaty with Satan will be nullified:

Therefore thus saith the Lord GOD, Behold, I lay in Zion for a foundation a stone, a tried stone, a precious corner stone, a sure foundation: he that believeth shall not make haste. Judgment also will I lay to the line, and righteousness to the plummet: and the hail shall sweep away the refuge of lies, and the waters shall overflow the hiding place. And your covenant with death shall be disannulled, and your agreement with hell shall not stand; when the overflowing scourge shall pass through, then ye shall be trodden down by it.

All this is further supported in Daniel 7:21–22 and 2 Thessalonians 2:8–10. Both passages foretell the Messiah's future victory over Israel's greatest enemy, the son of perdition, the Antichrist:

- **Daniel 7:21–22:** "I beheld, and the same horn made war with the saints, and prevailed against them; Until the Ancient of days came, and

judgment was given to the saints of the most High; and the time came
that the saints possessed the kingdom."

- **2 Thessalonians 2:8–10:** "And then shall that Wicked be revealed, whom
the Lord shall consume with the spirit of his mouth, and shall destroy
with the brightness of his coming: Even him, whose coming is after the
working of Satan with all power and signs and lying wonders, And with
all deceivableness of unrighteousness in them that perish; because they
received not the love of the truth, that they might be saved."

Luke 23:34 records one of the last things Jesus said before He died so hor-
ribly. He said, "Father, forgive them; for they know not what they do." In
spite of Christ's terrible torment and death, there can be no doubt that
He loves His people. In John 15:13 He also said, "Greater love hath no
man than this, that a man lay down his life for his friends." Jesus paid the
price for the sins of His people as well as the sins of the Gentiles. The Bible
teaches that it was He who established the New Covenant by which all of
us can be reconciled to our beloved Creator. Upon a person's acknowledge-
ment that Jesus is Lord and Savior, as well as their confession that God
raised Him from the dead, they are assured everlasting life.

In Matthew 23:39, Jesus tells the Jews: "Ye shall not see me henceforth,
till ye shall say, Blessed is he that cometh in the name of the Lord." Zechariah 12:9–10 indicates that there will come a day when all nations come
against Jerusalem to battle, and Israel looks upon Him who was pierced,
and they will mourn for Him as one mourns for his only son. In that day,
their veil of understanding will be removed, repentance will take place, and
sins will be forgiven. This will all be accomplished through King Messiah,
the stone described in Isaiah 28:16. Jesus Christ will return as King of
Kings and destroy anyone who comes against His people. The following
verses provide insurmountable proof that this precious cornerstone called
the Messiah will be the primary source of both the removal of sin in the
land and the execution of judgment on the earth:

- **Zechariah 3:8–9**—*The Messiah, the Stone, removes sin:* "Hear now, O
Joshua the high priest, thou, and thy fellows that sit before thee: for

they are men wondered at: for, behold, I will bring forth my servant the BRANCH. For behold the **stone** that I have laid before Joshua; upon one stone shall be seven eyes: behold, I will engrave the graving thereof, saith the LORD of hosts, and I will remove the iniquity of that land in one day."

* **Daniel 2:44–45**—*The Messiah, the Stone, executes judgment on the earth:* "And in the days of these kings shall the God of heaven set up a kingdom, which shall never be destroyed: and the kingdom shall not be left to other people, but it shall break in pieces and consume all these kingdoms, and it shall stand for ever. Forasmuch as thou sawest that the **stone** was cut out of the mountain without hands, and that it brake in pieces the iron, the brass, the clay, the silver, and the gold; the great God hath made known to the king what shall come to pass hereafter: and the dream is certain, and the interpretation thereof sure."

VIII. The Six Prophecies of Daniel 9:24

According to Daniel 9:24, there are six separate and distinct portions of prophecy that must be fulfilled by the end of the seventy-week period. They are as follows:

1. To finish the transgression,
2. To make an end of sins,
3. To make reconciliation for iniquity,
4. To bring in everlasting righteousness,
5. To seal up the vision and prophecy,
6. To anoint the most Holy [place].

1. To finish the transgression

This portion of the prophecy will be fulfilled at the end of the seventieth week, at Jesus' Second Coming. Ezekiel 37:23 and Joel 3:17 teach that, during the messianic reign, there will be no transgressions because Israel will be holy:

* **Ezekiel 37:23**—*regarding Israel:* "Neither shall they defile themselves any

more with their idols, nor with their detestable things, nor with any of their transgressions: but I will save them out of all their dwellingplaces, wherein they have sinned, and will cleanse them: so shall they be my people, and I will be their God."

• **Joel 3:17:** "So shall ye know that I am the LORD your God dwelling in Zion, my holy mountain: then shall Jerusalem be holy, and there shall no strangers pass through her any more."

2. To make an end of sins

Further confirmation that there will be no more sins and Israel will be holy during the messianic reign can be found in Zephaniah 3:13 and Isaiah 62:11–12. This portion of Daniel's prophecy will also be fulfilled at the end of the seventieth week, when Jesus returns:

• **Zephaniah 3:13;** "The remnant of Israel shall not do iniquity, nor speak lies; neither shall a deceitful tongue be found in their mouth: for they shall feed and lie down, and none shall make them afraid."

• **Isaiah 62:11–12:** "Behold, the LORD hath proclaimed unto the end of the world, Say ye to the daughter of Zion, Behold, thy salvation cometh; behold, his reward is with him, and his work before him. And they shall call them, The holy people, The redeemed of the LORD: and thou shalt be called, Sought out, A city not forsaken."

3. To make reconciliation for iniquity

As we have seen, this was fulfilled after the sixty-ninth week when Jesus poured His blood upon the heavenly altar shortly after His death and resurrection (Heb. 9:11–14).

4. To bring in everlasting righteousness

This will be fulfilled at Jesus' Second Coming, at the end of the seventieth week. Isaiah 11:1,4–5 and Jeremiah 33:14–16 tell us that the Messiah, the BRANCH, will bring everlasting righteousness:

• **Isaiah 11:1,4–5:** "And there shall come forth a rod out of the stem of Jesse, and a Branch shall grow out of his roots. . . . But with righteousness shall he judge the poor, and reprove with equity for the meek of the earth: and he shall smite the earth with the rod of his mouth, and with the breath of his lips shall he slay the wicked. And righteousness shall be the girdle of his loins, and faithfulness the girdle of his reins."

+ **Jeremiah 33:14–16:** "Behold, the days come, saith the LORD, that I will perform that good thing which I have promised unto the house of Israel and to the house of Judah. In those days, and at that time, will I cause the Branch of righteousness to grow up unto David; and he shall execute judgment and righteousness in the land. In those days shall Judah be saved, and Jerusalem shall dwell safely: and this is the name wherewith she shall be called, The LORD our righteousness."

5. To seal up the vision and prophecy

It will be totally impossible for unbelieving Jews to fully comprehend this seventy-week prophecy until all seventy weeks are completed and God removes their veil of understanding. This is clearly established in Daniel 12:8–9, where God tells Daniel that "the words are closed up and sealed till the time of the end:

And I [Daniel] heard, but I understood not: then said I, O my Lord, what shall be the end of these things? And he said, Go thy way, Daniel: for the words are closed up and sealed till the time of the end.

The New Testament supports this understanding with passages such as Romans 11:25–27 that tell us that blindness "in part" has happened to Israel. But this blindness or absence of understanding will only remain until the fullness of the Gentiles and the church age is completed. After Israel's blindness is removed they will say, "Blessed is he that cometh in the name of the Lord." Upon Jesus' return, Daniel's entire seventy-week prophecy will be finished.

6. To anoint the most Holy [place]

When Jesus' returns, He will build the temple in fulfillment of passages such as Zechariah 6:12–13 which tell us that the Messiah, the BRANCH, will build the temple:

> . . . Behold the man whose name is The BRANCH; and he shall grow up out of his place, and he shall build the temple of the LORD: Even he shall build the temple of the LORD; and he shall bear the glory, and shall sit and rule upon his throne; and he shall be a priest upon his throne: and the counsel of peace shall be between them both.

According to the Law of Moses, all articles inside the tabernacle were anointed with anointing oil. Exodus 30:22–29 explains:

> Moreover the LORD spake unto Moses, saying, Take thou also unto thee principal spices, of pure myrrh five hundred shekels, and of sweet cinnamon half so much, even two hundred and fifty shekels, and of sweet calamus two hundred and fifty shekels, And of cassia five hundred shekels, after the shekel of the sanctuary, and of oil olive an hin: And thou shalt make it an oil of holy ointment, an ointment compound after the art of the apothecary: it shall be an holy anointing oil. And thou shalt anoint the tabernacle of the congregation therewith, and the ark of the testimony, And the table and all his vessels, and the candlestick and his vessels, and the altar of incense, And the altar of burnt offering with all his vessels, and the laver and his foot. And thou shalt sanctify them, that they may be most holy: whatsoever toucheth them shall be holy.

Similar to the Law of Moses, when the Messiah builds the temple [the most holy place], in Hebrew *qodesh* (*Strong's,* #6944), Daniel's seventy-week prophecy instructs that all articles within the house will be anointed [with oil] according to the Law of Moses.

Naturally this will not take place until Jesus returns, builds the temple, and the seventieth week of Daniel is completed.

Chapter Two

The Curse of Jeconiah
and the Virgin Birth

Introduction

When God promised Abraham and Sarah a son, Genesis 17:17 records Abraham's reaction, "Then Abraham fell upon his face, and laughed, and said in his heart, Shall a child be born unto him that is an hundred years old? and shall Sarah, that is ninety years old, bear?" As promised, Sarah had a son named Isaac, and it was through this miraculous birth between a hundred-year-old man and a ninety-year-old woman that the LORD established His everlasting covenant with Abraham. Similarly, it would be through another miraculous birth that God would establish His covenant with all of mankind, through the virgin birth of Jesus, His only begotten Son.

For some, the justification for Jesus' virgin birth is difficult to understand. However, we need to remember one important thing: the Messiah's virgin birth became necessary due to the spiritual downfall of King Solomon and his descendents. Because of their continued rebellion against God's laws, commandments, and statutes, their progeny was cut off. As a result, the Messiah could not have had a human father, only a heavenly Father. Therefore, Jesus' virgin birth was not only a New Testament miracle, but also a fulfillment of the Hebrew scriptures. It became

God's solution to the disqualification of Solomon's heirs from sitting on the throne of David.

Part 1

I. Israel Wants a King

When Samuel was old, his sons became judges over Israel. The Bible teaches that they were corrupt, dishonest, and accepted bribes. Because of this, 1 Samuel 8:5 states that the elders came to Samuel with a request as follows: ". . . Behold, thou art old, and thy sons walk not in thy ways: now make us a king to judge us like all the nations."

Samuel was concerned because, although God was Israel's King, the people wanted an earthly ruler much like the other nations. The LORD had provided all of Israel's needs since the exodus from Egypt. Seemingly, they had rejected Him. When Samuel informed God about their request, according to 1 Samuel 8:7, the LORD told him the following: ". . . Hearken unto the voice of the people in all that they say unto thee: for they have not rejected thee, but they have rejected me, that I should not reign over them."

God honored Israel's request for a king. However, because of His concern for the nation's righteousness, He demanded that all its kings set an example that everyone should follow. This included obedience to His laws and statutes. As punishment, if these kings were unfaithful, they were cut off and consumed. According to 1 Samuel 12:25, this is what the LORD told Israel regarding its kings: "But if ye shall still do wickedly, ye shall be consumed, both ye and your king."

Saul became the first king of Israel. As its ruler, he was disobedient to God's commandments and statutes. For example, he offered burnt offerings for sacrifice. Because he was a member of the tribe of Benjamin, this was forbidden. According to 1 Chronicles 6:1–32, this was a responsibility set aside strictly for the descendents of Aaron of the tribe of Levi. After Saul's continued rebellion, 1 Samuel 13:13–14 records the words spoken to him by Samuel:

> . . . Thou hast done foolishly: thou hast not kept the commandment
> of the LORD thy God, which he commanded thee: for now would the

LORD have established thy kingdom upon Israel for ever. But now thy
kingdom shall not continue: the LORD hath sought him a man after his
own heart, and the LORD hath commanded him to be captain over his
people, because thou hast not kept that which the LORD commanded
thee.

According to this passage Saul was informed that because of his rebellion,
he was cut off as king. As a result, his heirs would not be allowed to rule
as kings of Israel.

II. David, Israel's Next King

David became Israel's next king. Remembering God's demands to Israel's
kings and the punishment inflicted upon Saul for his disobedience, in
order to demonstrate how the Messiah's virgin birth became necessary, it
is important to understand the LORD's special relationship with David.
God loved David so much that He vowed that his seed would endure
forever. According to Him, it would be through David's loins that the
Messiah would come. In these passages, God refers to David in the following manner:

- **2 Samuel 7:12–13:** "And when thy days be fulfilled, and thou shalt sleep
  with thy fathers, I will set up thy seed after thee, which shall proceed out
  of thy bowels, and I will establish his kingdom. He shall build an house
  for my name, and I will stablish the throne of his kingdom for ever."
- **Psalm 89:35–36:** "Once have I sworn by my holiness that I will not
  lie unto David. His seed shall endure for ever, and his throne as the sun
  before me."
- **Psalm 132:11:** "The LORD hath sworn in truth unto David; he will not
  turn from it; Of the fruit of thy body will I set upon thy throne."

God's Conditional Promise to David's Descendents

God's promise to David was clearly unconditional because, according to
Psalm 89:35–36 and Psalm 132:11, He swore that He would not change
His mind. In retrospect, God's promise to David's physical offspring was
conditional; it was an oath made with provisions.

In Psalm 132:12 the LORD pledged to David the following, "If thy children will keep my covenant and my testimony that I shall teach them, their children shall also sit upon thy throne for evermore." In this verse, God told David that his kingdom would be established through his loins if and only if they obeyed the covenant and testimony that He taught them. According to the Bible, though David had many sons, this conditional promise would only be filtered through Solomon, the one appointed to build the temple. First Chronicles 22:7–10 explains:

> And David said to Solomon, My son, as for me, it was in my mind to build an house unto the name of the LORD my God: But the word of the LORD came to me, saying, Thou hast shed blood abundantly, and hast made great wars: thou shalt not build an house unto my name, because thou hast shed much blood upon the earth in my sight. Behold, a son shall be born to thee, who shall be a man of rest; and I will give him rest from all his enemies round about: for his name shall be Solomon, and I will give peace and quietness unto Israel in his days. He shall build an house for my name; and he shall be my son, and I will be his father; and I will establish the throne of his kingdom over Israel for ever.

In this passage, David advised Solomon that he was the one God selected to build the temple. Moreover, it would be through him that Israel's kings would be established. However, it was also clear that the LORD would establish the throne of Solomon's kingdom over Israel as long as he and his heirs succeeded in meeting God's requirements provided in Psalm 132:12. Much like in the case with Saul, if Solomon and his heirs were disobedient, they too would be cut off and consumed.

We can find further verification of these provisions in other passages in the Bible. For example, 1 Kings 8 describes the time when King Solomon inaugurated the temple that was eventually built. In this chapter, he prayed to God and asked Him to verify the promise that He made to his father David. Solomon requested the LORD confirm that, through his seed, there would always be a man to sit upon Israel's throne. First Kings 8:22–28 states:

And Solomon stood before the altar of the LORD in the presence of all the congregation of Israel, and spread forth his hands toward heaven: And he said, LORD God of Israel, there is no God like thee, in heaven above, or on earth beneath, who keepest covenant and mercy with thy servants that walk before thee with all their heart: Who hast kept with thy servant David my father that thou promisedst him: thou spakest also with thy mouth, and hast fulfilled it with thine hand, as it is this day. Therefore now, LORD God of Israel, keep with thy servant David my father that thou promisedst him, saying, There shall not fail thee a man in my sight to sit on the throne of Israel; so that thy children take heed to their way, that they walk before me as thou hast walked before me. And now, O God of Israel, let thy word, I pray thee, be verified, which thou spakest unto thy servant David my father. But will God indeed dwell on the earth? behold, the heaven and heaven of heavens cannot contain thee; how much less this house that I have builded? Yet have thou respect unto the prayer of thy servant, and to his supplication, O LORD my God, to hearken unto the cry and to the prayer, which thy servant prayeth before thee to day.

Solomon's prayer ended at 1 Kings 8:54. It would be in the following chapter, in 1 Kings 9:3–5, that the LORD replied to Solomon's prayer and repeated the same stipulations made in Psalm 132:12:

And the LORD said unto him, I have heard thy prayer and thy supplication, that thou hast made before me: I have hallowed this house, which thou hast built, to put my name there for ever; and mine eyes and mine heart shall be there perpetually. And if thou wilt walk before me, as David thy father walked, in integrity of heart, and in uprightness, to do according to all that I have commanded thee, and wilt keep my statutes and my judgments: Then I will establish the throne of thy kingdom upon Israel for ever, as I promised to David thy father, saying, There shall not fail thee a man upon the throne of Israel.

Here, God repeats the demands on Solomon and his heirs. They were required to follow His statutes and judgments. These had to be met! If they kept them, then and only then would the LORD establish David's throne through Solomon's heirs forever.

First Kings 2:1–4 provides additional evidence of the provisions placed on Solomon and his descendents. Here, near the time of his death, David reminds Solomon of God's conditional promise as follows:

> Now the days of David drew nigh that he should die; and he charged Solomon his son, saying, I go the way of all the earth: be thou strong therefore, and shew thyself a man; And keep the charge of the LORD thy God, to walk in his ways, to keep his statutes, and his commandments, and his judgments, and his testimonies, as it is written in the law of Moses, that thou mayest prosper in all that thou doest, and whithersoever thou turnest thyself: That the LORD may continue his word which he spake concerning me, saying, If thy children take heed to their way, to walk before me in truth with all their heart and with all their soul, there shall not fail thee (said he) a man on the throne of Israel.

III. Solomon's Spiritual Downfall

As we have seen, the Bible demonstrates God's instructions to Solomon and his heirs to keep all His commandments and statutes in order for their kingdom to be established forever. However the Scriptures also reveal that, beginning with Solomon, David's descendents failed to comply. For example, when Solomon was old, he turned away from the God of his fathers and followed the pagan gods and goddesses of his many wives and concubines. He even made sacrifices and burnt incense offerings to them. First Kings 11:1–10 describes the details of Solomon's spiritual downfall:

> But king Solomon loved many strange women, together with the daughter of Pharaoh, women of the Moabites, Ammonites, Edomites, Zidonians, and Hittites; Of the nations concerning which the LORD said unto the children of Israel, Ye shall not go in to them, neither shall they come in unto you: for surely they will turn away your heart after their gods: Solomon clave unto these in love. And he had seven hundred wives, princesses, and three hundred concubines: and his wives turned

away his heart. For it came to pass, when Solomon was old, that his wives turned away his heart after other gods: and his heart was not perfect with the LORD his God, as was the heart of David his father. For Solomon went after Ashtoreth the goddess of the Zidonians, and after Milcom the abomination of the Ammonites. And Solomon did evil in the sight of the LORD, and went not fully after the LORD, as did David his father. Then did Solomon build an high place for Chemosh, the abomination of Moab, in the hill that is before Jerusalem, and for Molech, the abomination of the children of Ammon. And likewise did he for all his strange wives, which burnt incense and sacrificed unto their gods. And the LORD was angry with Solomon, because his heart was turned from the LORD God of Israel, which had appeared unto him twice. And had commanded him concerning this thing, that he should not go after other gods: but he kept not that which the LORD commanded.

As we can see, Solomon failed miserably! He eventually turned to pagan gods and goddesses. As a result of his rebellion against God, he was punished. His kingdom was rent in two and Israel became divided into two kingdoms, the House of Israel and the House of Judah. Shortly after Solomon's death it was Jeroboam, the son of Nebat and not a descendent of David, who became the House of Israel's first king. And Rehoboam, Solomon's only son according to 1 Chronicles 3:10, became the House of Judah's first king. First Kings 11:11–13 records the LORD's punishment upon Solomon as follows: His kingdom would be rent in two after his death and almost completely taken away from his only son Rehoboam:

Wherefore the LORD said unto Solomon, Forasmuch as this is done of thee, and thou hast not kept my covenant and my statutes, which I have commanded thee, I will surely rend the kingdom from thee, and will give it to thy servant. Notwithstanding in thy days I will not do it for David thy father's sake: but I will rend it out of the hand of thy son. Howbeit I will not rend away all the kingdom; but will give one tribe to thy son for David my servant's sake, and for Jerusalem's sake which I have chosen.

As of this moment, although the messianic line began with David and continued through Solomon, it could only continue through Rehoboam since Jeroboam was Nebat's son and not David's offspring. Therefore, the genealogy of the House of Israel's kings that began with Jeroboam must be considered ineligible with respect to the messianic promise because they were not descendents of David through Solomon. Regarding this matter, it is important to remember that God still had an unconditional promise to David which would be kept because He "swore by his holiness" that his seed would endure forever.

If Solomon had any other sons besides Rehoboam, the Bible would have recorded their names. It is interesting to note that the Scriptures specifically mention the names of Solomon's two daughters, Taphath and Basmath (1 Kings 4:11–15). So why would the Bible fail to mention that Solomon had other sons besides Rehoboam if this was the case? According to the Scriptures, there can only be one reason: Solomon had only one son and his name was Rehoboam. As a result, he and his heirs become the primary focus of attention as Judah's kings continually failed to meet God's requirements under His "conditional" promise.

IV. Continued Failures of Judah's Kings

It is important to realize that Solomon was not the only descendent of David who failed to meet the LORD's provisions. Of the twenty kings of Judah that followed Solomon, many did evil in the sight of the LORD. As a matter of record, regarding the last nine kings of Judah, seven were evil kings: Ahaz, Manasseh, Amon, Jehoahaz, Jehoiakim, Jeconiah also known as Jehoiachin or Coniah, and Zedekiah. Zedekiah was the last king of Judah. The following passages testify to the spiritual downfall of these kings:

* **2 Kings 16:2–3**—*regarding Ahaz:* "Twenty years old was Ahaz when he began to reign, and reigned sixteen years in Jerusalem, and did not that which was right in the sight of the LORD his God, like David his father. But he walked in the way of the kings of Israel, yea, and made his son to pass through the fire, according to the abominations of the heathen,

whom the Lord cast out from before the children of Israel."

- **2 Kings 21:1–2,6**—*regarding Manasseh:* "Manasseh was twelve years old when he began to reign, and reigned fifty and five years in Jerusalem. And his mother's name was Hephzibah. And he did that which was evil in the sight of the Lord, after the abominations of the heathen, whom the Lord cast out before the children of Israel. . . . And he made his son pass through the fire, and observed times, and used enchantments, and dealt with familiar spirits and wizards: he wrought much wickedness in the sight of the Lord, to provoke him to anger."

- **2 Kings 21:19–22**—*regarding Amon:* "Amon was twenty and two years old when he began to reign, and he reigned two years in Jerusalem. And his mother's name was Meshullemeth, the daughter of Haruz of Jotbah. And he did that which was evil in the sight of the Lord, as his father Manasseh did. And he walked in all the way that his father walked in, and served the idols that his father served, and worshipped them: And he forsook the Lord God of his fathers, and walked not in the way of the Lord."

- **2 Kings 23:31–32**—*regarding Jehoahaz:* "Jehoahaz was twenty and three years old when he began to reign; and he reigned three months in Jerusalem. And his mother's name was Hamutal, the daughter of Jeremiah of Libnah. And he did that which was evil in the sight of the Lord, according to all that his fathers had done."

- **2 Kings 23:36–37**—*regarding Jehoiakim:* "Jehoiakim was twenty and five years old when he began to reign; and he reigned eleven years in Jerusalem. And his mother's name was Zebudah, the daughter of Pedaiah of Rumah. And he did that which was evil in the sight of the Lord, according to all that his fathers had done."

- **2 Kings 24:8–9**—*regarding Jeconiah, also known as Jehoiachin or Coniah:* "Jehoiachin was eighteen years old when he began to reign, and he reigned in Jerusalem three months. And his mother's name was Nehushta, the daughter of Elnathan of Jerusalem. And he did that which was evil in the sight of the Lord, according to all that his father had done."

- **2 Kings 24:18–19**—*regarding Zedekiah:* "Zedekiah was twenty and one years old when he began to reign, and he reigned eleven years in Jerusalem. And his mother's name was Hamutal, the daughter of Jeremiah of Libnah. And he did that which was evil in the sight of the LORD, according to all that Jehoiakim had done."

Only two of Judah's last nine kings pleased God. According to 2 Kings 18:1–3 and 2 Kings 22:1–2, they were Hezekiah and Josiah. Josiah did all he could to restore Judah to righteousness and purge it from its sins. According to the Bible, he was the greatest of Judah's kings.

Though this was the case, God's conditional promise to David's descendents remained, and the Scriptures bear witness that many of them did evil in the LORD's sight by turning to other gods. And because they failed to meet the requirements that were stipulated in Psalm 132:12, 1 Kings 9:3–5, and 1 Kings 2:1–4, their punishment was that their progeny would be cut off, just like Saul's progeny was cut off.

Some may take the position that repentance of Judah's kings succeeded in soothing God's anger. However according to the Bible, this was not the case! Using Manasseh as an example, the Scriptures tell us that he reigned prior to Josiah and repented for his disobedience and sins. Second Chronicles 33:10–16 testifies to Manasseh's repentance as follows:

And the LORD spake to Manasseh, and to his people: but they would not hearken. Wherefore the LORD brought upon them the captains of the host of the king of Assyria, which took Manasseh among the thorns, and bound him with fetters, and carried him to Babylon. And when he was in affliction, he besought the LORD his God, and humbled himself greatly before the God of his fathers, And prayed unto him: and he was intreated of him, and heard his supplication, and brought him again to Jerusalem into his kingdom. Then Manasseh knew that the LORD he was God. Now after this he built a wall without the city of David, on the west side of Gihon, in the valley, even to the entering in at the fish gate, and compassed about Ophel, and raised it up a very great height, and put captains of war in all the fenced cities of Judah. And he took away the strange gods, and the idol out of the house of the LORD, and all the altars that he had built in the mount of the house of the LORD, and in Jerusalem, and cast them out of the city. And he repaired the altar of the LORD, and sacrificed thereon peace offerings and thank offerings, and commanded Judah to serve the LORD God of Israel.

This passage clearly shows that Manasseh repented for his sins. In spite of this, even though his successor Josiah was a great king, 2 Kings 23:25–27 explains that God remained outraged against Judah's kings in spite of Manassah's repentance and decided to remove them out of His sight:

And like unto him [Josiah] was there no king before him, that turned to the LORD with all his heart, and with all his soul, and with all his might, according to all the law of Moses; neither after him arose there any like him. Notwithstanding the LORD turned not from the fierceness of his great wrath, wherewith his anger was kindled against Judah, because of all the provocations that Manasseh had provoked him withal. And the LORD said, I will remove Judah also out of my sight, as I have removed Israel, and will cast off this city Jerusalem which I have chosen, and the house of which I said, My name shall be there.

Since Manasseh repented and God's anger remained, it is logical to conclude that any alleged or unrecorded repentance of other kings of Judah would also fail to soothe God's wrath.

Any claim that the LORD allowed the messianic line to continue through Solomon and his descendents in spite of their continued rebellion would certainly appear to be a far-reaching attempt to endorse a position that is baseless and without merit. It would blatantly defy the foundation God established with both Saul and David's heirs by alleging that His words are untrue. Even though some of Judah's kings could have repented for their sins, God's anger remained as demonstrated in Manasseh's case.

These are merely some of the Scriptures that record the defiance against God by Judah's kings. And as punishment for their rebellion, just as Saul's progeny was cut off and consumed by God, the offspring of Judah's kings would also be cut off and consumed. According to Ezekiel 43:7–9, God declares to Ezekiel the following:

. . . Son of man, the place of my throne, and the place of the soles of my feet, where I will dwell in the midst of the children of Israel for ever, and my holy name, shall the house of Israel no more defile, neither they, nor their kings, by their whoredom, nor by the carcases of their kings in their high places. In their setting of their threshold by my thresholds, and their post by my posts, and the wall between me and them, they have even defiled my holy name by their abominations that they have committed: **wherefore I have consumed them in mine anger.** Now let them put away their whoredom, and the carcases of their kings, far from me, **and I will dwell in the midst of them for ever."**

Author's note: This passage is critical for two reasons. First, it confirms that God consumed the royal line of kings. As a result, the foretold Messiah could not possibly be a physical descendent of human kings and must be born of a virgin. Secondly, it provides proof of the Messiah's deity since God Himself informs us that He will reign forever in their place.

Part 2
V. The Curse on Jeconiah's Descendents

Jeconiah, also known as Jehoiachin or Coniah, was the next to the last king of Judah who reigned before Zedekiah. According to the Bible, he was eighteen years old when he began to reign and he ruled for a total of three months. Second Kings 24:8–9 tells us that he did evil in the LORD's sight. Although the Bible provides some interesting facts about Jeconiah's life, God's words regarding his descendents have an even greater significance. In Jeremiah 22:24–30 the LORD announces a curse on all of Jeconiah's descendents, declaring them ineligible to sit upon the throne of David as Israel's king:

As I live, saith the LORD, though Coniah the son of Jehoiakim king of Judah were the signet upon my right hand, yet would I pluck thee thence; And I will give thee into the hand of them that seek thy life, and into the hand of them whose face thou fearest, even into the hand of Nebuchadrezzar king of Babylon, and into the hand of the Chaldeans.

And I will cast thee out, and thy mother that bare thee, into another country, where ye were not born; and there shall ye die. But to the land whereunto they desire to return, thither shall they not return. Is this man Coniah a despised broken idol? is he a vessel wherein is no pleasure? wherefore are they cast out, he and his seed, and are cast into a land which they know not? O earth, earth, earth, hear the word of the LORD. Thus saith the LORD, Write ye this man childless, a man that shall not prosper in his days: for no man of his seed shall prosper, sitting upon the throne of David, and ruling any more in Judah.

It is absolutely critical to understand the significance of this proclamation against Jeconiah's descendents when considering the necessity of the virgin birth. First of all, verse 28 states: "wherefore are they cast out, he and his seed." This tells us that God acknowledged that Jeconiah would have descendents, which he did! But according to verse 29, He makes a triple declaration against them as follows: "O earth, earth, earth, hear the word of the LORD," etc. And it is verse 30 that provides the greatest significance that "no man of his [Jeconiah's] seed shall prosper, sitting upon the throne of David, and ruling any more in Judah." This passage testifies that, although Jeconiah would have heirs, God disqualifies them from sitting on David's throne as king.

VI. Zedekiah and His Sons Are Cut Off

The Scriptures reveal that Zedekiah took Jeconiah's place as king and was the House of Judah's last earthly ruler. When he rebelled against the Babylonian king, the Chaldean armies pursued him and overtook him. The Bible reveals that Zedekiah and his sons were eventually captured in the plains of Jericho. Jeremiah 52:8–10 records their fate as follows:

But the army of the Chaldeans pursued after the king, and overtook Zedekiah in the plains of Jericho; and all his army was scattered from him. Then they took the king, and carried him up unto the king of Babylon to Riblah in the land of Hamath; where he gave judgment upon him. And the king of Babylon slew the sons of Zedekiah before his eyes: he slew also all the princes of Judah in Riblah.

The Hebrew scriptures now establish an interesting scenario: According to Jeremiah 52:8–10, all of Zedekiah's sons were killed. As a result, his progeny was completely cut off.

Additionally, Jeremiah 22:24–30 informs us that Jeconiah's progeny was cursed by God and declared ineligible to claim the throne of David. Because of these two facts, who can be the progenitor to the Messiah? Does Israel have an earthly candidate who would qualify? If so, does the Bible provide the name of such a person? The answer: No! Therefore, since the Hebrew scriptures fail to provide the name of a legitimate and qualified individual by which the messianic line could continue, the only logical conclusion is as follows: Israel's eternal King, Almighty God Himself, would have to intercede and become the Father of the Messiah. The result: a virgin birth!

VII. Zerubbabel, the Prince of Judah

As shown in the previous chapter, in approximately 607 b.c., Nebuchadnezzar king of Babylon took Israel into captivity. This period lasted for a total of seventy years. As a result of the decree made by Cyrus, king of Persia, immediately after this seventy-year exile, God's people were permitted to return to Jerusalem and rebuild the temple. Shortly following Cyrus' commandment, Ezra 1:8 mentions an individual by the name of Sheshbazzar and identifies him as "the prince of Judah": "Even those did Cyrus king of Persia bring forth by the hand of Mithredath the treasurer, and numbered them unto Sheshbazzar, the prince of Judah."

Sheshbazzar is the Babylonian name for Jeconiah's grandson, whose Hebrew name was Zerubbabel. His genealogy is recorded in 1 Chronicles 3:17–19 as follows, "And the sons of Jeconiah; Assir, Salathiel his son, Malchiram also, and Pedaiah, and Shenazar, Jecamiah, Hoshama, and Nedabiah. And the sons of Pedaiah were, Zerubbabel, and Shimei: and the sons of Zerubbabel; Meshullam, and Hananiah, and Shelomith their sister."

Since Zerubbabel was called the prince of Judah and was also Jeconiah's grandson, his descendents or offspring must also be cursed because all of Jeconiah's descendents were cursed. It is also significant to note that it is

Zerubbabel's genealogy that extends all the way past the official closing of the book of Chronicles, to his fifth and sixth generation. It begins in 1 Chronicles 3:19 and extends all the way to 1 Chronicles 3:24. His is the only genealogy provided in the Bible that proceeds from the genealogy of Judah's kings.

Therefore, it is of the utmost importance to remember that Zerubbabel, who is the only individual in the Bible that is called the prince of Judah after the return from the seventy-year captivity, descended from a cursed genealogy.

Zerubbabel Made a Signet

Prior to the return from Babylon, the prophets referred to the Messiah as David in the Scriptures.[30] A few examples of this can be found in Jeremiah 30:8–9, Ezekiel 34:22–25, Ezekiel 37:24–25, and Hosea 3:4–5:

- **Jeremiah 30:8–9:** "For it shall come to pass in that day, saith the LORD of hosts, that I will break his yoke from off thy neck, and will burst thy bonds, and strangers shall no more serve themselves of him: But they shall serve the LORD their God, and David their king, whom I will raise up unto them."
- **Ezekiel 34:22–25:** "Therefore will I save my flock, and they shall no more be a prey; and I will judge between cattle and cattle. And I will set up one shepherd over them, and he shall feed them, even my servant David; he shall feed them, and he shall be their shepherd. And I the LORD will be their God, and my servant David a prince among them; I the LORD have spoken it. And I will make with them a covenant of peace, and will cause the evil beasts to cease out of the land: and they shall dwell safely in the wilderness, and sleep in the woods."
- **Ezekiel 37:24–25:** "And David my servant shall be king over them; and they all shall have one shepherd: they shall also walk in my judgments, and observe my statutes, and do them. And they shall dwell in the land that I have given unto Jacob my servant, wherein your fathers have dwelt; and they shall dwell therein, even they, and their children,

and their children's children for ever: and my servant David shall be their prince for ever."

✦ **Hosea 3:4–5:** "For the children of Israel shall abide many days without a king, and without a prince, and without a sacrifice, and without an image, and without an ephod, and without teraphim: Afterward shall the children of Israel return, and seek the LORD their God, and David their king; and shall fear the LORD and his goodness in the latter days."

Jeremiah, Ezekiel, and Hosea all lived approximately three to four hundred years after King David died. Therefore, it is clear that the references made to David in these passages refer to the Messiah, and that God was actually calling the Messiah David. This is because the prophets continued to hold that the Messiah would be the offspring of David by God's eternal promise.

Though the prophets sometimes referred to the Messiah as David prior to the exile, there were times when the Messiah was actually called Zerubbabel in the Scriptures after the return from the Babylonian captivity. Haggai 2:21–23 provides an important illustration that demonstrates that the Messiah was actually called Zerubbabel:

Speak to Zerubbabel, governor of Judah, saying, I will shake the heavens and the earth; And I will overthrow the throne of kingdoms, and I will destroy the strength of the kingdoms of the heathen; and I will overthrow the chariots, and those that ride in them; and the horses and their riders shall come down, every one by the sword of his brother. In that day, saith the LORD of hosts, will I take thee, O Zerubbabel, my servant, the son of Shealtiel, saith the LORD, and will make thee as a signet: for I have chosen thee, saith the LORD of hosts.

Though Haggai 2:21–23 speaks of Zerubbabel, there are two reasons why he cannot be the subject of this passage and that this passage is actually messianic. First, Zerubbabel would not "destroy the strength of the kingdoms of the heathen" and "overthrow the chariots, and those that ride in them" in his lifetime. According to the prophets, this would be a responsibility set aside strictly for the Messiah. This is demonstrated in Zechariah 9:9–10 and Micah 5:2,4,10 as follows:

- **Zechariah 9:9–10:** "Rejoice greatly, O daughter of Zion; shout, O daughter of Jerusalem: behold, thy King cometh unto thee: he is just, and having salvation; lowly, and riding upon an ass, and upon a colt the foal of an ass. And I will cut off the chariot from Ephraim, and the horse from Jerusalem, and the battle bow shall be cut off: and he shall speak peace unto the heathen: and his dominion shall be from sea even to sea, and from the river even to the ends of the earth."
- **Micah 5:2,4,10:** "But thou, Bethlehem Ephratah, though thou be little among the thousands of Judah, yet out of thee shall he come forth unto me that is to be ruler in Israel; whose goings forth have been from of old, from everlasting. . . . And he shall stand and feed in the strength of the LORD, in the majesty of the name of the LORD his God; and they shall abide: for now shall he be great unto the ends of the earth. . . . And it shall come to pass in that day, saith the LORD, that I will cut off thy horses out of the midst of thee, and I will destroy thy chariots."

Secondly, the phrase in Haggai 2:21 "shake the heavens and the earth" is a reference to the day of the LORD. According to the prophets, the day of the LORD describes the time when all nations come against Jerusalem . . . a future event that has not yet taken place in our history. Zechariah 14:1–2 states,

Behold, the day of the LORD cometh, and thy spoil shall be divided in the midst of thee. For I will gather all nations against Jerusalem to battle; and the city shall be taken, and the houses rifled, and the women ravished; and half of the city shall go forth into captivity, and the residue of the people shall not be cut off from the city.

Since Zerubbabel died approximately twenty-five hundred years ago, the day of the LORD and the shaking of the heavens and the earth cannot possibly apply to him. Joel 2:10–11, Joel 3:16, and Isaiah 13:9–13 provide the proof that shaking the heavens and the earth will occur on the day of the LORD:

- **Joel 2:10–11:** "The earth shall quake before them; the heavens shall tremble: the sun and the moon shall be dark, and the stars shall withdraw their shining: And the LORD shall utter his voice before his army: for his camp is very great: for he is strong that executeth his word: for the day of the LORD is great and very terrible; and who can abide it?"

- **Joel 3:14,16:** "Multitudes, multitudes in the valley of decision: for the day of the LORD is near in the valley of decision. . . . The LORD also shall roar out of Zion, and utter his voice from Jerusalem; and the heavens and the earth shall shake: but the LORD will be the hope of his people, and the strength of the children of Israel."

- **Isaiah 13:9–13:** "Behold, the day of the LORD cometh, cruel both with wrath and fierce anger, to lay the land desolate: and he shall destroy the sinners thereof out of it. For the stars of heaven and the constellations thereof shall not give their light: the sun shall be darkened in his going forth, and the moon shall not cause her light to shine. And I will punish the world for their evil, and the wicked for their iniquity; and I will cause the arrogancy of the proud to cease, and will lay low the haughtiness of the terrible. I will make a man more precious than fine gold; even a man than the golden wedge of Ophir. Therefore I will shake the heavens, and the earth shall remove out of her place, in the wrath of the LORD of hosts, and in the day of his fierce anger."

During the day of the LORD, it is the Messiah who will come and rescue Jerusalem from her enemies. Meanwhile, when God disqualified Jeconiah's descendents as king, He removed Jeconiah as the signet on His right hand. Jeremiah 22:24 states, "As I live, saith the LORD, though Coniah the son of Jehoiakim king of Judah were the signet upon my right hand, yet would I pluck thee thence." According to Haggai 2:23, the Messiah, who is called Zerubbabel, was made as the signet. This indicates that the Jeconiah-Zerubbabel genealogy provides the arrow or direction to the Messiah even though Zerubbabel is subject to the curse of his grandfather.

As a result, the LORD has closed the doors on any imposter with an earthly father who would claim the throne of David. Therefore, the only eligible candidate for the Messiah is Jesus who was born of a virgin.

VIII. Joseph—Mary's Husband

In the New Testament, Matthew 1 records the genealogy of Joseph, Mary's husband. Matthew 1:6–16 states as follows:

> And Jesse begat David the king; and David the king begat Solomon of her that had been the wife of Urias; And Solomon begat Roboam; and Roboam begat Abia; and Abia begat Asa; And Asa begat Josaphat; and Josaphat begat Joram; and Joram begat Ozias; And Ozias begat Joatham; and Joatham begat Achaz; and Achaz begat Ezekias; And Ezekias begat Manasses; and Manasses begat Amon; and Amon begat Josias; And Josias begat Jechonias and his brethren, about the time they were carried away to Babylon: And after they were brought to Babylon, Jechonias begat Salathiel; and Salathiel begat Zorobabel; And Zorobabel begat Abiud; and Abiud begat Eliakim; and Eliakim begat Azor; And Azor begat Sadoc; and Sadoc begat Achim; and Achim begat Eliud; And Eliud begat Eleazar; and Eleazar begat Matthan; and Matthan begat Jacob; And Jacob begat Joseph the husband of Mary, of whom was born Jesus, who is called Christ.

This passage illustrates that Joseph was a direct descendent of the royal line of David through Solomon. According to verses 11–12, he was also a descendent of Jeconiah and Zerubbabel. Since Jeremiah 22:30 declares that all of Jeconiah's descendents are disqualified from claiming the throne of David as king, Joseph was also disqualified. Most importantly, if Jesus were the biological offspring of Joseph, He would also be ineligible to claim the throne of David because He would fall under the very same curse as His father.

In this chapter, the Gospel writer boldly addresses the curse on Jeconiah's descendents. Then he went on to explain how God circumvented this curse and resolved the matter by becoming the Father of the Messiah Himself. In other words, the Messiah, the Savior of the world, was born of a virgin! Matthew explained that while Joseph and Mary were espoused, before they came together as husband and wife, she became pregnant of the Holy Ghost. According to Matthew 1:18–23, this was the fulfillment of what was written by the prophet Isaiah:

- **Matthew 1:18–23:** "Now the birth of Jesus Christ was on this wise: When as his mother Mary was espoused to Joseph, before they came together, she was found with child of the Holy Ghost. Then Joseph her husband, being a just man, and not willing to make her a publick example, was minded to put her away privily. But while he thought on these things, behold, the angel of the Lord appeared unto him in a dream, saying, Joseph, thou son of David, fear not to take unto thee Mary thy wife: for that which is conceived in her is of the Holy Ghost. And she shall bring forth a son, and thou shalt call his name JESUS: for he shall save his people from their sins. Now all this was done, that it might be fulfilled which was spoken of the Lord by the prophet, saying, Behold, a virgin shall be with child, and shall bring forth a son, and they shall call his name Emmanuel, which being interpreted is, God with us."
- **Isaiah 7:14:** "Therefore the Lord himself shall give you a sign; Behold, a virgin shall conceive, and bear a son, and shall call his name Immanuel."

Heli: Mary's Father

The Bible provides the lineage of Heli, Mary's father[31] in Luke 3:23,31 as follows: "And Jesus himself began to be about thirty years of age, being (as was supposed) the son of Joseph, which was the son of Heli. . . . Which was the son of Melea, which was the son of Menan, which was the son of Mattatha, which was the son of Nathan, which was the son of David."

Many people get confused between this genealogy and the genealogy listed in Matthew 1 because Joseph's name appears in both sections and Mary's name does not appear in either section. The reason for this is as follows: According to Jewish tradition, it is not normally an acceptable practice to list a woman's name in a genealogy. When listing a woman's genealogy, it is better to use her husband's name instead. Such is the case in Luke's genealogy of Heli, the father of Mary.

Luke 3:23,31 informs us that God's eternal promise to David was fulfilled through Heli's [Mary's] genealogy because Heli was a descendent of David. As a result, his daughter [who was Jesus' mother] was also a descendent of David, but not from David through Solomon. She descended from David through another of his sons, Nathan.

IX. Tribal Affiliation by Adoption

According to Genesis 49:10, when Jacob blessed his sons, this is what he said to Judah: "The sceptre shall not depart from Judah, nor a lawgiver from between his feet, until Shiloh come; and unto him shall the gathering of the people be."

This messianic prophecy foretells that the Messiah, the one who would gather His people, would come from the tribe of Judah. Because of this, counter-missionaries attempt to disqualify Jesus as the Messiah since the New Testament instructs us that He is the begotten Son of God. According to them, Jesus could not be from Judah because his biological father was not a descendent from that tribe. In order to justify their position, Judaism's defenders cite the Torah, Numbers 1:18, which states: "And they [the children of Israel] assembled all the congregation together on the first day of the second month, and they declared their pedigrees after their families, by the house of their fathers, according to the number of the names, from twenty years old and upward, by their polls."

From this verse, it is apparent that those embracing Judaism are correct: a child's tribal affiliation depends solely upon the tribal affiliation of his or her father. But does it have to be the child's biological father?

Many who accept Jesus as the prophesied Messiah take the position that His tribal affiliation was established through His adopted father Joseph. However, the rabbis blatantly disagree. They claim that the Scriptures are absent of any evidence to support that a child's tribal affiliation is based upon the tribe of the adopted father. Well, they are wrong!

Jonathan, the son of Gershom, the son of Moses
Judges 17:7 states the following: "And there was a young man out of Beth-

lehemjudah of the family of Judah, who was a Levite, and he sojourned there."

This verse presents a problem for those embracing the rabbinical teaching that a child's tribal affiliation depends solely upon his or her biological father because it states that there was a man "of the family of Judah, who was a Levite." How can this be? In order to answer this question, it is important, if possible, to find this man's name as well as his genealogy. After reading from Judges 17:7 to Judges 18:30, his identity is revealed. Judges 18:30 states that he is "Jonathan, the son of Gershom" as follows: "And the children of Dan set up the graven image: and Jonathan, the son of Gershom, the son of Manasseh,* he and his sons were priests to the tribe of Dan until the day of the captivity of the land."

Exodus 2:1–10 reveals that Moses was a Levite. Therefore his son Gershom [see Exodus 2:21–22], must have also been a Levite. So why does the Bible describe Gershom's son Jonathan as a Levite from the family of Judah? The only logical explanation is as follows: Jonathan's biological father, though unidentified, was from the tribe of Judah. When he died, Gershom took Jonathan's mother as his wife and took in Jonathan as his adopted son. This would explain why Judges 17:7 describes Jonathan as a Levite from the family of Judah. His biological father was from the tribe of Judah, but his adopted father was a Levite.

This biblical precedent provides evidence that a child's adopted father can determine his or her tribal affiliation because, when Gershom married Jonathan's mother and took her child into his household, the boy became incorporated into Levi, Gershom's tribe.

These same circumstances are applied to Joseph, Mary, and Jesus. When Joseph [of the tribe of Judah] married Mary, and took Jesus into his household, the child became a member of Joseph's tribe. In other words, just as Jonathan became a Levite because his adopted father was a Levite, Jesus was of the tribe of Judah because Joseph was of the tribe of Judah.

Another interesting explanation for Judges 17:7 is provided by Rabbi Solomon ben Isaac, also known as Rashi, a highly respected Jewish sage

---

* Note: According to the 1917 JPS, evidence indicates another reading, "Moses," which is consistent with Exodus 2.

who lived from A.D. 1040–1105. Though he did not believe that Jesus is the Messiah, his commentary on this verse was quite interesting: He believed that Jonathan was called a Levite because his mother was a Levite. From this verse, Rashi concluded that there were occasions when the mother established her child's tribal affiliation.[32] As a result, Rashi would have certainly agreed that Jesus is from the tribe of Judah because Mary was from Judah.

In summary, Jonathan's case provides evidence that the adopted father determines a child's tribal affiliation. And even though Rashi's view on Judges 17:7 is quite different, believers in Jesus can remain confident that there is both biblical and Jewish support that He is from the tribe of Judah.

X. God Fulfills His Promise to David

As we have seen, because of the continued rebellion of Solomon and his descendants, God eliminated them from the paternal line to the Messiah. Remembering this, God's promise to David remained unconditional. How would He resolve it? The answer is clear: The Messiah would be the Son of God paternally, and the Son of David through Heli, Mary's father. Luke 1:30–35 records the words that the angel said to Mary:

And the angel said unto her, Fear not, Mary: for thou hast found favour with God. And, behold, thou shalt conceive in thy womb, and bring forth a son, and shalt call his name Jesus. He shall be great, and shall be called the Son of the Highest: and the Lord God shall give unto him the throne of his father David: And he shall reign over the house of Jacob for ever; and of his kingdom there shall be no end. Then said Mary unto the angel, How shall this be, seeing I know not a man? And the angel answered and said unto her, The Holy Ghost shall come upon thee, and the power of the Highest shall overshadow thee: therefore also that holy thing which shall be born of thee shall be called the Son of God.

Ever since mankind's spiritual downfall in the garden, God indicated that it would be through the seed of the woman that sin would be defeated. In

Genesis 3:15, He told the serpent who tempted Eve the following, "And I will put enmity between thee and the woman, and between thy seed and her seed; it shall bruise thy head, and thou shalt bruise his heel." It is generally believed that the seed of the serpent is sin; and the seed of the woman, Mary, is the Messiah.

In conclusion, Galatians 4:4–7 declares:

> But when the fulness of the time was come, God sent forth his Son, made of a woman, made under the law, To redeem them that were under the law, that we might receive the adoption of sons. And because ye are sons, God hath sent forth the Spirit of his Son into your hearts, crying, Abba, Father. Wherefore thou art no more a servant, but a son; and if a son, then an heir of God through Christ.

Chapter Three

Isaiah 7:14—Immanuel

I. Introduction

According to the previous chapter, the Hebrew scriptures lay the foundation for the Messiah's virgin birth. It explains that God cut off the genealogical pathway to the Messiah as a result of the continued rebellion by Solomon and his heirs.

Though the Messiah's virgin birth is clearly taught in the Hebrew scriptures, it was foretold in one single verse, Isaiah 7:14. Those who oppose this virgin birth prophecy openly challenge its Hebrew-to-English translation. In the King James Bible, Isaiah 7:14 reads, "Therefore the Lord himself shall give you a sign; Behold, a virgin [*almah*] shall conceive, and bear a son, and shall call his name Immanuel." Contrary to this translation, Jewish Bibles translate this same verse in a slightly different manner as follows, "Therefore the Lord Himself shall give you a sign: behold, the young woman [*almah*] shall conceive, and bear a son, and shall call his name Immanuel."

In order to establish which translation is more accurate, we should consider two things: the historical significance of the passage and the Hebrew definition of the word *almah*.

II. Historical Significance

Isaiah 7 chronicles the exchange between Isaiah and Ahaz during the prophet's visit to the king. It also bears witness to the king's disobedience and absence of faith during their meeting. Additionally, it records God's final judgment on the house of David [the House of Judah's kings] indicating that He would no longer consider them eligible progenitors to the Messiah.

During Isaiah's ministry as God's prophet, King Ahaz was one of Judah's reigning kings. His genealogy is found in 1 Chronicles 3:10–13 as follows: "And Solomon's son was Rehoboam, Abia his son, Asa his son, Jehoshaphat his son, Joram his son, Ahaziah his son, Joash his son, Amaziah his son, Azariah his son, Jotham his son, Ahaz his son, Hezekiah his son, Manasseh his son."

In 2 Kings 16:2–4, the Bible teaches that Ahaz was an evil king. It reads:

> Twenty years old was Ahaz when he began to reign, and reigned sixteen years in Jerusalem, and did not that which was right in the sight of the LORD his God, like David his father. But he walked in the way of the kings of Israel, yea, and made his son to pass through the fire, according to the abominations of the heathen, whom the LORD cast out from before the children of Israel. And he sacrificed and burnt incense in the high places, and on the hills, and under every green tree.

This passage describes some of the king's sins as he sacrificed and burnt incense to pagan gods. He also made his son pass through the fire. Second Chronicles 28:3 further testifies to Ahaz's spiritual rebellion as follows: "Moreover he burnt incense in the valley of the son of Hinnom, and burnt his children in the fire, after the abominations of the heathen whom the LORD had cast out before the children of Israel." Based on this evidence, regarding God's demands to David's descendents to be morally upright, there can be no doubt that Ahaz was a complete and utter failure.

During Ahaz's reign as Judah's king, there came a time when both Rezin, king of Syria, and Pekah, the son of Remaliah, king of Israel, joined forces against him. They came to Jerusalem in an attempt to overthrow him, but had not been successful. He was extremely concerned about not only this life-threatening circumstance, but also the future of the house of David. Second Kings 16:5 and Isaiah 7:1 confirm this situation confronting Ahaz:

- **2 Kings 16:5:** "Then Rezin king of Syria and Pekah son of Remaliah king of Israel came up to Jerusalem to war: and they besieged Ahaz, but could not overcome him."
- **Isaiah 7:1:** "And it came to pass in the days of Ahaz the son of Jotham, the son of Uzziah, king of Judah, that Rezin the king of Syria, and Pekah the son of Remaliah, king of Israel, went up toward Jerusalem to war against it, but could not prevail against it."

Isaiah 7 begins with God commanding Isaiah to take his son Shearjashub and meet with the king. God instructed Isaiah to tell him not to be discouraged or concerned about those who were opposing him. According to the LORD, Rezin and Pekah's attempts would fail. In Isaiah 7:3–7, Isaiah was there to encourage the king that the LORD God was with him:

Then said the LORD unto Isaiah, Go forth now to meet Ahaz, thou, and Shearjashub thy son, at the end of the conduit of the upper pool in the highway of the fuller's field. And say unto him, Take heed, and be quiet; fear not, neither be fainthearted for the two tails of these smoking firebrands, for the fierce anger of Rezin with Syria, and of the son of Remaliah. Because Syria, Ephraim, and the son of Remaliah, have taken evil counsel against thee, saying, Let us go up against Judah, and vex it, and let us make a breach therein for us, and set a king in the midst of it, even the son of Tabeal: Thus saith the Lord GOD, It shall not stand, neither shall it come to pass.

According to the prophet, although Rezin and Pekah were coming against him, the House of Israel, represented by Ephraim, would eventually be defeated. The Bible reveals God's words in Isaiah 7:8–9 that this defeat would occur within a sixty-five–year period:

For the head of Syria is Damascus, and the head of Damascus is Rezin; and within threescore and five years shall Ephraim be broken, that it be not a people. And the head of Ephraim is Samaria, and the head of Samaria is Remaliah's son. If ye will not believe, surely ye shall not be established.

According to Isaiah 7:9, Isaiah gives Ahaz an ultimatum as follows: "If ye will not believe, surely ye shall not be established." In other words, the condition for Ahaz' throne to continue was his belief in the LORD.

It was now time to test Ahaz's faith! Isaiah 7:10–11 explains that the LORD, through Isaiah, asked Ahaz the following, "Ask thee a sign of the LORD thy God; ask it either in the depth, or in the height above." In defiance against God, Ahaz tells Isaiah in Isaiah 7:12, "I will not ask, neither will I tempt the LORD."

Ahaz's demonstration of defiance, unbelief, and absence of cooperation with the prophet resulted in the LORD's immediate response against the house of David and the Judaic line of kings as follows: Since Ahaz failed to meet the requirement stipulated in Isaiah 7:9 by not believing God, his throne would *not* be established. The result was the LORD's final judgment against the house of David. Because David's heirs beginning with Solomon failed to meet God's conditions, the LORD's unconditional promise to David would be fulfilled in a sign: a virgin would conceive and bear a son. In other words, God Himself would become the Father of the Messiah! In Isaiah 7:13–14, the prophet's words reveal: "Hear ye now, O house of David; Is it a small thing for you to weary men, but will ye weary my God also? Therefore the Lord himself shall give you a sign; Behold, a virgin shall conceive, and bear a son, and shall call his name Immanuel."

III. Almah—Rebekah Provides the Definition

Since the historical context of Isaiah 7 has now been explained, there is one other matter to consider: the true translation of the Hebrew word *almah*. According to the Scriptures, which is correct? Is an *almah* a virgin or a young woman? The answer: based on the context when this word is used in the Bible, both are correct because an *almah* is a young woman who is a virgin.

It is important to keep in mind that the prophets use the word *almah* on six other occasions besides Isaiah's usage in Isaiah 7:14. This word is used in Genesis 24:43 to describe Rebekah; can be found in Exodus 2:8 to define Moses' sister Miriam; and is also found in Psalm 68:25, Proverbs 30:19, Song of Songs 1:3, and Song of Songs 6:8. Isaiah was the last prophet to use this word. Since it is only used seven times in the Hebrew scriptures, it is obviously a very unique word.

In order to understand the true meaning of an *almah,* we should refer to the first time it is used in the Scriptures and consider God's everlasting covenant that would continue through Abraham's son Isaac. Genesis 17:19 testifies to God's promise to Abraham as follows: "And God said, Sarah thy wife shall bear thee a son indeed; and thou shalt call his name Isaac: and I will establish my covenant with him for an everlasting covenant, and with his seed after him."

At Isaac's birth, Abraham was obviously aware that his son was someone special. As Isaac approached manhood and became of age to take a wife, his father expressed a legitimate concern because they lived in the land of the Canaanites. According to Leviticus 18, these were people who were idol worshippers and practiced all types of sexual immorality. Naturally, Abraham preferred that the everlasting covenant between God and himself would not continue by his son's marriage to a pagan Canaanite woman. To the contrary, he preferred that Isaac marry a pure and virtuous young woman. The LORD God felt the same way. This is where the story of Rebekah begins!

Genesis 24 begins with Abraham commanding his eldest servant to go to his home country in Mesopotamia, to the city of Nahor, to find a respectable wife for Isaac. Upon his arrival, the servant prayed to God and asked Him to bless Abraham. Genesis 24:12–14 records the prayer of Abraham's servant as follows:

And he said, O LORD God of my master Abraham, I pray thee, send me good speed this day, and shew kindness unto my master Abraham.

Behold, I stand here by the well of water; and the daughters of the men of the city come out to draw water: And let it come to pass, that the damsel to whom I shall say, Let down thy pitcher, I pray thee, that I may drink; and she shall say, Drink, and I will give thy camels drink also: let the same be she that thou hast appointed for thy servant Isaac; and thereby shall I know that thou hast shewed kindness unto my master.

Genesis 24:15 tells us that Rebekah came out with a pitcher on her shoulder before Abraham's servant was finished praying. The following verse, Genesis 24:16, describes Rebekah in the following manner: "And the damsel [*naarah*] was very fair to look upon, a virgin [*betulah*], neither had any man known her: and she went down to the well, and filled her pitcher, and came up."

Genesis 24:16 tells us that Rebekah was called a *naarah*. *Strong's Concordance* (#5291) defines a *naarah* as a girl from the age of infancy to adolescence. Additionally in the same verse, she was called a *betulah*. *Strong's Concordance* (#1330) defines a *betulah* as a virgin of any age.

Abraham's servant became elated because he had found the perfect wife for Isaac, an adolescent girl who was a virgin. In Genesis 24:43, the same chapter, he was recalling the incident back at the well. Regarding Rebekah, he stated as follows, "Behold, I stand by the well of water; and it shall come to pass, that when the virgin [*almah*] cometh forth to draw water, and I say to her, Give me, I pray thee, a little water of thy pitcher to drink." This verse provides the foundational use of the word *almah,* which is also translated virgin. Because a *betulah* is defined as a virgin of any age, and since Rebekah was also called a *naarah,* the conclusion is rather obvious: Genesis 24:16,43 provides the basis that an *almah* is a *naarah* who is a *betulah*. In other words, an *almah* is a young woman of marriageable age who is a virgin. The equation: *naarah* + *betulah* = *almah*.

In conclusion, Rebekah is the prototype *almah*. Isaiah understood this and used this word in Isaiah 7:14 to describe the character and attributes of the future mother of the Messiah. She too would adhere to the qualities of a pure and virtuous young virgin of marriageable age . . . just like Rebekah.

IV. Countering Rabbinic Judaism

Even though Genesis 24:16,43 provides the Bible's definition of an *almah,* those embracing rabbinic teachings constantly challenge its meaning. After all, if Isaiah 7:14 foretells a virgin birth, they must reconsider their position regarding Jesus of Nazareth. Obviously, this is something that they are not willing to do.

On occasion, Judaism's defenders refer to Proverbs 30:18–20 to try to build a case against an *almah* always being a virgin. This passage reads as follows:

> There are three things which are too wonderful for me, yea, four which I know not: The way of an eagle in the air; the way of a serpent upon a rock; the way of a ship in the midst of the sea; and the way of a man with a young woman [*almah*]. So is the way of an adulterous woman; she eateth, and wipeth her mouth, And saith: "I have done no wickedness."

This translation was taken from the 1917 Jewish Publication Society Bible. Here, the proverb writer describes wonderful and majestic things, like the way of an eagle in the air, the way of a ship in the midst of the sea, the way of a serpent upon a rock, and the way of a man with an *almah,* translated as young woman.

Judaism's counter-missionaries attempt to challenge the context of Proverbs 30:18–19 by using the next verse, "So is the way of an adulterous woman; she eateth, and wipeth her mouth, And saith: 'I have done no wickedness.'" They claim that the adulterous woman in verse 20 is the *almah* in verse 19. Then they use this as their justification that an *almah* does not always describe a virtuous and chaste young woman. However, their position is seriously flawed since verses 18–19 depict wonderful things. Certainly the way of a man with an adulterous woman cannot be described as wonderful. According to the Bible, it is sin! Exodus 20:14 states, "Thou shalt not commit adultery."

In reality, according to Proverbs 30:18–19, the proverb writer describes wonderful things. In verse 20, he portrays sin. As a result, the sin described in verse 20 provides the contrast to the wonderful things depicted in verses 18–19. Things that are wonderful to a man include his way of courting an *almah,* a young woman who is a virgin, just like Rebekah was before she married Isaac.

Seeking Other Candidates

In another effort to resist the Isaiah 7:14 virgin birth prophecy, Judaism's followers seek other candidates for the foretold child born to an *almah.* Some of them claim that King Ahaz was the child's father. However, Ahaz could only be the father of a child conceived with a queen or concubine, **not** an *almah.* Song of Songs 6:8 provides an important distinction as follows, "There are threescore queens, and fourscore concubines, and virgins [in Hebrew *alamot,* the plural for *almah*] without number." This verse alone eliminates King Ahaz as the father of the child conceived by an *almah.* By Bible definition, he could only be the father of a child conceived by a queen or concubine. But there is another reason to disqualify King Ahaz:

According to 2 Kings 16:2–3 and 2 Chronicles 28:1–3, Ahaz was an evil king who offered his children through the fires of pagan gods. Apparently, his heirs who survived these atrocities died from other causes without having sons of their own. For these reasons, 1 Chronicles 3:13 reveals that by the time Ahaz died, his son Hezekiah was the sole qualified heir to the throne.

Remembering this, when Isaiah came to visit the king in Isaiah 7 which ultimately resulted in the virgin birth prophecy of a child not yet born, Hezekiah was already at least nine years of age. This is demonstrated by referring to the following verses:

- **2 Kings 16:2:** "Twenty years old was Ahaz when he began to reign, and reigned sixteen years in Jerusalem, and did not that which was right in the sight of the LORD his God, like David his father."
- **2 Kings 16:20:** "And Ahaz slept with his fathers, and was buried with his fathers in the city of David: and Hezekiah his son reigned in his stead."

- **2 Kings 18:2**—*regarding Hezekiah:* "Twenty and five years old was he when he began to reign; and he reigned twenty and nine years in Jerusalem. His mother's name also was Abi, the daughter of Zachariah."

According to 2 Kings 16:2, the Bible tells us that Ahaz was twenty years old when he began to reign and he ruled for sixteen years. Therefore, his kingship ended at the age of thirty-six (20 + 16 = 36). We also see that 2 Kings 16:20 indicates that his son Hezekiah took the throne as king immediately upon Ahaz' death. Moreover, 2 Kings 18:2 provides critical information that Hezekiah was twenty-five years old when his kingship began. Therefore, since Ahaz died at the age of thirty-six and Hezekiah took the throne at the age of twenty-five, Hezekiah was eleven years younger than Ahaz (36 – 25 = 11). Since Isaiah 7 records Isaiah's visit to King Ahaz, and Ahaz began his reign at age twenty, his son Hezekiah must have been at least nine years of age at the time of Isaiah's visit (20 – 11 = 9). Once again, this proves that Ahaz' son Hezekiah could not possibly be the subject of Isaiah 7:14 since the verse foretells the birth of a child not yet born.

Regarding Isaiah 7:14, Judaism's counter-missionaries attempt to place one final candidate into the equation: Isaiah's wife, the prophetess mentioned in Isaiah 8. In Isaiah 8:3, Isaiah states: "And I [Isaiah] went unto the prophetess; and she conceived, and bare a son. Then said the Lord to me, Call his name Mahershalalhashbaz."

Unfortunately for Judaism's defenders, Isaiah's son Mahershalalhashbaz cannot be the subject of Isaiah 7:14 for two reasons. First, an *almah* never applies to a married woman in the Bible. Secondly, it never applies to a woman who already has a child. We need to remember that Isaiah and the prophetess already had a son. According to Isaiah 7:3, when Isaiah went to meet King Ahaz, he took his son Shearjashub with him.

In summary, the Scriptures reveal that Ahaz was an evil king. He demonstrated his defiance, unbelief, and absence of faith in God and failed to meet the requirement stipulated in Isaiah 7:9. As the Lord promised, his throne would not be established, and his progeny was cut off and consumed in God's anger. It should also be remembered that he clearly failed to meet the conditions God gave to David's heirs described in Psalm 132:12, etc. Hence, the LORD Himself would become the Father of the Messiah. The result: Isaiah 7:14's virgin birth prophecy!

Author's note: Regarding the context of Isaiah 7:14 and the prophet's use of the word *almah,* it is clear that his intention was to inform us that a miraculous birth would someday take place . . . a virgin would conceive. But because of this prophecy's fulfillment by Jesus the Messiah, Judaism's rabbis consistently remain in denial by openly challenging the definition of this Hebrew word. Perhaps they should refer to Rashi, their own highly-acclaimed Jewish sage. In his commentary on Song of Songs 1:3, he indicated that *alamot* [the Hebrew plural for *almah*] were *betulot* [the Hebrew plural for virgins].[33]

Chapter Four

Messiah—Son of David and Begotten Son of God

I. Introduction

The New Testament, as a fulfillment of the Hebrew scriptures, tells us that not only is the Messiah the son of David, He is also God's only begotten Son. But those adhering to the teachings of rabbinic Judaism are instructed differently. They are taught that the Messiah would never be God's literal Son. So they seek a messiah who is a physical descendent of human kings.

II. God's Chosen Sons

Regarding the LORD's words to David's descendents beginning with Solomon, they were considered to be His chosen sons. In other words they would be types of the Messiah, God's only begotten Son. As proof, in 1 Chronicles 28:4–6, King David declares that Solomon would succeed him as king. In this passage, he indicates that Solomon would sit on the throne as God's chosen son:

> Howbeit the LORD God of Israel chose me before all the house of my
> father to be king over Israel for ever: for he hath chosen Judah to be the
> ruler; and of the house of Judah, the house of my father; and among the

sons of my father he liked me to make me king over all Israel: And of all my sons, (for the LORD hath given me many sons,) he hath chosen Solomon my son to sit upon the throne of the kingdom of the LORD over Israel. And he said unto me, Solomon thy son, he shall build my house and my courts: for I have chosen him to be my son, and I will be his father.

The Bible also records God's promise to David in 2 Samuel 7:13–16. Regarding David's throne, it confirms two important things. First, the LORD would set up His everlasting kingdom through one of David's descendents. Secondly and more importantly, He calls this descendent His own son. Regarding David's son:

He shall build an house for my name, and I will stablish the throne of his kingdom for ever. I will be his father, and he shall be my son. If he commit iniquity, I will chasten him with the rod of men, and with the stripes of the children of men: But my mercy shall not depart away from him, as I took it from Saul, whom I put away before thee. And thine house and thy kingdom shall be established for ever before thee: thy throne shall be established for ever.

In this passage, God tells David that His son, one of David's descendents, would eternally reign as king. But logic tells us that since Solomon and his heirs died without fulfilling this prophecy, none of them are the cause of its fulfillment. Though these chosen sons of God failed, the Messiah as God's only begotten Son (and the son of David) will fulfill the LORD's unconditional promise to David and reign forever as King over the entire world.

And in fulfillment of the Hebrew scriptures, the New Testament stresses that it was Jesus Christ, both the Son of God and son of David, who will reign over the descendents of Jacob forever. Luke 1:30–33 states:

And the angel said unto her, Fear not, Mary: for thou hast found favour with God. And, behold, thou shalt conceive in thy womb, and bring forth a son, and shalt call his name JESUS. He shall be great, and shall be called the Son of the Highest: and the Lord God shall give unto him the throne of his father David: And he shall reign over the house of Jacob for ever; and of his kingdom there shall be no end.

III. Countering Rabbinic Judaism

Judaism's rabbis blatantly deny that the Messiah is God's begotten Son even though this is clearly taught in the Hebrew scriptures. These are the words in Psalm 2:6–9:

> Yet have I set my king upon my holy hill of Zion. I will declare the decree: the LORD hath said unto me, Thou art my Son; this day have I begotten thee. Ask of me, and I shall give thee the heathen for thine inheritance, and the uttermost parts of the earth for thy possession. Thou shalt break them with a rod of iron; thou shalt dash them in pieces like a potter's vessel.

This section of the Bible provides the evidence that God has a begotten son. In verse 7, the Hebrew word *yalad* is used (*Strong's*, #3205). It translates "to beget." Throughout the centuries, the subject of this passage has been debated or argued between Christians (who believe that this is the Messiah) and Judaism's defenders (who believe that this is King David).

Using the Bible as our source of reference, it is easy to prove that the person spoken of in Psalm 2:6–9 is not David. For instance, verse 7 tells us that he would be begotten of God. This could not be David who, according to 1 Chronicles 2:13–15 and Ruth 4:22, was begotten of Jesse:

+ **1 Chronicles 2:13–15:** "And Jesse begat his firstborn Eliab, and Abinadab the second, and Shimma the third, Nethaneel the fourth, Raddai the fifth, Ozem the sixth, David the seventh"
+ **Ruth 4:22:** "And Obed begat Jesse, and Jesse begat David."

Secondly, Psalm 2:8 tells us that this individual would be given the uttermost parts of the earth for his possession. This never happened to David, whose kingdom was restricted only to Israel.

And finally, Psalm 2:9 reveals that the subject would break the kingdoms of the earth in pieces "like a potter's vessel." David never accomplished this . . . but the Messiah will!

The prophet Daniel himself tells us that Psalm 2:6–9 is about the Messiah. As a reminder, Psalm 2:8 states that God's King would be given the entire world for His possession. And according to Daniel's vision described in Daniel 7:13–14, it would be King Messiah, called the Son of man, who is given the entire world for an everlasting kingdom:

> I [Daniel] saw in the night visions, and, behold, one like the Son of man came with the clouds of heaven, and came to the Ancient of days, and they brought him near before him. And there was given him dominion, and glory, and a kingdom, that all people, nations, and languages, should serve him: his dominion is an everlasting dominion, which shall not pass away, and his kingdom that which shall not be destroyed.

As a final reminder, Psalm 2:9 informs us that God's begotten Son would destroy the kingdoms of the earth "like a potter's vessel." Remembering this, when the LORD revealed to Daniel the understanding of Nebuchadnezzar's dream of a great image representing the future kingdoms of the earth being destroyed by a stone, Daniel 2:44–45 tells us what Daniel told the king:

> And in the days of these kings shall the God of heaven set up a kingdom, which shall never be destroyed: and the kingdom shall not be left to other people, but it shall break in pieces and consume all these kingdoms, and it shall stand for ever. Forasmuch as thou sawest that the stone was cut out of the mountain without hands, and that it brake in pieces the iron, the brass, the clay, the silver, and the gold; the great God hath made known to the king what shall come to pass hereafter: and the dream is certain, and the interpretation thereof sure.

In this passage, Daniel reveals to the king of Babylon that God's kingdom on earth (the messianic reign) would begin immediately after a great stone, cut out of the mountain without hands, "breaks in pieces" the final kingdoms of the earth described as "iron mixed with clay" (see Dan. 2:43). This wording clearly parallels the language used in Psalm 2:9 and the breaking of the kingdoms in pieces like "a potter's vessel." And according to Jeremiah 23:5, this is exactly what the Messiah would accomplish when He executes judgment and justice in the earth. As a result, Daniel 2:44–45 provides the perfect cross-reference to Psalm 2:9, proving once and for all that it is the Messiah, God's begotten Son (Ps. 2:7), who is the subject of the Psalm 2:6–9 passage.

IV. The New Testament and the Son of God

Those who place their faith in rabbinical teachings believe much differently from the Israelites who lived approximately two thousand years ago. For example, at the time Jesus raised Lazarus from the dead, Lazarus' sister Martha knew that the Messiah would be the Son of God. According to John 11:27, her confession of faith was in line with the Hebrew scriptures: "She saith unto him, Yea, Lord: I believe that thou art the Christ, the Son of God, which should come into the world."

Additionally in Matthew 16:15, Jesus asked Peter, "But whom say ye that I am?" In the following verse Peter responded, ". . . Thou art the Christ, the Son of the living God." Peter's answer testifies that he was also aware that the Messiah would be the Son of God.

Finally, when Jesus was arrested and tried, the high priest asked Him about His identity. Jesus did not answer him until the high priest confronted Him with the following question in Matthew 26:63, ". . . I adjure thee by the living God, that thou tell us whether thou be the Christ, the Son of God." In asking this question, it is also quite clear that the high priest was aware that the Messiah would be the Son of God.

The Son of God, Beaten for Sin

After Jesus was questioned by the high priest, the chief priests and elders wanted Him killed. But at that moment, Jesus was at the height of His popularity. As a result of all His miracles and wonderful teachings, many believed He was the Messiah. Consequently, since He had many followers and the priests and elders were concerned about their own popularity, they preferred the Roman government make the decision to destroy Him. So according to Matthew 27:1–2, the following morning Jesus was sent to Pilate the Roman governor.

Pilate eventually gave the Jews a choice to free either Jesus or Barabbas. Matthew 27:20 states: "But the chief priests and elders persuaded the multitude that they should ask Barabbas, and destroy Jesus."

Because the chief priests and the elders had an influence over the people, they chose to free Barabbas. It was then when Jesus was taken away to be beaten again. As further punishment, John 19:2 states that they placed a crown of thorns on His head. Even though this was done, John 19:4 attests that Pilate believed that Jesus was innocent of any wrongdoing, "Pilate therefore went forth again, and saith unto them, Behold, I bring him forth to you, that ye may know that I find no fault in him."

John 19:6 continues to explain that, "When the chief priests therefore and officers saw him, they cried out, saying, Crucify him, crucify him. Pilate saith unto them, Take ye him, and crucify him: for I find no fault in him." The Jews responded in the following verse, in John 19:7, as follows, ". . . We have a law, and by our law he ought to die, because he made himself the Son of God."

It is important to remember that the Messiah as the Son of God is clearly taught in the Hebrew scriptures. Though the chief priests and elders were certainly aware of this, it seems they were depending on Pilate's ignorance of this fact so that Jesus could be put to death.

When Pilate heard these accusations against Jesus, he returned to the judgment hall to ask Him who He was claiming to be. After all, if Jesus was claiming to be the Son of God and therefore the Son of Israel's heavenly King, the Roman governor had a responsibility to make sure that He was not plotting any insurrection or rebellion to overthrow Caesar. If Jesus was found guilty of rebelling against the Roman Empire and their king, He would most assuredly be put to death. Jesus initially provided no response to Pilate's questioning until Pilate said in John 19:10, ". . . Speakest thou not unto me? knowest thou not that I have power to crucify thee, and have power to release thee?" In the following verse, Jesus answers, ". . . Thou couldest have no power at all against me, except it were given thee from above: therefore he that delivered me unto thee hath the greater sin." After further questioning, Pilate remained convinced that Jesus was innocent of any wrongdoing. John 19:12 records: "And from thenceforth Pilate sought to release him: but the Jews cried out, saying, If thou let this man go, thou art not Caesar's friend: whosoever maketh himself a king speaketh against Caesar."

When the Roman governor heard that the Jews were threatening to challenge his loyalty to Caesar, he made the wrongful decision to put this innocent man to death by refusing to deal with the matter any further. He became just as guilty as anyone else! He then ordered Jesus brought before the crowd. John 19:14 tells us that, ". . . it was the preparation of the passover, and about the sixth hour: and he saith unto the Jews, Behold your King!" In the following passage, John 19:15–16 states: "But they cried out, Away with him, away with him, crucify him. Pilate saith unto them, Shall I crucify your King? The chief priests answered, We have no king but Caesar. Then delivered he him therefore unto them to be crucified. And they took Jesus, and led him away."

John 19:17 explains that they placed a cross on Jesus' back and forced Him to carry it to a place called Golgotha. It was there where they drove nails into His hands and His feet and hung Him on a cross to die a criminal's death. Though He was innocent, He was crucified!

John 19:19 informs us that, ". . . Pilate wrote a title, and put it on the cross. And the writing was, JESUS OF NAZARETH THE KING OF THE JEWS." John 19:21 tells us that the chief priests told Pilate, ". . . Write not, The King of the Jews; but that he said, I am King of the Jews." In the following verse, Pilate responded, ". . . What I have written I have written." Matthew 27:51–53 records the events that took place immediately after Jesus' death:

And, behold, the veil of the temple was rent in twain from the top to the bottom; and the earth did quake, and the rocks rent; And the graves were opened; and many bodies of the saints which slept arose, And came out of the graves after his resurrection, and went into the holy city, and appeared unto many.

In the following verse, Matthew 27:54 describes the reaction of those who witnessed what had taken place, "Now when the centurion, and they that were with him, watching Jesus, saw the earthquake, and those things that were done, they feared greatly, saying, Truly this was the Son of God."

Returning to 2 Samuel 7:13–16 and the words from the prophet Nathan to David, "He shall build an house for my name, and I will stablish the throne of his kingdom for ever. I will be his father, and he shall be my son. If he commit iniquity, I will chasten him with the rod of men, and with the stripes of the children of men."

As we have seen in chapter two, 1 Kings 11:1–10 testifies to Solomon's sins when he turned to the heathen gods of his many pagan wives and concubines. Though the Bible records his sins, he could never be the subject of 2 Samuel 7:13–16 because he was *never* beaten. However the Messiah, the only begotten Son of God and our sin-bearer, took the punishment that Solomon deserved. And as a result, He became the fulfillment of Nathan's prophecy to David. Regarding Jesus, 2 Corinthians 5:21 states: "For he hath made him to be sin for us, who knew no sin; that we might be made the righteousness of God in him."

Not only did Jesus take the punishment Solomon deserved, He took the punishment we all deserve as the result of our own sins. Although Hebrews 4:15 informs us that He never sinned, Isaiah 53:6 explains that He became our sin-bearer: "All we like sheep have gone astray; we have turned every one to his own way; and the LORD hath laid on him the iniquity of us all."

As prophesied in Isaiah 53:7–9, Jesus was innocent of any wrongdoing but never said a word in His defense. He was cut off or killed for the sins of God's people:

> He was oppressed, and he was afflicted, yet he opened not his mouth: he is brought as a lamb to the slaughter, and as a sheep before her shearers is dumb, so he openeth not his mouth. He was taken from prison and from judgment: and who shall declare his generation? for he was cut off out of the land of the living: for the transgression of my people was he stricken. And he made his grave with the wicked, and with the rich

in his death; because he had done no violence, neither was any deceit in his mouth.

Jesus of Nazareth, as both the son of David and the begotten Son of God, became the ultimate offering for sin. Through Him, mankind is reconciled to the Holy God of Israel. And with a final emphasis upon His ascension into Heaven, Acts 13:32–33 tells us: "And we declare unto you glad tidings, how that the promise which was made unto the fathers, God hath fulfilled the same unto us their children, in that he hath raised up Jesus again; as it is also written in the second psalm, Thou art my Son, this day have I begotten thee."

Chapter Five

Isaiah 9:6—
The Prophesied Birth of the Messiah

For unto us a child is born, unto us a son is given: and the government shall be upon his shoulder: and his name shall be called Wonderful, Counsellor, The mighty God, The everlasting Father, The Prince of Peace. Of the increase of his government and peace there shall be no end, upon the throne of David, and upon his kingdom, to order it, and to establish it with judgment and with justice from henceforth even for ever. The zeal of the LORD of hosts will perform this.

—Isaiah 9:6–7

Introduction

This chapter has five major objectives. They are as follows:

1. To refute Judaism's claim that the subject of Isaiah 9:6–7 is King Hezekiah, who was one of the kings of Judah who reigned during Isaiah's lifetime.
2. To establish the time period described in this verse. Was Isaiah referring to an event that had already taken place, was he describing a present condition, or was he prophesying a future event?
3. To prove that the Messiah is the subject of Isaiah 9:6–7.

4. To respond to Judaism's claim that Isaiah 9:6 is properly translated, from Hebrew to English, in the past tense and therefore translated incorrectly in Christian Bibles. This theory is used to support their position that King Hezekiah, who was already born at the time this was written, is the subject of the passage.

5. To illustrate that the names and characteristics of the child foretold in Isaiah 9:6 can only refer to the Messiah.[34]

I. Eliminating King Hezekiah

Counter-missionaries claim that Isaiah 9:6 was written in order to inspire and encourage King Hezekiah. During his reign, the Assyrians came to destroy the cities of Judah and capture Jerusalem. It was a very discouraging time for him as well as the entire nation because Assyria was a world empire. Using the Scriptures, let us determine Hezekiah's age when all this took place.

Second Kings 18:1–2 tells us that Hezekiah was twenty-five years old when he became king. Additionally, 2 Kings 18:13 informs us that Sennacherib, king of Assyria, came against Judah during the fourteenth year of Hezekiah's kingship. Therefore, Hezekiah must have been thirty-nine years old (25 + 14 = 39) when the Assyrians came against Judah. The applicable Scriptures follow:

- ✦ **2 Kings 18:1–2:** "Now it came to pass in the third year of Hoshea son of Elah king of Israel, that Hezekiah the son of Ahaz king of Judah began to reign. Twenty and five years old was he when he began to reign; and he reigned twenty and nine years in Jerusalem. His mother's name also was Abi, the daughter of Zachariah."
- ✦ **2 Kings 18:13:** "Now in the fourteenth year of king Hezekiah did Sennacherib king of Assyria come up against all the fenced cities of Judah, and took them."

Could the phrase "for unto us a child is born" apply to a person who was thirty-nine years old and the king of Judah for fourteen years? After coming to this realization, even the most devout counter-missionary should find this difficult to believe. It is illogical to apply this verse to King Hezekiah because his age at the time this was written should eliminate him as the subject of this passage.

There are many other ways to show that Hezekiah could not be the subject of Isaiah 9:6–7. For example, according to Isaiah 39, the LORD became infuriated with his display of pride and foolishness when he opened his doors to pagan Babylonians and showed them all the treasures in his house. This should certainly disqualify him as a Wonderful Counsellor which is one of the names given to the child in Isaiah 9:6.

Additionally, Judaism's claim that Isaiah 9:6–7 was written to encourage Hezekiah that, through him, the throne of David would be eternally established is baseless for the following reason: As punishment for Hezekiah's stupidity, the prophet Isaiah informs him that all of his descendents would be taken into prison and made eunuchs by the king of Babylon. Since eunuchs are castrated men and incapable of fathering children, this shows that Hezekiah's throne would not be eternally established:

> [Isaiah informs Hezekiah] ". . . Hear the word of the LORD of hosts: Behold, the days come, that all that is in thine house, and that which thy fathers have laid up in store until this day, shall be carried to Babylon: nothing shall be left, saith the LORD. And of thy sons that shall issue from thee, which thou shalt beget, shall they take away; and they shall be eunuchs in the palace of the king of Babylon.
>
> —Isaiah 39:5–7

Admittedly, the Bible neglects to mention all the names of Hezekiah's descendents who were taken away captive over a hundred years later and made eunuchs in Babylon. But at the time of the eventual Babylonian captivity, Daniel 1:3 tells us: "And the king [Nebuchadnezzar] spake unto Ashpenaz the master of his eunuchs, that he should bring certain of the children of Israel, and of the king's seed, and of the princes."

According to this verse, there were certainly eunuchs of the king's seed present at Babylon. And according to Daniel 1:6, Daniel and his three friends were among them: "Now among these were of the children of Judah, Daniel, Hananiah, Mishael, and Azariah."

God's punishment to Hezekiah became a reality at Babylon when his heirs became eunuchs. But those adhering to rabbinic teachings respond with the fact that Jeconiah, one of Hezekiah's descendents according to 1 Chronicles 3:13–17, had children after he was taken away captive into Babylon (citing 2 Kings 24:12 and 1 Chronicles 3:17–24). According to them, this is proof that he never became a eunuch. Though they are correct, it is important for them to understand that Jeremiah 22:24–30 shows that God already declared Jeconiah's descendents ineligible to sit on David's throne as king. As a result, whether or not Jeconiah became a eunuch is irrelevant since his descendents were already disqualified.

According to 1 Chronicles 3:13–15, Hezekiah had another descendent named Zedekiah. The Scriptures reveal that he took Jeconiah's place on the throne and was the last king of Judah. When he rebelled against the king of Babylon, the Chaldean armies pursued him and overtook him. Jeremiah 52:8–10 tells us what befell Zedekiah and his sons shortly after they were captured at the plains of Jericho:

> But the army of the Chaldeans pursued after the king, and overtook Zedekiah in the plains of Jericho; and all his army was scattered from him. Then they took the king, and carried him up unto the king of Babylon to Riblah in the land of Hamath; where he gave judgment upon him. And the king of Babylon slew the sons of Zedekiah before his eyes: he slew also all the princes of Judah in Riblah.

Because of God's curse on Jeconiah's descendents, Zedekiah's sons being killed at Riblah, and Hezekiah's descendents becoming eunuchs at Babylon, the Hebrew scriptures fail to mention anyone who is an eligible progenitor to the Messiah after the Babylonian captivity. As a result, Hezekiah is not the subject of Isaiah 9:7 since the throne of David could not possibly be established through him. Only the Messiah, born of a virgin, can qualify!

Finally, Isaiah 9:6 tells us that this child is called Prince of Peace. Isaiah 9:7 adds that he would bring everlasting peace. Such was not the case with Hezekiah. As we have already seen, 2 Kings 18:13 reveals that there were battles fought with the Assyrians during his lifetime. Second Kings 18:8 tells us that he also "smote the Philistines." History bears witness that since Hezekiah's death, Israel had been under the authority of many world powers such as the Babylonian Empire, Persian Empire, Greek Empire, and Roman Empire. Quite obviously, Hezekiah failed to establish peace and, as a result, could not be rightfully called Prince of Peace.

Regarding Isaiah 9:7, there is one other matter to consider. Hezekiah never established the earth "with judgment and with justice from henceforth even forever." Accordingly, Jeremiah 23:5 reveals that this precise responsibilty is set aside strictly for the Branch, the Messiah, as follows: "Behold, the days come, saith the LORD, that I will raise unto David a righteous Branch, and a King shall reign and prosper, and shall execute judgment and justice in the earth."

In summary, the subject of Isaiah 9:7 could not be King Hezekiah. He did not establish judgment and justice in the earth and he failed to establish everlasting peace. Further, his descendents were cut off from Judah's kingly line. It is the Messiah who will completely fulfill this prophecy.

II. What time period does Isaiah 9:2–7 reference? Who is the subject of Isaiah 9:2–7?

The people that walked in darkness have seen a great light: they that dwell in the land of the shadow of death, upon them hath the light shined. Thou hast multiplied the nation, and not increased the joy: they joy before thee according to the joy in harvest, and as men rejoice when they divide the spoil. For thou hast broken the yoke of his burden, and the staff of his shoulder, the rod of his oppressor, as in the day of Midian. For every battle of the warrior is with confused noise, and garments rolled in blood; but this shall be with burning and fuel of fire. For unto us a child is born, unto us a son is given: and the government shall be upon his shoulder: and his name shall be called Wonderful, Counsellor, The mighty God, The everlasting Father, The Prince of Peace. Of the increase of his government and peace there shall be no end, upon the throne of David, and upon his kingdom, to order it, and to establish it with judgment and with justice from henceforth even for ever. The zeal of the LORD of hosts will perform this.

—Isaiah 9:2–7

The next set of objectives is to uncover the time period described in this passage and to further support the Messiah as its subject. In order to accomplish this, the following questions need to be asked: Did Isaiah refer to an event or series of events that already happened, was he referring to Israel's present condition, or was he prophesying a future event? After reading this passage in its context, there is only one logical conclusion that can be made: Isaiah 9:2–7 not only foretells an event after Isaiah's lifetime, it describes a time period that has not yet taken place in our history.

This passage prophesies the day when all nations come against Jerusalem and the eventual defeat of those nations. It also describes the Messiah setting up His everlasting kingdom of peace. In order to confirm this is true, let us examine each verse beginning with Isaiah 9:2, which states: "The people that walked in darkness have seen a great light: they that dwell in the land of the shadow of death, upon them hath the light shined."

Earlier in his book, Isaiah has already identified Israel as the people who walked in darkness. When the prophet was commissioned by God to speak to the people, this is what the LORD told him:

. . . Go, and tell this people, Hear ye indeed, but understand not; and see ye indeed, but perceive not. Make the heart of this people fat, and make their ears heavy, and shut their eyes; lest they see with their eyes, and hear with their ears, and understand with their heart, and convert, and be healed.

—Isaiah 6:9–10

The great light that Israel will see is revealed in other passages in the Bible. This concept is fully developed in Isaiah 42, the first of Isaiah's Servant Songs. In Isaiah 42:18–20, Israel is referred to as the servant who lives in spiritual darkness. Meanwhile, according to Isaiah 42:6–7, the Messiah is called "a light of the Gentiles." Upon His return, He will be Israel's source of understanding and knowledge:

- **Isaiah 42:6–7**—*regarding the Messiah:* "I the LORD have called thee in righteousness, and will hold thine hand, and will keep thee, and give thee for a covenant of the people, for a light of the Gentiles. To open the blind eyes, to bring out the prisoners from the prison, and them that sit in darkness out of the prison house."
- **Isaiah 42:18–20**—*regarding Israel:* "Hear, ye deaf; and look, ye blind, that ye may see. Who is blind, but my servant? or deaf, as my messenger that I sent? who is blind as he that is perfect, and blind as the LORD's servant? Seeing many things, but thou observest not; opening the ears, but he heareth not."

Isaiah 9:2 describes the beginning of wonderful things for God's chosen people. Though they have walked in darkness, they will see a Great Light when the Messiah arrives. The Messiah's reign is about to commence and Israel is about to be exalted and glorified by every other nation.

The entire world will bear witness that the LORD's everlasting covenant with Abraham, Isaac, and Jacob was not forgotten. Though the nations of the world will come against Jerusalem to lay siege against it, they will fail! The Day of the LORD is about to begin, and Judgment Day has arrived!

Isaiah 9:3

Thou hast multiplied the nation, and not increased the joy: they joy before thee according to the joy in harvest, and as men rejoice when they divide the spoil.

The children of Israel have endured tremendous hardships throughout the centuries. It is safe to say that their joy as a people and a nation has been relatively nonexistent. The reason for Israel's sufferings is explained in Deuteronomy 31:16–17: their forefathers had broken the covenant with God and turned to other gods. As a result, the LORD had punished them:

And the LORD said unto Moses, Behold, thou shalt sleep with thy fathers; and this people will rise up, and go a whoring after the gods of the strangers of the land, whither they go to be among them, and will forsake me, and break my covenant which I have made with them. Then my anger shall be kindled against them in that day, and I will forsake them, and I will hide my face from them, and they shall be devoured, and many evils and troubles shall befall them; so that they will say in that day, Are not these evils come upon us, because our God is not among us?

The Bible teaches that there will come a time when Israel's suffering will come to an end. On that day, God will no longer hide His face from His people. According to Zechariah 12:9–10, this will happen at the battle of Armageddon, when Israel looks upon Him who was pierced and God pours out His Spirit upon the nation. This future event is also foretold in Ezekiel 39:29:

- **Zechariah 12:9–10:** "And it shall come to pass in that day, that I will seek to destroy all the nations that come against Jerusalem. And I will pour upon the house of David, and upon the inhabitants of Jerusalem, the spirit of grace and of supplications: and they shall look upon me whom they have pierced, and they shall mourn for him, as one mourneth for his only son, and shall be in bitterness for him, as one that is in bitterness for his firstborn."
- **Ezekiel 39:29:** "Neither will I hide my face any more from them: for I have poured out my spirit upon the house of Israel, saith the Lord GOD."

When Israel's enemies are defeated, the Messiah will establish His everlasting kingdom of peace on earth and Isaiah 9:2–7 will be fulfilled.

Isaiah 9:4

For thou hast broken the yoke of his burden, and the staff of his shoulder, the rod of his oppressor, as in the day of Midian.

In this verse, the eventual defeat of Israel's enemies is likened to their miraculous victory over the Midianites described in the Book of Judges, chapters six and seven. In Judges 6:6–7, Israel was greatly impoverished because of the Midianites. They became victorious when they cried out to the LORD and were delivered. In similar fashion, according to Zechariah 14:1, Israel's spoil will be divided by their enemies and they will again be greatly impoverished. Zechariah 13:9 and Joel 2:32 reveal that, just like in the days of Midian, they will call on the name of the LORD. And just like what befell the Midianites, there will be deliverance and Israel will be victorious. The following passages and verses apply:

- **Judges 6:6–7:** "And Israel was greatly impoverished because of the Midianites; and the children of Israel cried unto the LORD. And it came to pass, when the children of Israel cried unto the LORD because of the Midianites."
- **Zechariah 14:1:** "Behold, the day of the LORD cometh, and thy spoil shall be divided in the midst of thee."
- **Zechariah 13:9:** "And I will bring the third part through the fire, and will refine them as silver is refined, and will try them as gold is tried: they shall call on my name, and I will hear them: I will say, It is my people: and they shall say, The LORD is my God."
- **Joel 2:32:** "And it shall come to pass, that whosoever shall call on the name of the LORD shall be delivered: for in mount Zion and in Jerusalem shall be deliverance, as the LORD hath said, and in the remnant whom the LORD shall call."

Isaiah 9:5

For every battle of the warrior is with confused noise, and garments rolled in blood; but this shall be with burning and fuel of fire.

How will Israel become triumphant? Isaiah 9:5 is clear: victory will be achieved by "burning and fuel of fire." Once again, the cross-reference is supplied in Zechariah 14. According to Zechariah 14:3–4, when the LORD fights for His people, His feet will stand on the Mount of Olives.

Zechariah 14:12 describes the destruction of Israel's enemies caused by intense heat, i.e. with "burning and fuel of fire:"

> Then shall the LORD go forth, and fight against those nations, as when he fought in the day of battle. And his feet shall stand in that day upon the mount of Olives, which is before Jerusalem on the east. . . . And this shall be the plague wherewith the LORD will smite all the people that have fought against Jerusalem; Their flesh shall consume away while they stand upon their feet, and their eyes shall consume away in their holes, and their tongue shall consume away in their mouth.
>
> —Zechariah 14:3–4,12

When the LORD stands on the Mount of Olives and defeats Israel's enemies, He will be present in Jerusalem. Psalm 97:1–6 states that fire will go before Him and burn up all His enemies. Further, "the hills melt like wax at the presence of the LORD." Everyone will see His glory:

> The LORD reigneth; let the earth rejoice; let the multitude of isles be glad thereof. Clouds and darkness are round about him: righteousness and judgment are the habitation of his throne. A fire goeth before him, and burneth up his enemies round about. His lightnings enlightened the world: the earth saw, and trembled. The hills melted like wax at the presence of the LORD, at the presence of the Lord of the whole earth. The heavens declare his righteousness, and all the people see his glory.

Isaiah 9:7

> Of the increase of his government and peace there shall be no end, upon the throne of David, and upon his kingdom, to order it, and to establish it with judgment and with justice from henceforth even for ever. The zeal of the LORD of hosts will perform this.

According to this verse, after the Messiah establishes the earth with judgment and justice by destroying His enemies, He will set up His everlasting kingdom of peace. Psalm 2:6–9 and Psalm 110:2 provide the connection.

The Messiah, God's only begotten Son, will eternally rule as King over the entire world:

- **Psalm 2:6–9:** "Yet have I set my king upon my holy hill of Zion. I will declare the decree: the LORD hath said unto me, Thou art my Son; this day have I begotten thee. Ask of me, and I shall give thee the heathen for thine inheritance, and the uttermost parts of the earth for thy possession. Thou shalt break them with a rod of iron; thou shalt dash them in pieces like a potter's vessel."
- **Psalm 110:2:** "The LORD shall send the rod of thy strength out of Zion: rule thou in the midst of thine enemies."

Other passages in the Bible agree! As previously shown, the Book of Ezekiel was written approximately four hundred years after King David died. Ezekiel 37:22 describes the day when Israel will have one king. The reference to David in Ezekiel 37:24–25 is made to the Messiah, who would be the Son of David.[30] These passages confirm that He will be their eternal Shepherd, Prince, and King:

- **Ezekiel 37:22:** "And I will make them one nation in the land upon the mountains of Israel; and one king shall be king to them all: and they shall be no more two nations, neither shall they be divided into two kingdoms any more at all."
- **Ezekiel 37:24–25:** "And David my servant shall be king over them; and they all shall have one shepherd: they shall also walk in my judgments, and observe my statutes, and do them. And they shall dwell in the land that I have given unto Jacob my servant, wherein your fathers have dwelt; and they shall dwell therein, even they, and their children, and their children's children for ever: and my servant David shall be their prince for ever."

According to Isaiah 9:7, it is the Messiah who will establish everlasting peace. In the Bible, there are a number of other messianic verses and passages that support this position. They are:

- **Isaiah 11:8–10:** "And the sucking child shall play on the hole of the asp, and the weaned child shall put his hand on the cockatrice' den. They shall not hurt nor destroy in all my holy mountain: for the earth shall be full of the knowledge of the LORD, as the waters cover the sea, And in that day there shall be a root of Jesse, which shall stand for an ensign of the people; to it shall the Gentiles seek: and his rest shall be glorious."

- **Psalm 72:3:** "The mountains shall bring peace to the people, and the little hills, by righteousness."

- **Isaiah 2:4:** "And he shall judge among the nations, and shall rebuke many people: and they shall beat their swords into plowshares, and their spears into pruninghooks: nation shall not lift up sword against nation, neither shall they learn war any more."

- **Ezekiel 37:26:** "Moreover I will make a covenant of peace with them; it shall be an everlasting covenant with them: and I will place them, and multiply them, and will set my sanctuary in the midst of them for evermore."

- **Micah 5:2–5 (KJV)*:** "But thou, Bethlehem Ephratah, though thou be little among the thousands of Judah, yet out of thee shall he come forth unto me that is to be ruler in Israel; whose goings forth have been from of old, from everlasting. Therefore will he give them up, until the time that she which travaileth hath brought forth: then the remnant of his brethren shall return unto the children of Israel. And he shall stand and feed in the strength of the LORD, in the majesty of the name of the LORD his God; and they shall abide: for now shall he be great unto the ends of the earth. And this man shall be the peace, when the Assyrian shall come into our land: and when he shall tread in our palaces, then shall we raise against him seven shepherds, and eight principal men."

- **Zechariah 9:9–10:** "Rejoice greatly, O daughter of Zion; shout, O daughter of Jerusalem: behold, thy King cometh unto thee: he is just, and having salvation; lowly, and riding upon an ass, and upon a colt the foal of an ass. And I will cut off the chariot from Ephraim, and the horse from Jerusalem, and the battle bow shall be cut off: and he shall

---

* The KJV is indicated because this actually corresponds with Micah 5:1-4 in the Hebrew scriptures.

speak peace unto the heathen: and his dominion shall be from sea even to sea, and from the river even to the ends of the earth."

These passages certainly support the Messiah as the subject of Isaiah 9:7. World peace will be accomplished by Him.

III. Isaiah 9:6 (KJV) (Past, Present or Future Tense?)

For unto us a child is born, unto us a son is given: and the government shall be upon his shoulder: and his name shall be called Wonderful, Counsellor, The mighty God, The everlasting Father, The Prince of Peace.

Counter-missionaries, those who defend rabbinic Judaism, teach that this verse should properly be translated in the past tense, not the present tense. They insist it should read: "For unto us a child has been born," etc. This assertion is made in an attempt to qualify King Hezekiah as the subject of the passage by claiming that the child was already born. However, according to the Soncino translation of Isaiah, a highly respected Jewish translation, Isaiah 9:5, which is the equivalent of Isaiah 9:6 in the King James Bible, translates as follows, "For to us a child is born, to us a son is given, and the government is upon his shoulder."

According to the Soncino translation, this verse is in the present tense. In other words, it agrees with the Christian translations! Additionally, the 1917 Jewish Publication Society Bible's Hebrew-to-English translation agrees with the Soncino, also translating this verse in the present tense as, "For a child is born unto us, a son is given unto us," etc. Therefore, Christianity's response to the counter-missionaries is that their claim is without merit, citing their own Jewish sources against them.

It should also be mentioned that believers in Jesus as the subject of Isaiah 9:2–7 should have no problem countering Judaism's past tense theory. As we have seen, Isaiah 9:2–7 foretells an event that has not yet taken place in our history. "For unto us a child has been born, unto us a son has been given" can certainly apply to Jesus. When He returns, Israel's declaration, "For unto us a child has been born," etc. will be true. He *was* born two thousand years ago, in the little town of Bethlehem (Micah 5:2 and Matthew 2:1, KJV).

IV. The Names of the Child

According to Isaiah 9:6, the names of the child are as follows: Wonderful, Counsellor, The mighty God, The everlasting Father, and The Prince of Peace. Wonderful and Counsellor are certainly qualities directly associated with the Messiah. In Isaiah 11, only two chapters later, Isaiah refers to the rod out of the stem of Jesse, the Messiah, in the following manner: "And there shall come forth a rod out of the stem of Jesse, and a Branch shall grow out of his roots: And the spirit of the Lord shall rest upon him, the spirit of wisdom and understanding, the spirit of counsel and might, the spirit of knowledge and of the fear of the Lord."

This passage depicts the Messiah, referred to as a "rod out of the stem of Jesse, and a Branch," as having the Lord's spirit of counsel, understanding, and wisdom. Therefore, He must be a Wonderful Counsellor.

The prophesied child in Isaiah 9:6 is also called "the mighty God," in Hebrew *el gibbor*. This is a title reserved only for the Lord. Only one chapter later, Isaiah refers to God in the same manner. Isaiah 10:20–21 states:

> And it shall come to pass in that day, that the remnant of Israel, and such as are escaped of the house of Jacob, shall no more again stay upon him that smote them; but shall stay upon the Lord, the Holy One of Israel, in truth. The remnant shall return, even the remnant of Jacob, unto the mighty God (*el gibbor*).

In the Hebrew scriptures, only the Lord is called *el gibbor*. This clearly establishes this child's deity. He is also the same prophesied child foretold in Isaiah 7:14 who would be born of a virgin. According to that verse, He is called Immanuel, meaning God with us. He is the mighty God!

In Isaiah 9:6, the child is also called "The everlasting Father" (in Hebrew *'abi 'ad*). This title further verifies the Messiah's deity as follows: According to Exodus 4:22, the Lord calls Israel His firstborn son: "And thou shalt say unto Pharaoh, Thus saith the LORD, Israel is my son, even my firstborn."

Exodus 4:22 emphasizes God's Father-son relationship with Israel. Since Isaiah 9:6 indicates that they will call the Messiah "The everlasting Father," He must be the LORD Himself. After all, how many fathers can a son have? Malachi 2:10 states, "Have we not all one father? hath not one God created us?"

According to Malachi, Israel has one father, not two! Isaiah 9:6 indicates that the child to be born will be called "The everlasting Father." Therefore, He must be the LORD!

Finally, according to Isaiah 9:6, the child will be called, The Prince of Peace. As we have seen, it is the Messiah who will establish world peace.

In closing, the evidence that Isaiah 9:2–7 refers to the Messiah is overwhelming. Likewise, the proof that Hezekiah is not the subject is equally significant. This passage foretells an event that will take place in the future, when all nations come against Jerusalem. According to the Bible, these nations will be defeated with burning and fuel of fire as the Messiah executes judgment and justice in the earth. Immediately after, He will set up His everlasting kingdom of peace. These are things that Hezekiah *never* accomplished. And this will all be fulfilled at Jesus' Second Coming as revealed in the Book of Revelation:

♦ **Revelation 11:15:** "And the seventh angel sounded; and there were great voices in heaven, saying: The kingdoms of this world are become the kingdoms of our LORD, and of His Christ; and He shall reign for ever and ever"

♦ **Revelation 19:11–16:** "And I saw heaven opened, and behold a white horse; and he that sat upon him was called Faithful and True, and in righteousness he doth judge and make war. His eyes were as a flame of fire, and on his head were many crowns; and he had a name written, that no man knew, but he himself. And he was clothed with a vesture dipped in blood: and his name is called The Word of God. And the armies which were in heaven followed him upon white horses, clothed in fine linen, white and clean. And out of his mouth goeth a sharp sword, that with it he should smite the nations: and he shall rule them with a rod of iron: and he treadeth the winepress of the fierceness and wrath of Almighty God. And he hath on his vesture and on his thigh a name written, KING OF KINGS, AND LORD OF LORDS."

Author's note: **See chapter 16 in this book, which is titled "The Second Coming of Jesus Christ," for further information.**

Part Two

Isaiah's Servant Songs

Chapter Six

Isaiah 42:1–7:
Isaiah's First Servant Song

In the Hebrew scriptures, God's plan for mankind's redemption is found within Isaiah's four Servant Songs: Isaiah chapters 42, 49, 50, and 53. In Isaiah 42, the prophet presents two servants, Israel and the Messiah, whose profiles are quite diiferent from one another. In Isaiah 49, the second Servant Song, Isaiah foretells Israel's abhorrence and rejection of its Messiah, who is called the Holy One of Israel. In Isaiah 50, the third Servant Song, Isaiah provides the details of a Messiah who is viciously beaten yet not rebellious. Finally in Isaiah 53, the fourth Servant Song, the prophet describes the Messiah's rejection, suffering, and death, and explains why His death became necessary.

Isaiah 42:1–7

Behold my servant, whom I uphold; mine elect, in whom my soul delighteth; I have put my spirit upon him: he shall bring forth judgment to the Gentiles. He shall not cry, nor lift up, nor cause his voice to be heard in the street. A bruised reed shall he not break, and the smoking flax shall he not quench: he shall bring forth judgment unto truth. He shall not fail nor be discouraged, till he have set judgment in the earth: and the isles shall wait for his law. Thus saith God the LORD, he that created the heavens, and stretched them out; he that spread forth the earth, and that which cometh out of it; he that giveth breath unto the people upon it, and spirit to them that walk therein: I the LORD have called thee in righteousness, and will hold thine hand, and will keep thee, and give thee for a covenant of the people, for a light of the Gentiles; To open the blind eyes, to bring out the prisoners from the prison, and them that sit in darkness out of the prison house.

In Isaiah 42, the prophet introduces two servants. Isaiah 42:6–7 describes one that is a "light of the Gentiles" and opens the eyes of those who are blind. Meanwhile, Isaiah 42:18–20 describes a blind servant who sees many things yet does not understand.[35] The Scriptures showing the contrast between these two servants follow:
The servant that gives light:

I the LORD have called thee in righteousness, and will hold thine hand, and will keep thee, and give thee for a covenant of the people, for a light of the Gentiles; To open the blind eyes, to bring out the prisoners from the prison, and them that sit in darkness out of the prison house.

—Isaiah 42:6–7

The blind servant:

Hear, ye deaf; and look, ye blind, that ye may see. Who is blind, but my servant? or deaf, as my messenger that I sent? who is blind as he that is perfect, and blind as the LORD's servant? Seeing many things, but thou observest not; opening the ears, but he heareth not.

—Isaiah 42:18–20

It is obvious that these two passages describe different servants. After all, how can a blind servant be a light? If an individual does not understand, would he or she be qualified to teach others? If someone walks in darkness, would they have the ability to lead the way? Of course not!
Isaiah identifies these two servants in previous chapters in his book.

For example, Isaiah 41:8 refers to Israel as God's servant. And according to Isaiah 6:9–10, it is described as a blind servant whose knowledge has been taken away. Isaiah 29:13–14 explains why God removed much of their understanding: it was because of their continued rebellion. The applicable scriptures follow:

- **Isaiah 41:8:** "But thou, Israel, art my servant, Jacob whom I have chosen, the seed of Abraham my friend."
- **Isaiah 6:9–10:** "And he said, Go, and tell this people, Hear ye indeed, but understand not; and see ye indeed, but perceive not. Make the heart of this people fat, and make their ears heavy, and shut their eyes; lest they see with their eyes, and hear with their ears, and understand with their heart, and convert, and be healed."
- **Isaiah 29:13–14:** "Wherefore the Lord said, Forasmuch as this people draw near me with their mouth, and with their lips do honour me, but have removed their heart far from me, and their fear toward me is taught by the precept of men: Therefore, behold, I will proceed to do a marvellous work among this people, even a marvellous work and a wonder: for the wisdom of their wise men shall perish, and the understanding of their prudent men shall be hid."

After viewing these passages, it is clear that Israel must be the blind servant described in Isaiah 42:18–20.

As previously mentioned, Isaiah 42 portrays a different servant. In another book in the Bible, Zechariah 3:8 calls the Messiah, known as the BRANCH, God's servant. Unlike Israel, Isaiah advises us that this Branch [the Messiah], called "a rod out of the stem of Jesse," will possess the spirit of wisdom, understanding, and knowledge. As a result, the Messiah is the one who qualifies as the "light of the Gentiles." The applicable Scriptures follow:

- **Zechariah 3:8:** "Hear now, O Joshua the high priest, thou, and thy fellows that sit before thee: for they are men wondered at: for, behold, I will bring forth my servant the BRANCH."

- **Isaiah 11:1–2:** "And there shall come forth a rod out of the stem of Jesse, and a Branch shall grow out of his roots: And the spirit of the LORD shall rest upon him, the spirit of wisdom and understanding, the spirit of counsel and might, the spirit of knowledge and of the fear of the LORD."

After viewing these passages, it is clear that Isaiah discloses two distinct servants in his first Servant Song, the Messiah and Israel, yet only the Messiah qualifies as the light. This is further verified by the fact that Isaiah 11:10 refers to Him, the root of Jesse, as an ensign or banner of the people: "And in that day there shall be a root of Jesse, which shall stand for an ensign of the people; to it shall the Gentiles seek: and his rest shall be glorious."

After introducing both servants, Isaiah 42:22 describes the blind servant [Israel] as robbed and spoiled, snared in holes, and hid in prison houses. Meanwhile, Isaiah 42:7 reveals that the Messiah, who is the light, as the one bringing out the prisoners from the prison, and them that sit in darkness out of the prison house:

- **Isaiah 42:22**—*regarding Israel:* "But this is a people robbed and spoiled; they are all of them snared in holes, and they are hid in prison houses: they are for a prey, and none delivereth; for a spoil, and none saith, Restore."
- **Isaiah 42:7**—*regarding the Messiah:* "To open the blind eyes, to bring out the prisoners from the prison, and them that sit in darkness out of the prison house."

The conclusion is the following: In Isaiah's first Servant Song, the prophet refers to two servants, the Messiah and Israel. He prophesies a time when the Messiah, who has wisdom, understanding and knowledge, will open the eyes and ears of God's blind and deaf servant Israel. He will also be a light of the Gentiles.

Since the foundation of this chapter is now established, let us examine Isaiah's first Servant Song in its proper context.

Isaiah 42:1

> Behold my servant, whom I uphold; mine elect, in whom my soul delighteth; I have put my spirit upon him: he shall bring forth judgment to the Gentiles.

Though the name of God's servant is not mentioned in this verse, who can it be, the Messiah or Israel? By referring to other verses and passages in the Bible, this servant's identity is easily uncovered. When reading Isaiah 42:1, it is important to recognize that this servant has three qualities:

1. God's soul delights in him.
2. God places His spirit upon him.
3. He brings forth judgment to the Gentiles.

Regarding the first qualification, does God's soul delight in Israel? Regarding Israel, Jeremiah 5:7–9 provides the answer in the negative:

> How shall I pardon thee for this? thy children have forsaken me, and sworn by them that are no gods: when I had fed them to the full, they then committed adultery, and assembled themselves by troops in the harlots' houses. They were as fed horses in the morning: every one neighed after his neighbour's wife. Shall I not visit for these things? saith the LORD: and shall not my soul be avenged on such a nation as this?

With respect to the second qualification, does Isaiah reveal the identity of the servant who God has placed His Spirit upon? The answer is provided in Isaiah 11:1–2. It is the "rod out of the stem of Jesse," the Messiah: "And there shall come forth a rod out of the stem of Jesse, and a Branch shall grow out of his roots: And the spirit of the LORD shall rest upon him, the spirit of wisdom and understanding, the spirit of counsel and might, the spirit of knowledge and of the fear of the LORD."

Finally, regarding the third qualification, who will bring forth judgment to the Gentiles? Once again, Isaiah and Jeremiah foretell that this is a responsibility strictly for the Messiah:

- **Isaiah 11:1,4:** "And there shall come forth a rod out of the stem of Jesse, and a Branch shall grow out of his roots: . . . But with righteousness shall he judge the poor, and reprove with equity for the meek of the earth: and he shall smite the earth with the rod of his mouth, and with the breath of his lips shall he slay the wicked."
- **Jeremiah 23:5:** "Behold, the days come, saith the LORD, that I will raise unto David a righteous Branch, and a King shall reign and prosper, and shall execute judgment and justice in the earth."

The identity of God's servant in Isaiah 42:1 has now become clear. Since the Scriptures reveal that God's soul does not delight in Israel, it is automatically eliminated as the subject of this verse. Further, since God's Spirit rests on the Messiah, and He will bring forth judgment to the Gentiles, He must be the subject of Isaiah 42:1. Remembering this, the prophet's message throughout the rest of the first Servant Song becomes much clearer.

Isaiah 42:2–3

He shall not cry, nor lift up, nor cause his voice to be heard in the street. A bruised reed shall he not break, and the smoking flax shall he not quench: he shall bring forth judgment unto truth.

Since the identity of the servant in Isaiah 42:1 has been established as the Messiah, this passage merely repeats the message that He will bring forth judgment. It also adds that He will be gentle and kind. These qualities are directly related to fearing or revering the LORD. Isaiah 11:2 illustrates that the the Messiah would possess the fear of the LORD and, according to Hebrews 5:7 in the New Testament, Jesus qualifies:

- **Isaiah 11:2:** "And the spirit of the LORD shall rest upon him, the spirit of wisdom and understanding, the spirit of counsel and might, the spirit of knowledge and of the fear of the LORD."
- **Hebrews 5:7**—*regarding Jesus:* "Who in the days of his flesh, when he had offered up prayers and supplications with strong crying and tears unto him that was able to save him from death, and was heard in that he feared."

Isaiah 42:4

> He shall not fail nor be discouraged, till he have set judgment in the
> earth: and the isles shall wait for his law.

Once again, the point is stressed that the Messiah will bring judgment.
And further confirming that He is the subject of this verse, Isaiah 2:2–3
teaches that when He sets up His everlasting kingdom, the law will proceed
out of Zion. It will come from Him, the King over all the earth:

> And it shall come to pass in the last days, that the mountain of the
> LORD's house shall be established in the top of the mountains, and shall
> be exalted above the hills; and all nations shall flow unto it. And many
> people shall go and say, Come ye, and let us go up to the mountain of
> the LORD, to the house of the God of Jacob; and he will teach us of his
> ways, and we will walk in his paths: for out of Zion shall go forth the
> law, and the word of the LORD from Jerusalem.

Isaiah 42:5–6

> Thus saith God the LORD, he that created the heavens, and stretched
> them out; he that spread forth the earth, and that which cometh out
> of it; he that giveth breath unto the people upon it, and spirit to them
> that walk therein: I the LORD have called thee in righteousness, and will
> hold thine hand, and will keep thee, and give thee for a covenant of the
> people, for a light of the Gentiles.

According to this passage, the LORD calls the Messiah in righteousness.
Isaiah 11:4–5 and Jeremiah 23:5–6 describe Him as righteous. In contrast,
there are a number of verses and passages in the Bible that tell us that Israel
is not righteous. Isaiah 48:1,8 describes Israel as "a transgressor from the
womb." The applicable verses and passages follow:

Regarding the Messiah:
- **Isaiah 11:4–5:** "But with righteousness shall he judge the poor, and
  reprove with equity for the meek of the earth: and he shall smite the

earth with the rod of his mouth, and with the breath of his lips shall he slay the wicked. And righteousness shall be the girdle of his loins, and faithfulness the girdle of his reins."

- **Jeremiah 23:5–6:** "Behold, the days come, saith the LORD, that I will raise unto David a righteous Branch, and a King shall reign and prosper, and shall execute judgment and justice in the earth. In his days Judah shall be saved, and Israel shall dwell safely: and this is his name whereby he shall be called, THE LORD OUR RIGHTEOUSNESS."

Regarding Israel:

- **Deuteronomy 9:4–6:** "Speak not thou in thine heart, after that the LORD thy God hath cast them out from before thee, saying, For my righteousness the LORD hath brought me in to possess this land: but for the wickedness of these nations the LORD doth drive them out from before thee. Not for thy righteousness, or for the uprightness of thine heart, dost thou go to possess their land: but for the wickedness of these nations the LORD thy God doth drive them out from before thee, and that he may perform the word which the LORD sware unto thy fathers, Abraham, Isaac, and Jacob. Understand therefore, that the LORD thy God giveth thee not this good land to possess it for thy righteousness; for thou art a stiffnecked people."

- **Isaiah 1:4:** "Ah sinful nation, a people laden with iniquity, a seed of evildoers, children that are corrupters: they have forsaken the LORD, they have provoked the Holy One of Israel unto anger, they are gone away backward."

- **Isaiah 48:1,8:** "Hear ye this, O house of Jacob, which are called by the name of Israel, and are come forth out of the waters of Judah, which swear by the name of the LORD, and make mention of the God of Israel, but not in truth, nor in righteousness. . . . Yea, thou heardest not; yea, thou knewest not; yea, from that time that thine ear was not opened: for I knew that thou wouldest deal very treacherously, and wast called a transgressor from the womb."

From these verses and passages, it is clear that the Messiah is righteous while Israel is unrighteous. All of this supports that the Messiah is the subject of Isaiah 42:1–6. Isaiah 42:6 also states that He is given as a covenant of the people.

Though Israel is called sinful and unrighteous in the Scriptures, it is important to remember that all of the nations are sinful. Israel is no exception! As the result of our sins, all of us are unclean before the holy God of Israel.

+ **Psalm 51:3,5**—*the words of King David:* "For I acknowledge my transgressions: and my sin is ever before me. . . . Behold, I was shapen in iniquity; and in sin did my mother conceive me."

+ **Isaiah 64:6:** "But we are all as an unclean thing, and all our righteousnesses are as filthy rags; and we all do fade as a leaf; and our iniquities, like the wind, have taken us away."

+ **Romans 3:23**—*the words of the apostle Paul:* "For all have sinned, and come short of the glory of God."

Isaiah 42:7

To open the blind eyes, to bring out the prisoners from the prison, and them that sit in darkness out of the prison house.

As we have seen, Isaiah 6:9–10 and Isaiah 29:13–14 reveal that Israel is the blind servant in spiritual darkness. According to the New Testament, Romans 11:25–27 indicates that their blindness will continue "until the fullness of the Gentiles:"

For I would not, brethren, that ye should be ignorant of this mystery, lest ye should be wise in your own conceits; that blindness in part is happened to Israel, until the fulness of the Gentiles be come in. And so all Israel shall be saved: as it is written, There shall come out of Sion the Deliverer, and shall turn away ungodliness from Jacob: For this is my covenant unto them, when I shall take away their sins.

In agreement with Romans 11:26, Isaiah 42:6–7 indicates that Israel's blindness will continue until it is removed by the Messiah [Sion the Deliverer], who is the light of the world.

Isaiah 42:16

And I will bring the blind by a way that they knew not; I will lead them in paths that they have not known: I will make darkness light before them, and crooked things straight. These things will I do unto them, and not forsake them.

This verse tells us that the LORD will redeem Israel by a way that is unexpected, i.e. "a way that they knew not." For them, redemption and salvation will arrive in a surprising fashion. As explained in Isaiah 9:2, Israel who walked in darkness will see the great light when Jesus their Messiah arrives: "The people that walked in darkness have seen a great light: they that dwell in the land of the shadow of death, upon them hath the light shined."

According to the Scriptures, there will come a time when the Messiah sets up His everlasting kingdom of peace. However, it will not be established until that day when all nations come against Jerusalem and victory is obtained through Him. Once again, Israel's victory is foretold in Isaiah 9:5 and Zechariah 14:12:

- **Isaiah 9:5:** "For every battle of the warrior is with confused noise, and garments rolled in blood; but this shall be with burning and fuel of fire."
- **Zechariah 14:12:** "And this shall be the plague wherewith the LORD will smite all the people that have fought against Jerusalem; Their flesh shall consume away while they stand upon their feet, and their eyes shall consume away in their holes, and their tongue shall consume away in their mouth."

On this day, all people that come against Jerusalem will be destroyed and Israel will no longer walk in darkness. This has not yet occurred, but it will! In other words, Israel presently remains in spiritual darkness.

Isaiah 42:17

They shall be turned back, they shall be greatly ashamed, that trust in graven images, that say to the molten images, Ye are our gods.

In this verse, the subject is Israel. It is they who will be greatly ashamed after God brings them back. They will come to realize that they had been wrong all along about their Messiah. Here, the prophet also makes reference to Israel as the servant who trusted in graven images, etc. This refers to their forefathers who built the golden calf when Moses went up to Mount Sinai to receive the tablets of the covenant. Exodus 32:35 states, "And the LORD plagued the people, because they made the calf, which Aaron made."

Ezekiel 36:31–32 supports Israel's eventual shame when God brings them back and they finally come to a complete understanding. According to this passage, God will not bring them back because of anything good they will do. Micah 7:18–20 explains why God brings them back: He will do it because of His mercy and love for His people, and to honor the covenant He made with Abraham, Isaac, and Jacob:

- **Ezekiel 36:31–32:** "Then shall ye remember your own evil ways, and your doings that were not good, and shall lothe yourselves in your own sight for your iniquities and for your abominations. Not for your sakes do I this, saith the Lord GOD, be it known unto you: be ashamed and confounded for your own ways, O house of Israel."

- **Micah 7:18–20:** "Who is a God like unto thee, that pardoneth iniquity, and passeth by the transgression of the remnant of his heritage? he retaineth not his anger for ever, because he delighteth in mercy. He will turn again, he will have compassion upon us; he will subdue our iniquities; and thou wilt cast all their sins into the depths of the sea. Thou wilt perform the truth to Jacob, and the mercy to Abraham, which thou hast sworn unto our fathers from the days of old."

Chapter Seven

Isaiah 49:1–8:
Isaiah's Second Servant Song

And he said, It is a light thing that thou shouldest be my servant to raise
up the tribes of Jacob, and to restore the preserved of Israel: I will also
give thee for a light to the Gentiles, that thou mayest be my salvation
unto the end of the earth.

—Isaiah 49:6

In Isaiah 49, Isaiah's second Servant Song, the prophet begins to describe
the Messiah's mission. He is called to complete all the things Israel failed
to accomplish. For example, at Sinai, Israel was called to be a kingdom of
priests. Because of their rebellion, their priesthood was taken away. As a
result, the Messiah would fill that responsibility. In addition, the Messiah
would reconcile Israel to God by providing the final offering for sin.

The Bible teaches that the Messiah would not only be Israel's physical
Redeemer, He would also provide their spiritual redemption. Through
Him, Israel will also be glorified! Isaiah 62:11–12 states:

Behold, the LORD hath proclaimed unto the end of the world, Say ye
to the daughter of Zion, Behold, thy salvation cometh; behold, his
reward is with him, and his work before him. And they shall call them,

The holy people, The redeemed of the LORD: and thou shalt be called, Sought out, A city not forsaken.

Isaiah 49:1–2

Listen, O isles, unto me; and hearken, ye people, from far; The LORD hath called me from the womb; from the bowels of my mother hath he made mention of my name. And he hath made my mouth like a sharp sword; in the shadow of his hand hath he hid me, and made me a polished shaft; in his quiver hath he hid me.

In this passage, the Messiah speaks to the nations, [isles] of the earth. His words are likened to a sharp sword.[36] This is proven by Isaiah 11:1–2 which informs us that He has the spirit of wisdom, understanding, and knowledge. The fact that the LORD called Him from the womb and His mother's bowels is explained in the New Testament as follows:

And the angel said unto her, Fear not, Mary: for thou hast found favour with God. And, behold, thou shalt conceive in thy womb, and bring forth a son, and shalt call his name JESUS. He shall be great, and shall be called the Son of the Highest: and the Lord God shall give unto him the throne of his father David: And he shall reign over the house of Jacob for ever; and of his kingdom there shall be no end. Then said Mary unto the angel, How shall this be, seeing I know not a man? And the angel answered and said unto her, The Holy Ghost shall come upon thee, and the power of the Highest shall overshadow thee: therefore also that holy thing which shall be born of thee shall be called the Son of God.

—Luke 1:30–35

Isaiah 49:3

And said unto me, Thou art my servant, O Israel, in whom I will be glorified.

In this verse, the LORD speaks to the Messiah in the name of Israel stating that, through Him, He will be glorified. The Bible illustrates a similar example in which the LORD responds to a single individual in the name of the group he represents. This can be seen in Isaiah 7:10–14, which records a verbal exchange between King Ahaz and the LORD through the prophet Isaiah:

> Moreover the LORD spake again unto Ahaz, saying, Ask thee a sign of the LORD thy God; ask it either in the depth, or in the height above. But Ahaz said, I will not ask, neither will I tempt the LORD. And he said, Hear ye now, O house of David; Is it a small thing for you to weary men, but will ye weary my God also? Therefore the Lord himself shall give you a sign; Behold, a virgin shall conceive, and bear a son, and shall call his name Immanuel.

According to Isaiah 7:13, God addresses King Ahaz as "the house of David" because he, as Judah's king, was their highest representative. In similar fashion in Isaiah 49:3, the LORD calls King Messiah Israel since He would be the utmost representative of the nation.

Isaiah 49:4
> Then I said, I have laboured in vain, I have spent my strength for nought, and in vain; yet surely my judgment is with the LORD, and my work with my God.

In this verse the Messiah is speaking. He pours out His heart to God as He realizes that Israel would reject Him. His initial reaction is one of sadness and concern. He indicates that although His efforts may seemingly appear unsuccessful, the LORD is with Him.

Isaiah 49:5
> And now, saith the LORD that formed me from the womb to be his servant, to bring Jacob again to him, Though Israel be not gathered, yet shall I be glorious in the eyes of the LORD, and my God shall be my strength.

In this verse, the LORD provides His response to the Messiah's sadness by stating that He should not be discouraged. In fact, He encourages Him! Though Israel would not be immediately gathered as the result of the Messiah's rejection, God instructs Him that He will not fail in His ministry because He, the LORD Himself, will strengthen Him. Additionally, God reveals His utmost respect for the Messiah, proclaiming that He is glorious in His eyes.

> **Author's note: It is important to realize that because Israel would reject its Messiah at His first coming, He would not gather the people. Since the Bible teaches that it is His responsibility to gather the people (Gen. 49:10; Isa. 11:9–12; and Ezek. 37:21–24), this will be fulfilled at His Second Coming when Israel accepts Him.**

Isaiah 49:6

> And he said, It is a light thing that thou shouldest be my servant to raise up the tribes of Jacob, and to restore the preserved of Israel: I will also give thee for a light to the Gentiles, that thou mayest be my salvation unto the end of the earth.

This verse is clear: Since the LORD will be the source of the Messiah's strength, it would be a light thing, i.e. not a difficult thing, to "raise up the tribes of Jacob and to restore the preserved of Israel." Because the LORD will help Him, the Messiah will not only succeed in restoring Israel, He would be "a light of the Gentiles." Through Him, God would reveal His salvation to the ends of the earth, to all nations! This is confirmed in Isaiah 52:10 where the Messiah is referred to as the LORD's holy arm, i.e. the arm of the LORD (see chapter 9): "The LORD hath made bare his holy arm in the eyes of all the nations; and all the ends of the earth shall see the salvation of our God."

This has already been established in the first Servant Song where the prophet indicates that because the LORD is with Him, i.e., "holding his hand," the righteous Messiah would be given as a covenant of the people, for a light of the Gentiles: "I the LORD have called thee in righteousness, and will hold thine hand, and will keep thee, and give thee for a covenant of the people, for a light of the Gentiles" (Isa. 42:6).

Isaiah 49:7

> Thus saith the LORD, the Redeemer of Israel, and his Holy One, to him whom man despiseth, to him whom the nation abhorreth, to a servant of rulers, Kings shall see and arise, princes also shall worship, because of the LORD that is faithful, and the Holy One of Israel, and he shall choose thee.

This verse foretells that Israel would abhor and reject its Messiah, also known as the Holy One of Israel. The explanation for this is as follows: Because of their blindness and absence of understanding, they would not recognize Him. As a result, they would despise and reject Him. It is also important to realize that in this verse the Hebrew word *goy* (*Strong's*, #1471) is used, and refers to a single nation. Contextually, the nation that does the abhoring must be Israel. This precise Hebrew word is the same word used in Isaiah 1:4 regarding Israel, which refers to them as, "Ah sinful nation . . ."

Finally, Isaiah 49:7 ends with the phrase: "and he shall choose thee." The following verse, Isaiah 49:8, confirms that it is the Messiah who God has chosen for this responsibility, not Israel!

Isaiah 49:8

> Thus saith the LORD, In an acceptable time have I heard thee, and in a day of salvation have I helped thee: and I will preserve thee, and give thee for a covenant of the people, to establish the earth, to cause to inherit the desolate heritages.

Here, the LORD once again declares the Messiah being chosen and given as a covenant of the people. It is the LORD who will help Him (Isa. 42:6). The Messiah is not only chosen to bring back Jacob and to restore the preserved of Israel (Isa. 49:5–6), but the One who provides salvation and light to the Gentiles (Isa. 42:6; 49:6).

- **Isaiah 42:6:** "I the LORD have called thee in righteousness, and will hold thine hand, and will keep thee, and give thee for a covenant of the people, for a light of the Gentiles."
- **Isaiah 49:6:** "And he said, It is a light thing that thou shouldest be my servant to raise up the tribes of Jacob, and to restore the preserved of Israel: I will also give thee for a light to the Gentiles, that thou mayest be my salvation unto the end of the earth."

Isaiah 49:9–10

That thou mayest say to the prisoners, Go forth; to them that are in darkness, Shew yourselves. They shall feed in the ways, and their pastures shall be in all high places. They shall not hunger nor thirst; neither shall the heat nor sun smite them: for he that hath mercy on them shall lead them, even by the springs of water shall he guide them.

In this passage, the LORD instructs the Messiah to speak to the children of Israel. They are the ones described as prisoners in prison houses (Isa. 42:7; 42:22). They are also portrayed as being in spiritual darkness (Isa. 9:2; 42:16) whose understanding and knowledge has been removed (Isa. 6:9–10; 29:13–14; 42:18–22). In Isaiah 5:13, when God told Israel that they had no knowledge, He likened them to being famished and dried up with thirst. Therefore according to the Scriptures, there is a correlation between having no knowledge and being famished and dried up with thirst: "Therefore my people are gone into captivity, because they have no knowledge: and their honourable men are famished, and their multitude dried up with thirst."

Isaiah 49:9–10 brings a great promise from the Messiah to the children of Israel. The people who walked in darkness will see a great light (Isa. 9:2). He will be their Light! In that day, He will have mercy on them and lead them by the springs of water. They will no longer be famished, be hungry or thirsty. Through Him, Israel will be exalted and glorified above all the nations of the earth. Zechariah 8:23 declares: "Thus saith the LORD of hosts; In those days it shall come to pass, that ten men shall take hold out of all languages of the nations, even shall take hold of the skirt of him that is a Jew, saying, We will go with you: for we have heard that God is with you."

Though the children of Israel have endured tremendous torment and affliction throughout the centuries, the LORD vows that He has not completely turned away from His people. Through the Messiah, the Savior of the world, He will fulfill His promise to Abraham, Isaac and Jacob. Isaiah 49:14–16 states:

> But Zion said, The LORD hath forsaken me, and my Lord hath forgotten me. Can a woman forget her sucking child, that she should not have compassion on the son of her womb? yea, they may forget, yet will I not forget thee. Behold, I have graven thee upon the palms of my hands; thy walls are continually before me.

As the third and fourth Servant Songs come to light, it will become obvious to everyone how much love the Messiah has for His people. This is shown by the foretold beatings He would receive and the innocent blood He would shed for the forgiveness of their sins.

Chapter Eight

Isaiah 50:4–10:
Isaiah's Third Servant Song

The Lord GOD hath given me the tongue of the learned, that I should know how to speak a word in season to him that is weary: he wakeneth morning by morning, he wakeneth mine ear to hear as the learned. The Lord GOD hath opened mine ear, and I was not rebellious, neither turned away back. I gave my back to the smiters, and my cheeks to them that plucked off the hair: I hid not my face from shame and spitting. For the Lord GOD will help me; therefore shall I not be confounded: therefore have I set my face like a flint, and I know that I shall not be ashamed. He is near that justifieth me; who will contend with me? let us stand together: who is mine adversary? let him come near to me. Behold, the Lord GOD will help me; who is he that shall condemn me? lo, they all shall wax old as a garment; the moth shall eat them up. Who is among you that feareth the LORD, that obeyeth the voice of his servant, that walketh in darkness, and hath no light? let him trust in the name of the LORD, and stay upon his God.

When studying Isaiah's four Servant Songs, Isaiah 50 provides an abundance of additional information indicating that God's two servants, the

Messiah and Israel, have characteristics and qualities that are very different from one another.[37] Though this has been clearly taught in the first Servant Song, this third Servant Song confirms that God's suffering servant could not be Israel.

I. The Suffering Messiah

Isaiah 50:4–7 is not the only place in the Bible portraying a servant whose face is brutally beaten. The prophet Micah also foretells of such an individual. In his book, he describes the everlasting rule of King Messiah as Judge during a future time of world peace. During these days, all nations will come to Jerusalem and be taught. Micah 4:1–3 tells us that both the law and God's Word will come directly from Him as He sits and rules upon His throne in Jerusalem:

> But in the last days it shall come to pass, that the mountain of the house of the LORD shall be established in the top of the mountains, and it shall be exalted above the hills; and people shall flow unto it. And many nations shall come, and say, Come, and let us go up to the mountain of the LORD, and to the house of the God of Jacob; and he will teach us of his ways, and we will walk in his paths: for the law shall go forth of Zion, and the word of the LORD from Jerusalem. And he shall judge among many people, and rebuke strong nations afar off; and they shall beat their swords into plowshares, and their spears into pruninghooks: nation shall not lift up a sword against nation, neither shall they learn war any more.

Although Micah describes the glorious reign of the Messiah as Judge and King, he goes on to explain that He would first have to suffer. Micah 5:1 [KJV] states: "Now gather thyself in troops, O daughter of troops: he hath laid siege against us: they shall smite the judge of Israel with a rod upon the cheek."

Here, Micah explains that the Messiah would be stricken "with a rod upon the cheek." This is a clear connection to Isaiah 50:7 describing a servant setting his face like a flint. Together, these verses provide a powerful picture of the Messiah's suffering. The result of the beatings to His face is depicted in Isaiah 52:14. The applicable verses follow:

- **Isaiah 50:6:** "I gave my back to the smiters, and my cheeks to them that plucked off the hair: I hid not my face from shame and spitting."
- **Isaiah 52:14:** "As many were astonied at thee; his visage was so marred more than any man, and his form more than the sons of men."

Another reference to a suffering Messiah can be found in Zechariah 13:7 which states: "Awake, O sword, against my shepherd, and against the man that is my fellow, saith the LORD of hosts: smite the shepherd, and the sheep shall be scattered: and I will turn mine hand upon the little ones."

In the 1917 Jewish Publication Society Bible, this verse translates: "Awake, O sword, against My shepherd, And against the man that is near unto Me. . . ."

According to this verse, the one that God calls "my shepherd" and, "my fellow" is stricken. Who is this shepherd that is spoken of so fondly and with such deep admiration? As previously shown earlier in this book, the prophet Ezekiel provides the answer to this question. In Ezekiel 37:24, it is generally believed that the reference to David is made toward the Messiah who would be the Son of David.[30] Ezekiel 37:24 states: "And David my servant shall be king over them; and they all shall have one shepherd: they shall also walk in my judgments, and observe my statutes, and do them."

Although Zechariah 13:7 states that the LORD's shepherd would be stricken, Ezekiel 37:24 identifies Him as the Messiah. Why was He stricken? Zechariah 13:1 provides the answer. It states, "In that day there shall be a fountain opened to the house of David and to the inhabitants of Jerusalem for sin and for uncleanness."

The shepherd was stricken and His blood was shed "for sin and for uncleanness." But He was not beaten for anything He had done; He was punished for the sin and uncleanness of others. This is fully developed and explained in Isaiah's fourth Servant Song, Isaiah 53.

II. Further Qualifying the Messiah

Isaiah 50:4–7 reveals five facts about the suffering servant who sets his face like a flint. They are as follows:

1. He has been given the tongue of the learned,
2. The LORD God has opened his ears,
3. The LORD God will help him,
4. He was not rebellious, and
5. He shall not be confounded and ashamed.

It has already been shown that King Messiah has the spirit of wisdom, understanding, and knowledge. Therefore, He must have the tongue of the learned. This meets qualification #1. Regarding Him, Isaiah 11:1–2 states: "And there shall come forth a rod out of the stem of Jesse, and a Branch shall grow out of his roots: And the spirit of the LORD shall rest upon him, the spirit of wisdom and understanding, the spirit of counsel and might, the spirit of knowledge and of the fear of the LORD."

As proven by this passage, it is logical that the LORD has opened the Messiah's ears since He will possess full understanding of all things. This meets qualification #2. Additionally, Isaiah 42:6 reveals that the LORD God will hold His hand, i.e. help Him. This has also been established and verified in Isaiah 49:8 where God indicates that He would help the Messiah. This meets qualification #3. The applicable Scriptures follow:

- **Isaiah 42:6:** "I the LORD have called thee in righteousness, and will hold thine hand, and will keep thee, and give thee for a covenant of the people, for a light of the Gentiles."
- **Isaiah 49:8:** "Thus saith the LORD, In an acceptable time have I heard thee, and in a day of salvation have I helped thee: and I will preserve thee, and give thee for a covenant of the people, to establish the earth, to cause to inherit the desolate heritages."

As we have seen in Isaiah 11:2, the Messiah would also possess the fear of the LORD. This quality certainly relates to *not* being rebellious toward

God. This meets qualification #4.

The fifth and final qualification indicates that this individual would not be ashamed and confounded. Regarding the Messiah, Isaiah 49:5 teaches that He shall be glorious in God's eyes and be successful in His mission. This meets the final qualification: "And now, saith the LORD that formed me from the womb to be his servant, to bring Jacob again to him, Though Israel be not gathered, yet shall I be glorious in the eyes of the LORD, and my God shall be my strength."

As a result of this evidence, it is clear that the Messiah meets all five qualifications as the subject of Isaiah's third Servant Song. Therefore, it is He who sets His face like a flint and who gives His back to those who strike Him.

III. Disqualifying Israel

As we have seen, the Messiah meets all of the requirements in Isaiah 50:4–7. Let us further examine the Scriptures to see whether or not Israel qualifies.

Israel, No Knowledge

The Lord GOD hath given me the tongue of the learned, that I should know how to speak a word in season to him that is weary: he wakeneth morning by morning, he wakeneth mine ear to hear as the learned.

—Isaiah 50:4

According to this verse, the suffering servant must have the tongue and open ears of the learned. In other words, He will possess full understanding and knowledge of all things. But it has already been shown in the first Servant Song that Israel is blind and deaf (Isa. 42:18–20). Therefore, this cannot apply to Israel, whose understanding and knowledge has been taken away by God. As a result, it cannot qualify as the subject of this third Servant Song because it fails to meet the necessary criteria of having both understanding and knowledge.

As further confirmation of this, Isaiah 9:16 provides a firm warning to those who follow the teachings of Israel's spiritual leaders, "For the leaders of this people cause them to err; and they that are led of them are destroyed."

Israel, a Rebellious People

The Lord GOD hath opened mine ear, and I was not rebellious, neither turned away back.

—Isaiah 50:5

This verse indicates that the servant will not be rebellious against God. Regarding Israel, the Hebrew scriptures bear witness of their rebellion. Here are a few examples:

* **Deuteronomy 9:7**: "Remember, and forget not, how thou provokedst the LORD thy God to wrath in the wilderness: from the day that thou didst depart out of the land of Egypt, until ye came unto this place, ye have been rebellious against the LORD."
* **Isaiah 30:9**: "That this is a rebellious people, lying children, children that will not hear the law of the LORD."
* **Isaiah 65:2**: "I have spread out my hands all the day unto a rebellious people, which walketh in a way that was not good, after their own thoughts."
* **Jeremiah 5:3,23**: "O LORD, are not thine eyes upon the truth? thou hast stricken them, but they have not grieved; thou hast consumed them, but they have refused to receive correction: they have made their faces harder than a rock; they have refused to return. . . . But this people hath a revolting and a rebellious heart; they are revolted and gone."
* **Zechariah 7:11–12**: "But they refused to hearken, and pulled away the shoulder, and stopped their ears, that they should not hear. Yea, they made their hearts as an adamant stone, lest they should hear the law, and the words which the LORD of hosts hath sent in his spirit by the former prophets: therefore came a great wrath from the LORD of hosts."

As we can see, the prophets give testimony to Israel's continued rebellion. Deuteronomy 9:7 teaches that this has been the case ever since the days of

Moses. However, it needs to be mentioned that all of us have a tendency of being rebellious against God. In this respect, the children of Israel are no exception. Romans 3:23 declares, "For all have sinned, and come short of the glory of God."

Once again, as a result of the overwhelming evidence showing that Israel has been rebellious, it must be disqualified as the subject of Isaiah's third Servant Song.

Israel, ashamed and confounded

> For the Lord GOD will help me; therefore shall I not be confounded: therefore have I set my face like a flint, and I know that I shall not be ashamed.
>
> —Isaiah 50:7

According to this verse, the servant shall not be confounded and ashamed. But Isaiah 42:16–17 tells us that immediately after Israel's foretold redemption and salvation, they will be ashamed. Meanwhile, Ezekiel 36:28–32 reconfirms that Israel will be both ashamed and confounded for their ways after this has taken place:

* **Isaiah 42:16–17:** "And I will bring the blind by a way that they knew not; I will lead them in paths that they have not known: I will make darkness light before them, and crooked things straight. These things will I do unto them, and not forsake them. They shall be turned back, they shall be greatly ashamed, that trust in graven images, that say to the molten images, Ye are our gods."
* **Ezekiel 36:28–32:** "And ye shall dwell in the land that I gave to your fathers; and ye shall be my people, and I will be your God. I will also save you from all your uncleannesses: and I will call for the corn, and will increase it, and lay no famine upon you. And I will multiply the fruit of the tree, and the increase of the field, that ye shall receive no more reproach of famine among the heathen. Then shall ye remember your own evil ways, and your doings that were not good, and shall lothe yourselves in your own sight for your iniquities and for your abominations. Not

for your sakes do I this, saith the Lord GOD, be it known unto you: be ashamed and confounded for your own ways, O house of Israel."

Since Isaiah 50:7 indicates that the servant will not be ashamed and confounded, and these two passages foretell Israel will be ashamed and confounded, Israel is not the subject of this Servant Song.

As a result of the overwhelming evidence illustrating Israel's failures to meet these requirements, logic dictates that they could not possibly be the subject of Isaiah's third Servant Song. And as we have already seen, the Messiah qualifies!

IV. The Glorified Messiah

As we can see, Isaiah 50:7 tells us that God's suffering servant would not be confounded and ashamed. Such is the case with the Messiah! The Scriptures reveal that He will be highly exalted and glorified throughout the ends of the earth. Daniel 7:13–14 tells us that all people, nations, and languages shall serve him. Psalm 72:11, Isaiah 9:7, and Isaiah 11:10 all describe a highly glorified and exalted Messiah:

+ **Daniel 7:13–14:** "I saw in the night visions, and, behold, one like the Son of man came with the clouds of heaven, and came to the Ancient of days, and they brought him near before him. And there was given him dominion, and glory, and a kingdom, that all people, nations, and languages, should serve him: his dominion is an everlasting dominion, which shall not pass away, and his kingdom that which shall not be destroyed."
+ **Psalm 72:11:** "Yea, all kings shall fall down before him: all nations shall serve him."
+ **Isaiah 9:7**—*regarding King Messiah:* "Of the increase of his government and peace there shall be no end, upon the throne of David, and upon his kingdom, to order it, and to establish it with judgment and with justice from henceforth even for ever. The zeal of the LORD of hosts will perform this."
+ **Isaiah 11:10**—*regarding King Messiah:* "And in that day there shall be

a root of Jesse, which shall stand for an ensign of the people; to it shall the Gentiles seek: and his rest shall be glorious."

These verses and passages teach that the Messiah will be glorified. And as we will learn in chapter thirteen in this book, He is the only one given the distinction of being placed at the right hand of God Himself.

V. The Glorified Israel

When all nations come against Jerusalem to battle, it is the LORD who will fight for His people (Zech. 12:3; 14:1–4). After the enemy is defeated (Zech. 14:12), the Messiah will set up His everlasting kingdom in Zion (Zech. 14:16–17; Ps. 132:13–14). Zephaniah 3:17–20 not only confirms the LORD's joy and gladness when He reigns in the midst of His people, it also reveals that Israel will be exalted by every other nation. The applicable scriptures follow:

- **Psalm 132:13–14:** "For the LORD hath chosen Zion; he hath desired it for his habitation. This is my rest for ever: here will I dwell; for I have desired it."

- **Zechariah 14:16–17:** "And it shall come to pass, that every one that is left of all the nations which came against Jerusalem shall even go up from year to year to worship the King, the LORD of hosts, and to keep the feast of tabernacles. And it shall be, that whoso will not come up of all the families of the earth unto Jerusalem to worship the King, the LORD of hosts, even upon them shall be no rain."

- **Zephaniah 3:17–20:** "The LORD thy God in the midst of thee is mighty; he will save, he will rejoice over thee with joy; he will rest in his love, he will joy over thee with singing. I will gather them that are sorrowful for the solemn assembly, who are of thee, to whom the reproach of it was a burden. Behold, at that time I will undo all that afflict thee: and I will save her that halteth, and gather her that was driven out; and I will get them praise and fame in every land where they have been put to shame. At that time will I bring you again, even in the time that I gather you: for I will make you a name and a praise among all people of the earth, when I turn back your captivity before your eyes, saith the LORD."

There will come a day when Israel will be exalted, but not until they look upon Him who was pierced (Zech. 12:10). According to this verse, they will mourn for Him, as one mourns for his only son. All that remain in Jerusalem, "the remnant," will mourn for Him on that great and terrible day of the LORD when all nations come against them (Zech. 12:9–14). Zechariah 13:1 reveals that, in that day, there will be a fountain opened to the house of David and to the inhabitants of Jerusalem "for sin and for uncleanness." They will call on His name, and he will hear them. There will be complete forgiveness of sins in the land. Zechariah 13:9 declares: "And I will bring the third part through the fire, and will refine them as silver is refined, and will try them as gold is tried: they shall call on my name, and I will hear them: I will say, It is my people: and they shall say, The LORD is my God."

Summary

In summary, it is the Messiah who has been given the tongue of the learned (Isa. 50:4; 11:1–2). Additionally, He possesses the fear of the LORD and would not be rebellious against God (Isa. 50:5; 11:2; Heb. 5:7). In contrast, Israel has been called blind and deaf in the Scriptures (Isa. 6:9–10; 42:18–20, etc.), and a servant having no knowledge (Isa. 5:13; 29:13–14; Hos. 4:1,6). Israel has also been rebellious throughout its history and has not shown the fear of the LORD (Deut. 9:7; Isa. 1:5; 30:9, etc.).

The Bible also teaches that Israel will be confounded and ashamed immediately after their salvation has been achieved (Isa. 42:16–17; Ezek. 36:28–32). In contrast, not only will the Messiah *not* be confounded and ashamed, He would be highly exalted and glorified (Dan. 7:13–14; Ps. 72:11; Isa. 9:7; 11:10).

All of these verses prove that it is the Messiah's face that would be beaten and that He is the subject of Isaiah's third Servant Song. This provides the foundation for the fourth Servant Song, Isaiah 53.

Isaiah 50:10 states, "Who is among you that feareth the LORD, that obeyeth the voice of his servant, that walketh in darkness, and hath no light? let him trust in the name of the LORD, and stay upon his God." According to this verse, who is the servant we must obey? Is it the Messiah who has the spirit of wisdom, understanding, and knowledge and is a light of the Gentiles? Or is it Israel, who walks in spiritual darkness? Certainly it must be the Messiah! It is He whom we are commanded to obey!

Chapter Nine

Isaiah 53—The Suffering Messiah

He shall see of the travail of his soul, and shall be satisfied: by his knowledge shall my righteous servant justify many; for he shall bear their iniquities.

—Isaiah 53:11

Part 1—Introduction

As we have seen, the Messiah is the subject of Isaiah's first three Servant Songs: Isaiah 42, 49, and 50. There, the prophet provides the foundation for Isaiah 53, his fourth and final Servant Song. In this chapter, Isaiah foretells the fulfillment of the Messiah's mission by explaining how He would accomplish mankind's redemption for sin by His suffering and death. Because of this, it is one of the most important chapters in the Hebrew scriptures.[38]

In Isaiah 42, the first Servant Song, the prophet portrays two servants whose profiles are radically different from one another. One servant is Israel, depicted as the blind servant living in spiritual darkness (Isa. 42:18–20). The other is the Messiah, referred to as both a light of the Gentiles and a covenant of the people (Isa. 42:6).

Isaiah 49, the second Servant Song, prophesies the nation of Israel despising its Messiah (Isa. 49:7). And according to Isaiah 50, the third Servant Song, the despised and rejected Messiah is beaten. While whipped and flogged, He is not rebellious and voluntarily gives His back to those who strike Him. Moreover, He does not hide His face from shame and spitting; He sets it like a flint. Finally, He would not be ashamed. To the contrary, He is exalted and glorified.

In Isaiah 53, the prophet foretells the Messiah becoming our sin-bearer (Isa. 53:6,11–12). It is also important to mention that Isaiah actually begins his dialogue regarding this Suffering Servant in Isaiah 52:13, not Isaiah 53:1. Therefore, the analysis of this section of the Bible will begin there. At its conclusion, the Messiah's ministry and New Covenant will be firmly established and verified. It will be demonstrated that the fourth Servant Song beautifully connects with Isaiah 50, proving once and for all that the Messiah is the Suffering Servant portrayed in *all* four Servant Songs.

Part 2—The Exalted Servant

Isaiah 52:13

> Behold, my servant shall deal prudently, he shall be exalted and extolled, and be very high.

At the beginning of Isaiah's fourth Servant Song, the prophet introduces the Messiah as God's exalted Servant. As we have previously shown, the prophet mentions that the Messiah would be raised up and glorified in Isaiah 42:1 and Isaiah 11:1–2, when God places His Spirit upon Him. Isaiah 52:13 also tells us that the Messiah "shall deal prudently," since He will bring forth judgment to the Gentiles (Isa. 42:1, Jer. 23:5). Finally, according to Isaiah 42:6 and Isaiah 49:8, the Messiah's exaltation and glorification are shown by the fact that He is called "in righteousness," is a light to the nations, and is a covenant of the people.

Isaiah 52:14–15

> As many were astonied at thee; his visage was so marred more than any man, and his form more than the sons of men: So shall he sprinkle many nations; the kings shall shut their mouths at him: for that which had not been told them shall they see; and that which they had not heard shall they consider.

This passage is the entryway into Isaiah 53 and merits serious attention. Isaiah 52:14 reveals that the Messiah's visage or face is beaten to such a high extent that it becomes unrecognizable. It is also important to realize that both Isaiah 50:5–7 and Micah 5:1 support the idea of a suffering Messiah whose face is viciously beaten. There is therefore a clear connection between Isaiah 50:5–7, Micah 5:1, and Isaiah 52:14 since these scriptures foretell the beating and marring of His face.

- **Isaiah 50:5–7:** "The Lord GOD hath opened mine ear, and I was not rebellious, neither turned away back. I gave my back to the smiters, and my cheeks to them that plucked off the hair: I hid not my face from shame and spitting. For the Lord GOD will help me; therefore shall I not be confounded: therefore have I set my face like a flint, and I know that I shall not be ashamed."
- **Micah 5:1** (KJV): "Now gather thyself in troops, O daughter of troops: he hath laid siege against us: they shall smite the judge of Israel with a rod upon the cheek."

When someone's hair is pulled from his cheeks and his face is set like a flint, it is conceivable that a large amount of blood can be lost. And according to Isaiah 52:14–15, the shedding of this servant's blood will result in the sprinkling of many nations. Because of this shed blood, mankind's sins will be forgiven.

In Isaiah 52:15, the Hebrew word *yazeh,* a form of the verb *nazah,* is used (*Strong's,* #5137). Throughout the Hebrew scriptures, this word is used a total of twenty-four times. It always translates sprinkle. There is no place in the Bible where this word ever translates any other way. Besides Isaiah 52:15, this word is used in Exodus 29:21; Leviticus 4:6,17; 5:9; 6:27, twice; 8:11,30; 14:7,16,27,51; 16:14, twice, 16:15; 16:19; Numbers 8:7; 19:4,18–19,21; 2 Kings 9:33; and Isaiah 63:3.

In every instance in the Torah, this word translates sprinkle and is used with respect to the sprinkling of blood, water, and/or anointing oil for the purpose of purification and cleansing. As an example, on the Day of Atonement which is Yom Kippur, blood was sprinkled on the mercy seat

(Lev. 16:15) and used to atone for the sins of the people. In these verses, the Hebrew word *nazah*, or *yazeh*, is used:

> And he [the high priest] shall take of the blood of the bullock, and sprinkle it with his finger upon the mercy seat eastward; and before the mercy seat shall he sprinkle of the blood with his finger seven times. Then shall he kill the goat of the sin offering, that is for the people, and bring his blood within the vail, and do with that blood as he did with the blood of the bullock, and sprinkle it upon the mercy seat, and before the mercy seat. . . . And he shall sprinkle of the blood upon it with his finger seven times, and cleanse it, and hallow it from the uncleanness of the children of Israel.
>
> —Leviticus 16:14–15,19

It is also important to note that the definition of the word *yazeh* or *nazah* as sprinkle in Isaiah 52:15 makes perfect sense and fits contextually with the surrounding verses. Isaiah 52:14 foretells that the subject's visage or face would be, "marred more than any man, and his form more than the sons of men." The shedding of blood is also implied in Isaiah 53:5 which states that "he was wounded for our transgressions, he was bruised for our iniquities . . . and with his stripes we are healed." Additionally, Isaiah 53 prophesies this servant's death. Verse 9 indicates that, "he made his grave with the wicked, and with the rich in his death. . . ." It is clear that this individual would be beaten and brutalized to such a high degree that not only would his blood be shed, he would also die.

Though Yom Kippur provided atonement for the sins of the people by the blood and death of animals, Isaiah 53 teaches that they are now made clean by a new and better way, by the shed blood and death of God's righteous servant. This describes the New Covenant, the new way God forgives sins. According to Isaiah 52:15, the sprinkling of the blood of this Righteous Servant will provide complete and absolute redemption for the sins of the world, "So shall he sprinkle many nations."

The word sprinkle, *yazeh*, shows the connection between Leviticus 16 and Isaiah 53. This fourth Servant Song describes how the Messiah provides the final redemption for sin. The Day of Atonement described in Leviticus 16 was merely a type or foreshadow of better things . . . pointing to what He would ultimately accomplish. As we will see, God's servant establishes the New Covenant by providing mankind's ultimate forgiveness for their sins.

Isaiah 53:1

Who hath believed our report? and to whom is the arm of the LORD revealed?

It is important to realize that in Isaiah 52:10, the prophet already tells us that the LORD's arm would be revealed to all nations, so that everyone would see His salvation: "The LORD hath made bare his holy arm in the eyes of all the nations; and all the ends of the earth shall see the salvation of our God."

However in Isaiah 53:1, the prophet asks the question with the express purpose of explaining how God would bare His holy arm. In this verse, the report spoken of is not only Isaiah's, but the report of all the other prophets: the entire word of God.

After reading Isaiah 53:1, several questions need to be asked: First, who or what is the arm of the LORD? Secondly, to whom is the arm of the LORD revealed? As we will see, the LORD's arm is a figurative expression for God's spiritual and physical salvation for His people. Isaiah 52:10 teaches that God's holy arm will not only provide salvation for Israel, but the entire world. In Hebrew, the word for salvation is *yeshua* (*Strong's,* #3444).

How will God provide salvation to the world? The answer: Through the Messiah, His holy arm. It would be through Him that spiritual and physical salvation takes place.

Part 3—The Arm of the LORD: the Messiah

The Hebrew scriptures provide six clear connections between the arm of the LORD and the Messiah. They are as follows:

1. In Isaiah 59:16, the prophet likens the LORD's arm to an intercessor.

An intercessor is a priest. Accordingly, when Zechariah writes about the BRANCH, the Messiah, he foretells that He would be both King and Priest (Zech. 6:12–13). Psalm 110:4 calls Him the eternal priest by God's personal decree:

♦ **Isaiah 59:16:** "And he saw that there was no man, and wondered that there was no intercessor: therefore his arm brought salvation unto him. . . ."

♦ **Zechariah 6:12–13:** ". . . Behold the man whose name is The BRANCH; and he shall grow up out of his place, and he shall build the temple of the LORD: Even he shall build the temple of the LORD; and he shall bear the glory, and shall sit and rule upon his throne; and he shall be a priest upon his throne: and the counsel of peace shall be between them both."

♦ **Psalm 110:4:** "The LORD hath sworn, and will not repent, Thou art a priest for ever after the order of Melchizedek."

2. Isaiah 59:16 continues: ". . . therefore his arm brought salvation unto him." Though this verse indicates that the LORD's arm brought salvation to Him, Zechariah 9:9 foretells the Messiah riding into Jerusalem "having salvation": "Rejoice greatly, O daughter of Zion; shout, O daughter of Jerusalem: behold, thy King cometh unto thee: he is just, and having salvation; lowly, and riding upon an ass, and upon a colt the foal of an ass" (see also Matt. 21:4–9; John 12:12–15).

3. Isaiah 59:17 states, "For he [the LORD's arm] put on righteousness as a breastplate." Though this verse indicates that the LORD's arm put on righteousness as a breastplate, Jeremiah 23:5–6 and Isaiah 11:5 both state that the Messiah would do the same:

♦ **Jeremiah 23:5–6:** "Behold, the days come, saith the LORD, that I will raise unto David a righteous Branch, and a King shall reign and prosper, and shall execute judgment and justice in the earth. In his days Judah shall be saved, and Israel shall dwell safely: and this is his name whereby he shall be called, THE LORD OUR RIGHTEOUSNESS."

♦ **Isaiah 11:5**—*regarding the Messiah:* "And righteousness shall be the girdle of his loins. . . .

4. Isaiah 59:17–18 continues: ". . . he put on the garments of vengeance for clothing, and was clad with zeal as a cloke. According to their deeds, accordingly he will repay, fury to his adversaries, recompence to his enemies; to the islands he will repay recompence." Though this verse indicates that the LORD's arm will judge and punish the nations, Isaiah 11:4 and Jeremiah 23:5 both tell us that the Messiah would do the same:

- **Isaiah 11:4:** "But with righteousness shall he judge the poor, and reprove with equity for the meek of the earth: and he shall smite the earth with the rod of his mouth, and with the breath of his lips shall he slay the wicked."
- **Jeremiah 23:5:** "Behold, the days come, saith the LORD, that I will raise unto David a righteous Branch, and a King shall reign and prosper, and shall execute judgment and justice in the earth."

5. Isaiah 40:10 gives us further information about the LORD's arm. It states, "Behold, the Lord GOD will come with strong hand, and his arm shall rule for him: behold, his reward is with him, and his work before him." Though this verse indicates that the LORD's arm "shall rule for him," Daniel 7:13–14, Jeremiah 23:5, Zechariah 6:12–13 and 9:9 all teach that the Messiah will be King.

- **Daniel 7:13–14:** "I saw in the night visions, and, behold, one like the Son of man came with the clouds of heaven, and came to the Ancient of days, and they brought him near before him. And there was given him dominion, and glory, and a kingdom, that all people, nations, and languages, should serve him: his dominion is an everlasting dominion, which shall not pass away, and his kingdom that which shall not be destroyed."
- **Jeremiah 23:5:** "Behold, the days come, saith the LORD, that I will raise unto David a righteous Branch, and a King shall reign and prosper, and shall execute judgment and justice in the earth."
- **Zechariah 6:12–13:** ". . . Behold the man whose name is The BRANCH;

and he shall grow up out of his place, and he shall build the temple of the LORD: Even he shall build the temple of the LORD; and he shall bear the glory, and shall sit and rule upon his throne; and he shall be a priest upon his throne: and the counsel of peace shall be between them both."

- **Zechariah 9:9:** "Rejoice greatly, O daughter of Zion; shout, O daughter of Jerusalem: behold, thy King cometh unto thee: he is just, and having salvation; lowly, and riding upon an ass, and upon a colt the foal of an ass."

6. Isaiah 40:11 likens the LORD's arm to a shepherd by stating, "He shall feed his flock like a shepherd." Remembering this, Zechariah 13:7 and Ezekiel 37:24 refer to the Messiah as God's shepherd:

- **Zechariah 13:7:** "Awake, O sword, against my shepherd, and against the man that is my fellow, saith the LORD of hosts: smite the shepherd, and the sheep shall be scattered: and I will turn mine hand upon the little ones."
- **Ezekiel 37:24:** "And David my servant [with reference to the Messiah[30]] shall be king over them; and they all shall have one shepherd: they shall also walk in my judgments, and observe my statutes, and do them."

In conclusion, the Scriptures provide at least six important parallels between the LORD's arm and the Messiah. They are as follows:

1. The LORD's arm is likened to an intercessor, a priest (Isa. 59:16), and the Messiah will be a priest forever (Zech. 6:12–13; Ps. 110:4).
2. The LORD's arm would bring salvation unto Him (Isa. 59:16), and the Messiah would ride into Jerusalem having salvation (Zech. 9:9).
3. The LORD's arm put on righteousness as a breastplate (Isa. 59:17), and the Messiah would wear righteousness as the girdle of his loins (Isa. 11:5) and be called a righteous King and "THE LORD OUR RIGHTEOUSNESS" (Jer. 23:5–6).
4. The LORD's arm will judge the nations (Isa. 59:17–18), and the Messiah will judge the nations (Isa. 11:4; Jer. 23:5).

5. The LORD's arm shall rule for Him (Isa. 40:10), and the Messiah will be King (Dan. 7:13–14; Jer. 23:5; Zech. 6:12–13; 9:9).
6. The LORD's arm is likened to a shepherd (Isa. 40:11), and the Messiah is called God's shepherd (Zech. 13:7; Ezek. 37:24).

At this point it should be clear that the arm of the LORD is the Messiah. Just like the first three Servant Songs, He must be the subject of this fourth Servant Song, Isaiah 53!

Part 4—King Messiah: The Root Out of Dry Ground
Isaiah 53:2

> For he shall grow up before him as a tender plant, and as a root out of a dry ground: he hath no form nor comeliness; and when we shall see him, there is no beauty that we should desire him."

In this verse, Isaiah describes the Messiah as a root, in Hebrew *sheresh* (*Strong's*, #8328). It is significant to note that in Isaiah 11:10, He is also referred to as a root, a root of Jesse. Here, the same Hebrew word, *sheresh*, is used: "And in that day there shall be a root [*sheresh*] of Jesse, which shall stand for an ensign of the people; to it shall the Gentiles seek: and his rest shall be glorious."

In previous chapters in his book, Isaiah identifies the dry ground as the nation of Israel. This is portrayed in Isaiah 5:13 and Isaiah 44:1–3 which state:

* **Isaiah 5:13:** "Therefore my people are gone into captivity, because they have no knowledge: and their honourable men are famished, and their multitude dried up with thirst."
* **Isaiah 44:1–3:** "Yet now hear, O Jacob my servant; and Israel, whom I have chosen: Thus saith the LORD that made thee, and formed thee from the womb, which will help thee; Fear not, O Jacob, my servant; and thou, Jesurun, whom I have chosen. For I will pour water upon him that is thirsty, and floods upon the dry ground: I will pour my spirit upon thy seed, and my blessing upon thine offspring."

According to these scriptures, Israel is the dry ground. Therefore, Isaiah 53:2 teaches that the Messiah (the root) will come forth out of the dry ground (Israel). In other words, He would be an Israelite, a Jew!

Israel will remain a dry ground until the LORD pours out His Spirit upon the nation. The prophet Joel foretells that this will not happen until the Day of the LORD, a future event, when all nations come against Jerusalem. The prophet Zechariah agrees:

+ **Joel 2:28–32:** "And it shall come to pass afterward, that I will pour out my spirit upon all flesh; and your sons and your daughters shall prophesy, your old men shall dream dreams, your young men shall see visions: And also upon the servants and upon the handmaids in those days will I pour out my spirit. And I will shew wonders in the heavens and in the earth, blood, and fire, and pillars of smoke. The sun shall be turned into darkness, and the moon into blood, before the great and the terrible day of the LORD come. And it shall come to pass, that whosoever shall call on the name of the LORD shall be delivered: for in mount Zion and in Jerusalem shall be deliverance, as the LORD hath said, and in the remnant whom the LORD shall call."

+ **Zechariah 12:9–10:** "And it shall come to pass in that day, that I will seek to destroy all the nations that come against Jerusalem. And I will pour upon the house of David, and upon the inhabitants of Jerusalem, the spirit of grace and of supplications: and they shall look upon me whom they have pierced, and they shall mourn for him, as one mourneth for his only son, and shall be in bitterness for him, as one that is in bitterness for his firstborn."

Regarding Isaiah 53:2, we have shown the following: the root is the Messiah, the root of Jesse (Isa. 11:10), and the dry ground is Israel (Isa. 5:13; 44:1–3). When placing the proper noun next to the pronouns in Isaiah 53:2, it is now much easier to understand what the prophet is saying. He states as follows:

For he [the Messiah] shall grow up before him [Israel] as a tender plant, and as a root [the Messiah, see Isa. 11:10] out of a dry ground [Israel]:

he [the Messiah] hath no form nor comeliness; and when we [Israel, Isaiah's people] shall see him [the Messiah], there is no beauty that we [Isaiah's people, Israel] should desire him [the Messiah].

One other note: Isaiah 53:2 concludes with the phrase: ". . . and when we shall see him, there is no beauty that we should desire him." In fulfillment of this verse it is important to realize that when Jesus came into the world approximately two thousand years ago, it was the majority of his own people, the Jews, who rejected him. John 1:11 states, "He came unto his own, and his own received him not."

Isaiah 53:3

He is despised and rejected of men; a man of sorrows, and acquainted with grief: and we hid as it were our faces from him; he was despised, and we esteemed him not."

Isaiah 53:3 stresses the Messiah's rejection by His own people. In Isaiah 49, the second Servant Song, it was prophesied that He would be despised and rejected by a single nation, the nation of Israel. Isaiah 49:7 states:

Thus saith the LORD, the Redeemer of Israel, and his Holy One, to him whom man despiseth, to him whom the nation abhorreth, to a servant of rulers, Kings shall see and arise, princes also shall worship, because of the LORD that is faithful, and the Holy One of Israel, and he shall choose thee.

The Messiah's rejection comes to its climax when He is severely beaten (Isa. 50:5–7; 52:14; Mic. 5:1 KJV) and killed (Isa. 53:8). When placing the proper noun next to the pronouns in Isaiah 53:3, the prophet's message is clear. It reads:

He [the Messiah] is despised and rejected of men; a man of sorrows, and acquainted with grief: and we [Isaiah's people, Israel] hid as it were our faces [Isaiah's people, Israel] from him [the Messiah]; he [the Messiah] was despised, and we [Isaiah's people, Israel] esteemed him [the Messiah] not.

Isaiah 53:4–6

Surely he hath borne our griefs, and carried our sorrows: yet we did esteem him stricken, smitten of God, and afflicted. But he was wounded [pierced] for our transgressions, he was bruised for our iniquities: the chastisement of our peace was upon him; and with his stripes we are healed. All we like sheep have gone astray; we have turned every one to his own way; and the LORD hath laid on him the iniquity of us all.

These verses tell us the reasons for the Messiah's rejection and eventual death. According to verse 4, the children of Israel would originally believe that God punished Him because of what He had done. However, verses 5 and 6 state that there will come a day when Israel will realize that they had been wrong. In reality, the Messiah was wounded and pierced for their transgressions, He was bruised for their iniquities, and with His stripes they are healed. He was not punished for His sins; He was punished for their sins! By the LORD laying Israel's iniquities and sins upon the Messiah, He became their sin-bearer.

According to Leviticus 16:21, when Aaron placed his hands on the head of the live goat and confessed all of the iniquities, transgressions, and sins of the people over it, the scapegoat was Israel's sin-bearer: "And Aaron shall lay both his hands upon the head of the live goat, and confess over him all the iniquities of the children of Israel, and all their transgressions in all their sins, putting them upon the head of the goat, and shall send him away by the hand of a fit man into the wilderness."

This sacrificial system was the original way provided by God through which Israel received atonement for their sins. The Bible instructs that the penalty for sin is death (Gen. 2:17; Rom. 6:23). By these sacrifices, God was demonstrating that animals had to pay the price and die in place of sinners. This is called a vicarious sacrifice. During the days of Moses, this became necessary because sinners needed to be saved from their own deaths, which is the penalty for sin. Instead of people dying, innocent and clean animals paid the penalty.

In Isaiah 53:4–6 the prophet shows that God's righteous servant, the Messiah, would become mankind's sin-bearer and pay the penalty for sin by His suffering and death. The Messiah's death for sin becomes critical in mankind's relationship with God and is the basis and foundation for the New Testament, the new way by which God forgives sins. Jeremiah 31:31–34 states:

> Behold, the days come, saith the LORD, that I will make a new covenant with the house of Israel, and with the house of Judah: Not according to the covenant that I made with their fathers in the day that I took them by the hand to bring them out of the land of Egypt; which my covenant they brake, although I was an husband unto them, saith the LORD: But this shall be the covenant that I will make with the house of Israel; After those days, saith the LORD, I will put my law in their inward parts, and write it in their hearts; and will be their God, and they shall be my people. And they shall teach no more every man his neighbour, and every man his brother, saying, Know the LORD: for they shall all know me, from the least of them unto the greatest of them, saith the LORD: for I will forgive their iniquity, and I will remember their sin no more.

When an individual is wounded, pierced, bruised, and struck with a whip, much blood is shed. Through the New Covenant established by the shed blood of God's righteous Messiah, the children of Israel are now saved from their own deaths, the penalty for their sins.

Based on the conclusions resulting from this analysis, let us place the subject alongside the pronouns in Isaiah 53:4–6. The passage now reads:

> Surely he [the Messiah] hath borne our [Isaiah's people, Israel] griefs, and carried our [Isaiah's people, Israel] sorrows: yet we [Isaiah's people, Israel] did esteem him [the Messiah] stricken, smitten of God, and afflicted. But he [the Messiah] was wounded [pierced] for our [Isaiah's people, Israel] transgressions, he [the Messiah] was bruised for our [Isaiah's people, Israel] iniquities: the chastisement of our [Isaiah's people, Israel] peace was upon him [the Messiah]; and with his [the Messiah's] stripes

we [Isaiah's people, Israel] are healed. All we [Isaiah's people, Israel] like sheep have gone astray; we [Isaiah's people, Israel] have turned every one to his [Isaiah's people, Israel] own way; and the LORD hath laid on him [the Messiah] the iniquity of us [Isaiah's people, Israel] all.

Isaiah 53:7

He was oppressed, and he was afflicted, yet he opened not his mouth: he is brought as a lamb to the slaughter, and as a sheep before her shearers is dumb, so he openeth not his mouth.

This verse prophesies the Messiah would not complain or resist when under oppression and affliction. He would willingly suffer for mankind's sins. This was previously foretold in Isaiah 50:5–7 which states as follows:

The Lord GOD hath opened mine ear, and I was not rebellious, neither turned away back. I gave my back to the smiters, and my cheeks to them that plucked off the hair: I hid not my face from shame and spitting. For the Lord GOD will help me; therefore shall I not be confounded: therefore have I set my face like a flint, and I know that I shall not be ashamed.

Did Jesus complain when He was oppressed and afflicted? Did He go willingly to His death? The answer: He went to His death just as Isaiah 50:5–7 and Isaiah 53:7 foretold. He was not rebellious! In the New Testament, Jesus stated:

- **John 10:11:** "I am the good shepherd: the good shepherd giveth his life for the sheep."
- **John 10:15:** "As the Father knoweth me, even so know I the Father: and I lay down my life for the sheep."
- **John 10:17:** "Therefore doth my Father love me, because I lay down my life, that I might take it again."
- **John 15:13:** "Greater love hath no man than this, that a man lay down his life for his friends."

According to Matthew 26:50–54, when they took Jesus away from the garden of Gethsemane to be tried and ultimately crucified, He never complained:

> And Jesus said unto him, Friend, wherefore art thou come? Then came they, and laid hands on Jesus, and took him. And, behold, one of them which were with Jesus stretched out his hand, and drew his sword, and struck a servant of the high priest's, and smote off his ear. Then said Jesus unto him, Put up again thy sword into his place: for all they that take the sword shall perish with the sword. Thinkest thou that I cannot now pray to my Father, and he shall presently give me more than twelve legions of angels? But how then shall the scriptures be fulfilled, that thus it must be?

From these passages, it is clear that Jesus told His friends to put their swords away. According to Him, the time had arrived for the Scriptures to be fulfilled. He never complained, and went willingly to His death. When He was taken from near the garden and placed into prison, the following events took place: They whipped Him and scourged Him. They made Him a crown of thorns, mocked Him, spat at Him, and drove nails into His hands and His feet. Finally, they hung Him on a cross to die a criminal's death.

Did Jesus demonstrate anger toward those who persecuted Him? Did He curse them? One of the last things Jesus said before He died such a horrible death is recorded in Luke 23:34, which states, "Then said Jesus, Father, forgive them; for they know not what they do."

Based on this evidence, placing the appropriate subject alongside the pronouns in Isaiah 53:7, it now reads:

> He [the Messiah] was oppressed, and he [the Messiah] was afflicted, yet he [the Messiah] opened not his [the Messiah's] mouth: he [the Messiah] is brought as a lamb to the slaughter, and as a sheep before her shearers is dumb, so he [the Messiah] openeth not his [the Messiah's] mouth.

Isaiah 53:8-9

He was taken from prison and from judgment: and who shall declare his generation? for he was cut off out of the land of the living: for the transgression of my people was he stricken. And he made his grave with the wicked, and with the rich in his death; because he had done no violence, neither was any deceit in his mouth.

—Isaiah 53:8–9

This portion of Isaiah 53 teaches that the Messiah would be "cut off out of the land of the living," a clear reference to being killed. According to this passage, the reason for His death was "for the transgression of my people." In other words, the Messiah would die to pay the penalty for the sins of His people, not for Himself.

The Scriptures instruct that God would only accept a pure and unblemished offering for sin. It has also been shown that all of us sin. But according to Hebrews 4:15, Jesus was without sin. John 1:29 advises us that He was the perfect and spotless Lamb of God who takes away the sin of the world. The applicable scriptures follow:

- **John 10:11:** "I am the good shepherd: the good shepherd giveth his life for the sheep."
- **John 1:29:** "The next day John seeth Jesus coming unto him, and saith, Behold the Lamb of God, which taketh away the sin of the world."
- **Hebrews 4:15:** "For we have not an high priest which cannot be touched with the feeling of our infirmities; but was in all points tempted like as we are, yet without sin."

As we have seen, the arm of the LORD is a clear reference to the Messiah and, according to Isaiah 52:10, the Lord's arm is holy. Therefore, the Messiah must also be holy. Since Jesus was without sin, He certainly qualifies as the holy arm of the LORD.

In addition to being holy, the Bible teaches us that the Messiah would be righteous. Jeremiah 23:5–6 calls the Branch a righteous King and *"the Lord our Righteousness."* Furthermore regarding the Messiah, Isaiah 11:5

teaches that righteousness shall be the girdle of his loins:

- **Isaiah 52:10:** "The LORD hath made bare his holy arm in the eyes of all the nations; and all the ends of the earth shall see the salvation of our God."
- **Jeremiah 23:5–6:** "Behold, the days come, saith the LORD, that I will raise unto David a righteous Branch, and a King shall reign and prosper, and shall execute judgment and justice in the earth. In his days Judah shall be saved, and Israel shall dwell safely: and this is his name whereby he shall be called, THE LORD OUR RIGHTEOUSNESS."
- **Isaiah 11:5:** "And righteousness shall be the girdle of his loins, and faithfulness the girdle of his reins."

Regarding Isaiah 53:8, the prophet also speaks of a servant who would be cut off for "my people." Isaiah's people are Israel; God's people are Israel. In the Scriptures, the term "my people" refers to Israel. Further, Isaiah calls Israel my people just a few verses prior to this fourth Servant Song. Regarding Israel, Isaiah 52:4–6 states:

> For thus saith the Lord GOD, My people went down aforetime into Egypt to sojourn there; and the Assyrian oppressed them without cause. Now therefore, what have I here, saith the LORD, that my people is taken away for nought? they that rule over them make them to howl, saith the LORD; and my name continually every day is blasphemed. Therefore my people shall know my name: therefore they shall know in that day that I am he that doth speak: behold, it is I.

It is apparent that Isaiah 53:8 foretells the Messiah would suffer and die for the iniquities, transgressions, and sins of God's people Israel. Therefore based on these conclusions, placing the appropriate subject alongside the pronouns in Isaiah 53:8, it now reads:

> He [the Messiah] was taken from prison and from judgment: and who shall declare his generation? for he [the Messiah] was cut off out of the

land of the living: for the transgression of my people [Israel] was he [the Messiah] stricken.

Regarding Isaiah 53:9, the Messiah would possess no deceit. Additionally, Isaiah 11:2 reveals that He would fear the LORD. Certainly those who truly fear God are absent of any deceit and, because of this, the Messiah would further qualify as the subject of Isaiah 53:9. In the New Testament, 1 Peter 2:22, and Hebrews 5:7 [KJV] teach that Jesus had no deceit and feared God. Because of this, He is the fulfillment of both Isaiah 11:2 and Isaiah 53:9:

- **Isaiah 11:2**—*regarding the Messiah*: "And the spirit of the LORD shall rest upon him, the spirit of wisdom and understanding, the spirit of counsel and might, the spirit of knowledge and of the fear of the LORD."
- **1 Peter 2:22**—*regarding Jesus*: "Who did no sin, neither was guile [deceit] found in his mouth."
- **Hebrews 5:7**—*regarding Jesus*: "Who in the days of his flesh, when he had offered up prayers and supplications with strong crying and tears unto him that was able to save him from death, and was heard in that he feared."

Based on these illustrations, placing the appropriate subject alongside the pronouns in Isaiah 53:9, it now reads:

And he [the LORD] made his [the Messiah's] grave with the wicked, and with the rich in his death; because he [the Messiah] had done no violence, neither was any deceit in his [the Messiah's] mouth.

Author's note: Those who deny that Jesus is the subject of this chapter might ask a challenging question: "Who is the rich in this verse?" Here, the Hebrew word for "rich" is *ashiyr,* (*Strong's* #6223). In the Bible, this same word is used on many occasions and translated "rich man." A couple of examples are found in 2 Samuel 12:2 and 2 Samuel 12:4: "The rich man [*ashiyr*] had exceeding many flocks and herds" (2 Sam. 12:2). "And there came a traveller unto the rich man [*ashiyr*], and he spared to take of his own flock and of his own herd, to dress for the wayfaring man that was come unto him; but took the poor man's lamb, and dressed it for the man that was come to him" (2 Sam. 12:4).

Keeping this in mind, we can use the NASB translation which translates *ashiyr* in the same manner as does the KJV in the above two verses: "His grave was assigned with wicked men, Yet He was with a rich *man* [*ashiyr*] in His death, Because He had done no violence, Nor was there any deceit in His mouth."

It is generally believed that Joseph of Arimathaea was the foretold rich man since he was the individual responsible for providing the tomb or sepulchre where Jesus was buried. Matthew 27:57–60 testifies: "When the even was come, there came a rich man of Arimathaea, named Joseph, who also himself was Jesus' disciple: He went to Pilate, and begged the body of Jesus. Then Pilate commanded the body to be delivered. And when Joseph had taken the body, he wrapped it in a clean linen cloth, And laid it in his own new tomb, which he had hewn out in the rock: and he rolled a great stone to the door of the sepulchre, and departed."

Isaiah 53:10

Yet it pleased the LORD to bruise him; he hath put him to grief: when thou shalt make his soul an offering for sin, he shall see his seed, he shall prolong his days, and the pleasure of the LORD shall prosper in his hand.

Why would it please the LORD to bruise the Messiah and put Him to grief? The answer is clear: Through His shed blood, suffering, and death, mankind is now reconciled to the holy God of Israel. Though sin entered into the world and succeeded in separating us from our beloved Creator, the LORD has provided reconciliation through the New Covenant by which sins are forgiven. God sent the righteous Messiah to redeem mankind from its sins. In John 3:16 we read, "For God so loved the world, that he gave his only begotten Son, that whosoever believeth in him should not perish, but have everlasting life."

When the covenant at Sinai was established, Exodus 24:5–10 records that the seventy of Israel went up with Moses, Aaron, Nadab, and Abihu and were permitted to enter into Almighty God's presence after they were sprinkled with the blood of the covenant. In similar fashion, we are now allowed into God's presence through the precious blood of the New Covenant, the Messiah's blood. Hebrews 10:17–20 states:

> And their sins and iniquities will I remember no more. Now where remission of these is, there is no more offering for sin. Having therefore, brethren, boldness to enter into the holiest by the blood of Jesus, By a new and living way, which he hath consecrated for us, through the veil, that is to say, his flesh.

Regarding Isaiah 53:10 and prolonging His days, it is the LORD who shall see His son, His seed, and shall prolong His days. Hence, the resurrection! As we have already seen in chapter four of this book, the Messiah is God's only begotten Son and can rightfully claim that God is His Father. God refers to Him as His Son in Psalm 2:6–7: "Yet have I set my king upon my holy hill of Zion. I will declare the decree: the LORD hath said unto me, Thou art my Son; this day have I begotten thee."

In Isaiah 53:10, the Hebrew word *zera* is used (*Strong's*, #2233). It is translated seed. Although this word can refer to a physical seed, it also translates child or offspring. Examples of this can be found in Leviticus 22:13 and 1 Samuel 1:11:

- **Leviticus 22:13:** "But if the priest's daughter be a widow, or divorced, and have no child [*zera*], and is returned unto her father's house, as in her youth, she shall eat of her father's meat: but there shall no stranger eat thereof."
- **1 Samuel 1:11:** "And she vowed a vow, and said, O LORD of hosts, if thou wilt indeed look on the affliction of thine handmaid, and remember me, and not forget thine handmaid, but wilt give unto thine handmaid

a man child [*zera*], then I will give him unto the LORD all the days of his life, and there shall no razor come upon his head."

Regarding Isaiah 53:10, the LORD sees His seed, His Son, and prolongs His days. This can certainly apply to Jesus' resurrection where it states in Acts 13:33, Romans 1:4, and Romans 10:9 the following:

- **Acts 13:33:** "God hath fulfilled the same unto us their children, in that he hath raised up Jesus again; as it is also written in the second psalm, Thou art my Son, this day have I begotten thee."
- **Romans 1:4:** "And declared to be the Son of God with power, according to the spirit of holiness, by the resurrection from the dead."
- **Romans 10:9:** "That if thou shalt confess with thy mouth the Lord Jesus, and shalt believe in thine heart that God hath raised him from the dead, thou shalt be saved."

Based on the evidence, placing the appropriate subject alongside the pronouns in Isaiah 53:10, it now reads:

Yet it pleased the LORD to bruise him [the Messiah]; he [the LORD] hath put him [the Messiah] to grief: when thou [the LORD] shalt make his [the Messiah's] soul an offering for sin, he [the LORD] shall see his [the LORD's] seed, he [the LORD] shall prolong his [the Messiah's] days, and the pleasure of the LORD shall prosper in his [the Messiah's] hand.

Isaiah 53:11

He shall see of the travail of his soul, and shall be satisfied: by his knowledge shall my righteous servant justify many; for he shall bear their iniquities.

According to this verse the Messiah would bear our iniquities. This has already been shown in Isaiah 53:5–6. This verse also teaches that God's suffering Messiah would have two attributes: righteousness and knowledge.

His righteousness has already been established in Isaiah's first Servant Song. Isaiah 42:6 refers to Him as called "in righteousness": "I the LORD have called thee in righteousness, and will hold thine hand, and will keep thee, and give thee for a covenant of the people, for a light of the Gentiles."

Meanwhile, Isaiah 11:5 and Jeremiah 23:5–6 bear further witness to a righteous Messiah.

Regarding knowledge, Isaiah 11:1–2 foretells that the Messiah would have the spirit of wisdom and understanding, and the spirit of knowledge. As a result, He meets both qualifications as the subject of Isaiah 53:11.

According to the New Testament, Jesus possessed both of these characteristics. He was righteous before God, and He had the knowledge that Isaiah foretold the Messiah would have. The verses to show how He fulfilled Isaiah 53:11 follow:

- **1 John 2:1:** "My little children, these things write I unto you, that ye sin not. And if any man sin, we have an advocate with the Father, Jesus Christ the righteous."
- **Colossians 2:3:** "In whom [Jesus] are hid all the treasures of wisdom and knowledge."

One other note: The Hebrew word for righteous is *tsaddiyq* (*Strong's*, #6662). This word not only translates "righteous," it also translates "just." This precise Hebrew word is used in Zechariah 9:9 and refers to the Messiah coming into Jerusalem: ". . . he is just [righteous] [*tsaddiyq*], and having salvation; lowly, and riding upon an ass, and upon a colt the foal of an ass." And according to Matthew 21:4–9, Jesus fulfilled this prophecy.

Based on all of this evidence, placing the appropriate subject alongside the pronouns in Isaiah 53:11, it now reads:

He [the LORD] shall see of the travail of his [the Messiah's] soul, and shall be satisfied: by his [the Messiah's] knowledge shall my [the LORD's] righteous servant [the Messiah] justify many; for he [the Messiah] shall bear their [Israel's] iniquities.

Isaiah 53:12

> Therefore will I divide him a portion with the great, and he shall divide the spoil with the strong; because he hath poured out his soul unto death: and he was numbered with the transgressors; and he bare the sin of many, and made intercession for the transgressors.

In this chapter's final verse, the Messiah takes possession of the spoils in victory. Spoils are also mentioned in the Book of Zechariah, where the prophet foretells a great future battle when all nations come against Jerusalem. Zechariah 14:1–4 states:

> Behold, the day of the LORD cometh, and thy spoil shall be divided in the midst of thee. For I will gather all nations against Jerusalem to battle; and the city shall be taken, and the houses rifled, and the women ravished; and half of the city shall go forth into captivity, and the residue of the people shall not be cut off from the city. Then shall the LORD go forth, and fight against those nations, as when he fought in the day of battle. And his feet shall stand in that day upon the mount of Olives, which is before Jerusalem on the east, and the mount of Olives shall cleave in the midst thereof toward the east and toward the west, and there shall be a very great valley; and half of the mountain shall remove toward the north, and half of it toward the south.

Zechariah 14:12 describes the defeat of Israel's enemies as follows: "And this shall be the plague wherewith the LORD will smite all the people that have fought against Jerusalem; Their flesh shall consume away while they stand upon their feet, and their eyes shall consume away in their holes, and their tongue shall consume away in their mouth."

Zechariah 14:14 clearly shows the spoils obtained in Israel's victory, "And Judah also shall fight at Jerusalem; and the wealth of all the heathen round about shall be gathered together, gold, and silver, and apparel, in great abundance."

When the LORD Jesus goes forth and fights against the nations that come against Jerusalem, His feet will stand on the Mount of Olives. Zechariah 14:12 teaches that He will destroy Israel's enemies. Immediately after, all those who had fought on His side are rewarded. They are compensated with the spoils of victory, the same spoils referred to in Isaiah 53:12.

The following question could be asked: What does this great battle have to do with the suffering Messiah's spoils in Isaiah 53:12? The answer is provided in Zechariah 12:10–14 which explains that it would be the LORD, the Messiah Himself, the One who was pierced, who will return and fight for His people:

> And I will pour upon the house of David, and upon the inhabitants of Jerusalem, the spirit of grace and of supplications: and they shall look upon me [him] whom they have pierced, and they shall mourn for him, as one mourneth for his only son, and shall be in bitterness for him, as one that is in bitterness for his firstborn. In that day shall there be a great mourning in Jerusalem, as the mourning of Hadadrimmon in the valley of Megiddon. And the land shall mourn, every family apart; the family of the house of David apart, and their wives apart; the family of the house of Nathan apart, and their wives apart; The family of the house of Levi apart, and their wives apart; the family of Shimei apart, and their wives apart; All the families that remain, every family apart, and their wives apart.

All the children of Israel who remain will see Him, the One who was pierced, and will mourn for Him. What will happen after this mourning and repentance takes place? The answer is provided in the next verse. Zechariah 13:1 reveals that there will be forgiveness of sin: "In that day there shall be a fountain opened to the house of David and to the inhabitants of Jerusalem for sin and for uncleanness."

According to Isaiah 53:12, the Messiah poured out His soul unto death, was numbered with the transgressors, bore the sin of many, and made intercession for the transgressors. When Jesus rode into Jerusalem lowly and riding on a donkey (Matt. 21:4–9; Zech. 9:9) He was just, and having salvation. When He returns with the clouds of Heaven (Dan. 7:13–14; Zech. 12:10; 14:3–4) He will defeat Israel's enemies. He, as

King Messiah, will execute judgment and righteousness in the earth (Jer. 23:5–6; 33:15–16; Rev. 19:11–16) and establish His everlasting kingdom (Isa. 9:7; Dan. 2:44–45; 7:13–14; Mic. 4:7; Luke 1:30–33).

It is Jesus who redeemed mankind from their sins. As a result of His suffering, death, and humiliation, His reward is great. He can ask His Father for anything He wants because the entire world belongs to Him. Regarding Jesus, His Father tells Him in Psalm 2:8: "Ask of me, and I shall give thee the heathen for thine inheritance, and the uttermost parts of the earth for thy possession."

Additionally, Isaiah 53:12 states that the Messiah, as Priest, made intercession for transgressors. As we have seen, Zechariah 6:12–13, Psalm 110:4, and Psalm 2:6–7 foretold that He would also sit and rule upon His throne. Finally in the New Testament, Hebrews 5:5–6 teaches that it is Jesus Himself who fulfills these prophecies pointing to a King holding the office of a Priest: "So also Christ glorified not himself to be made an high priest; but he that said unto him, Thou art my Son, to day have I begotten thee. As he saith also in another place, Thou art a priest for ever after the order of Melchisedec."

Chapter Ten

Isaiah 53—Not About Israel

As we have seen, the entire prophecy provided in Isaiah 53 points to a Messiah who would suffer and die for our sins. But throughout the centuries, Judaism's rabbis have consistently attempted to deny this truth, and have taken the stance that the suffering servant in Isaiah 53 is not the Messiah, but Israel. According to them, when Isaiah writes, "Who hath believed our report? and to whom is the arm of the LORD revealed?," the prophet is quoting the Gentile kings who are speaking of the descendents of Jacob. In response to the rabbinic position, though Israel has suffered greatly throughout the centuries, it simply does not fit within the context of the chapter.[39]

Israel has certainly been tormented and afflicted throughout their history. However, the Bible teaches that these afflictions are not the result of the sins of the Gentile nations. To the contrary, Israel's sufferings have been the consequences for their own sins. In Deuteronomy 31:16–17, the LORD advised Moses that Israel would turn away from Him and become disobedient. He also told Moses how they would be punished:

> And the LORD said unto Moses, Behold, thou shalt sleep with thy fathers; and this people will rise up, and go a whoring after the gods of the strangers of the land, whither they go to be among them, and will forsake me, and break my covenant which I have made with them. Then my anger

shall be kindled against them in that day, and I will forsake them, and I will hide my face from them, and they shall be devoured, and many evils and troubles shall befall them; so that they will say in that day, Are not these evils come upon us, because our God is not among us?

In fulfillment of what the LORD told Moses, Judges 2:8–14 reveals that Israel immediately turned to other gods after Joshua's death. Their rebellion continued as they refused to heed the warnings of the prophets. And just as the LORD promised, they were punished for their hardness of heart. Regarding Israel's disobedience, Zechariah 7:11–14 states:

But they refused to hearken, and pulled away the shoulder, and stopped their ears, that they should not hear. Yea, they made their hearts as an adamant stone, lest they should hear the law, and the words which the LORD of hosts hath sent in his spirit by the former prophets: therefore came a great wrath from the LORD of hosts. Therefore it is come to pass, that as he cried, and they would not hear; so they cried, and I would not hear, saith the LORD of hosts: But I scattered them with a whirlwind among all the nations whom they knew not. Thus the land was desolate after them, that no man passed through nor returned: for they laid the pleasant land desolate.

Though this has been the case, the Scriptures provide some wonderful news for God's people. He will turn to them again, and honor the everlasting covenant He made with Abraham, Isaac, and Jacob.

I. Israel Disqualified

This chapter's primary objective is to provide twelve clear reasons why Israel cannot be the subject of Isaiah 53. Though there are probably more, these should satisfy any believer in Jesus as the suffering Messiah so that they can remain confident in their faith. The second objective is to address three of Judaism's far-reaching attempts to qualify Israel as the subject of Isaiah's fourth Servant Song.

These illustrations are as follows:

1. Israel's knowledge

Isaiah 53:11 states: "He shall see of the travail of his soul, and shall be satisfied: by his knowledge shall my righteous servant justify many; for he shall bear their iniquities."

According to this verse, God's suffering servant must have knowledge. This is not any knowledge, but understanding and wisdom of God and His Word. If this applied to Israel, the Scriptures would indicate that they have knowledge. However, this is not the case! To the contrary, the Scriptures reveal Israel's absence of knowledge. They are called a blinded servant having no knowledge and living in spiritual darkness (Isa. 5:13; 6:9–10; 9:2 (KJV); 29:13–14; 42:18–20; Mic. 3:5–6; Hos. 4:1,6; and Rom. 11:25–27). With all of this evidence, how can anyone claim that Israel is the subject of Isaiah 53:11 when it is obvious that this servant must have knowledge?

In retrospect, the Messiah is the perfect candidate as the subject of Isaiah 53:11 because Isaiah 11:1–2 indicates that He will have the spirit of wisdom, the spirit of understanding, and the spirit of knowledge. Furthermore, Isaiah 50:4 teaches that He will have the tongue of the learned.

Even though Israel does not qualify as the subject of Isaiah's fourth Servant Song because of their absence of knowledge (in part), there will come a day when they and the entire world will be filled with the knowledge of the LORD. However, this will not occur until the Messiah's reign:

> They shall not hurt nor destroy in all my holy mountain: for the earth shall be full of the knowledge of the LORD, as the waters cover the sea. And in that day there shall be a root of Jesse, which shall stand for an ensign of the people; to it shall the Gentiles seek: and his rest shall be glorious.
>
> —Isaiah 11:9–10

2. Is Israel righteous?

Isaiah 53:11 states: "He shall see of the travail of his soul, and shall be satisfied: by his knowledge shall my righteous servant justify many; for he shall bear their iniquities."

According to this verse, God's suffering servant must be righteous. Does righteousness apply to Israel according to the Bible? The following evidence answers this question in the negative:

- **Deuteronomy 9:5–6:** "Not for thy righteousness, or for the uprightness of thine heart, dost thou go to possess their land: but for the wickedness of these nations the LORD thy God doth drive them out from before thee, and that he may perform the word which the LORD sware unto thy fathers, Abraham, Isaac, and Jacob. Understand therefore, that the LORD thy God giveth thee not this good land to possess it for thy righteousness; for thou art a stiffnecked people."

- **Isaiah 1:4–5:** "Ah sinful nation, a people laden with iniquity, a seed of evildoers, children that are corrupters: they have forsaken the LORD, they have provoked the Holy One of Israel unto anger, they are gone away backward. Why should ye be stricken any more? ye will revolt more and more: the whole head is sick, and the whole heart faint."

- **Isaiah 30:1:** "Woe to the rebellious children, saith the LORD, that take counsel, but not of me; and that cover with a covering, but not of my spirit, that they may add sin to sin."

- **Zechariah 7:11–12:** "But they refused to hearken, and pulled away the shoulder, and stopped their ears, that they should not hear. Yea, they made their hearts as an adamant stone, lest they should hear the law, and the words which the LORD of hosts hath sent in his spirit by the former prophets: therefore came a great wrath from the LORD of hosts."

These are merely some of the many examples illustrating Israel's rebellion and unrighteousness. Additionally, Isaiah 48:1,8 refers to them as a "transgressor from the womb:"

Hear ye this, O house of Jacob, which are called by the name of Israel, and are come forth out of the waters of Judah, which swear by the name of the LORD, and make mention of the God of Israel, but not in truth, nor in righteousness. . . . Yea, thou heardest not; yea, thou knewest not; yea, from that time that thine ear was not opened: for I knew that thou wouldest deal very treacherously, and wast called a transgressor from the womb.

How can Israel be the subject of Isaiah 53:11 when this verse clearly stipulates that it must be righteous? According to the covenant at Sinai, the children of Israel were only righteous before God when every statute and commandment was observed. Deuteronomy 6:24–25 states:

> And the LORD commanded us to do all these statutes, to fear the LORD our God, for our good always, that he might preserve us alive, as it is at this day. And it shall be our righteousness, if we observe to do all these commandments before the LORD our God, as he hath commanded us.

This passage explains that as long as *all* of God's statutes and commandments were observed, Israel would be righteous. Since Yom Kippur is an everlasting statute (Lev. 16:34), and Israel has not had a temple since A.D. 70, the children of Israel remain unrighteous without the deaths of the animals as atonement for sin. They cannot observe Yom Kippur according to the instructions provided in Leviticus 16. Therefore, it is impossible for them to be righteous according to the covenant at Sinai. However, under the New Covenant provided by the shed blood and death of the Messiah, all can be righteous.

One final note: It is the Messiah who is righteous (Isa. 11:5; Jer. 23:5–6). He alone is the perfect candidate as the subject of Isaiah 53:11.

3. Isaiah 53:5

Isaiah 53:5 states: "But he was wounded for our transgressions, he was bruised for our iniquities: the chastisement of our peace was upon him; and with his stripes we are healed."

Since counter-missionaries believe that the Gentile kings are speaking of Israel in this verse, the phrase "and with his stripes we are healed" presents a problem for them. The reason is because the Bible does not teach that the Gentiles are healed as a result of Israel's sufferings. Is there evidence in today's world suggesting that this is true? Would it be reasonable to assert that somehow Almighty God has healed or restored the Gentile nations because they have been the source of Israel's pains and afflictions throughout the centuries? Of course not!

Unfortunately for Judaism's defenders, Isaiah 53:5 does not prophesy that the Gentile nations would be healed as a result of Israel's sufferings. To the contrary, it foretells that Israel would be forgiven for their sins as a result of the Messiah's afflictions.

4. Isaiah 53:7: Has Israel complained?

Isaiah 53:7 states: "He was oppressed, and he was afflicted, yet he opened not his mouth: he is brought as a lamb to the slaughter, and as a sheep before her shearers is dumb, so he openeth not his mouth."

Judaism claims that Israel is the subject of this verse. However, does the Bible reveal that Israel was mute and without complaint when under torment, oppression, and affliction? To the contrary, not only do the Scriptures record that Israel complained, they testify that there were times when they cried out to God for vengeance. Here are a few examples:

- **Psalm 79:10,12:** "Wherefore should the heathen say, Where is their God? let him be known among the heathen in our sight by the revenging of the blood of thy servants which is shed. . . . And render unto our neighbours sevenfold into their bosom their reproach, wherewith they have reproached thee, O Lord."
- **Jeremiah 15:15:** "O LORD, thou knowest: remember me, and visit me, and revenge me of my persecutors; take me not away in thy longsuffering: know that for thy sake I have suffered rebuke."
- **Lamentations 3:64–66:** "Render unto them a recompence, O LORD, according to the work of their hands. Give them sorrow of heart, thy curse unto them. Persecute and destroy them in anger from under the heavens of the LORD."

Once again, the Bible teaches that Israel fails to meet the requirements of Isaiah 53 since they complained while under affliction. However, it should be mentioned that all of us have a tendency to cry out to God when under torment and oppression. This is a human characteristic that all of us possess. These illustrations are not meant to fault Israel in any way, but to demonstrate that they fail to meet the contingencies, stipulations, and conditions of the entire chapter.

5. Isaiah 53:8: My people

Isaiah 53:8 states; "He was taken from prison and from judgment: and who shall declare his generation? for he was cut off out of the land of the living: for the transgression of my people was he stricken."

In this verse, the prophet reveals that God's servant would be cut off for "my people." God's people and Isaiah's people are Israel. In verses such as Zechariah 2:11 (KJV), which is the equivalent to Zechariah 2:15 in the 1917 JPS, the LORD calls other nations "my people," but only during the Messiah's reign.

Israel is called "my people" just a few verses prior to this fourth Servant Song. Isaiah 52:4–6 states, regarding Israel:

> For thus saith the Lord GOD, My people went down aforetime into Egypt to sojourn there; and the Assyrian oppressed them without cause. Now therefore, what have I here, saith the LORD, that my people is taken away for nought? they that rule over them make them to howl, saith the LORD; and my name continually every day is blasphemed. Therefore my people shall know my name: therefore they shall know in that day that I am he that doth speak: behold, it is I.

There is no indication that the speaker has changed between Isaiah 52:4–6 and Isaiah 53:8, where the LORD speaks and refers to Israel as my people. Therefore, the only logical conclusion that can be made is that Isaiah 53:8 foretells of someone who would be cut off and killed for the transgressions of "my people, Israel." Consequently the Gentiles cannot be the "my people" referred to in Isaiah 53:8.

6. Isaiah 53:8–9: The land of the living

Isaiah 53:8–9 states: "He was taken from prison and from judgment: and who shall declare his generation? for he was cut off out of the land of the living: for the transgression of my people was he stricken. And he made his grave with the wicked, and with the rich in his death; because he had done no violence, neither was any deceit in his mouth."

Though this passage seemingly teaches that this servant would be killed, i.e., "cut off out of the land of the living" since "he made his grave with the wicked," Judaism's counter-missionaries maintain an entirely different viewpoint. They claim that Isaiah is prophesying Israel's exile into Babylon and their separation from the land. According to them, Israel is the land of the living. Contrary to their position, the Book of Isaiah does not refer to Israel as the land of the living since he calls Israel a dry and thirsty ground in earlier passages:

- **Isaiah 5:13:** "Therefore my people are gone into captivity, because they have no knowledge: and their honourable men are famished, and their multitude dried up with thirst."
- **Isaiah 44:1–3:** "Yet now hear, O Jacob my servant; and Israel, whom I have chosen: Thus saith the LORD that made thee, and formed thee from the womb, which will help thee; Fear not, O Jacob, my servant; and thou, Jesurun, whom I have chosen. For I will pour water upon him that is thirsty, and floods upon the dry ground: I will pour my spirit upon thy seed, and my blessing upon thine offspring."

How can Israel be referred to as the land of the living in Isaiah 53:8 when the Scriptures teach that it is a dry ground? On a dry ground nothing can grow. It is lifeless! Therefore, Judaism's interpretation that the land of the living is Israel must be deemed incorrect since a dry ground cannot bear life.

In reality, when this servant is described as cut off from the land of the living, it means He would die. This is supported by the following verse, Isaiah 53:9, which states that "he made his grave with the wicked." Quite clearly, this servant would lose his life and be killed!

7. Isaiah 53:9: Israel's violence

Isaiah 53:9 states: "And he made his grave with the wicked, and with the rich in his death; because he had done no violence, neither was any deceit in his mouth."

Isaiah 53:9 testifies that this servant would do "no violence." Here, the Hebrew word for violence is *chamac* (*Strong's*, #2555). *Chamac* refers to false injustice and unrighteous violence. According to Ezekiel 12:19, Israel possessed *chamac*. Therefore, it is again disqualified!

> And say unto the people of the land, Thus saith the Lord GOD of the inhabitants of Jerusalem, and of the land of Israel; They shall eat their bread with carefulness, and drink their water with astonishment, that her land may be desolate from all that is therein, because of the violence [*chamac*] of all them that dwell therein.

Since Israel is once again disqualified as the subject of this chapter because of their unrighteous violence, or *chamac*, Judaism's counter-missionaries may respond by trying to disqualify Jesus as well by claiming that He was also violent, citing Matthew 21:12–13, Mark 11:15–17, and Luke 19:45–46. In response to their claim, when Jesus turned over the tables of the moneychangers in the temple, He did not exhibit "unrighteous violence." He said, "It is written, My house shall be called the house of prayer; but ye have made it a den of thieves." Jesus cited Isaiah 56:7 indicating that God's house should be a house of prayer, not a place for marketing and selling for profit. Therefore according to the Scriptures, Jesus' anger was justified and ***not*** unrighteous.

8. Isaiah 53:9: Israel's deceit

Isaiah 53:9 states: "And he made his grave with the wicked, and with the rich in his death; because he had done no violence, neither was any deceit in his mouth."

According to Isaiah 53:9, this servant would possess no deceit or deception. Do the Scriptures reveal that Israel has deceit? Jeremiah 5:27–31 speaks of Israel in the following manner:

> As a cage is full of birds, so are their houses full of deceit: therefore they are become great, and waxen rich. They are waxen fat, they shine: yea,

they overpass the deeds of the wicked: they judge not the cause, the cause of the fatherless, yet they prosper; and the right of the needy do they not judge. Shall I not visit for these things? saith the LORD: shall not my soul be avenged on such a nation as this? A wonderful and horrible thing is committed in the land; The prophets prophesy falsely, and the priests bear rule by their means; and my people love to have it so: and what will ye do in the end thereof?

Regarding Israel, Jeremiah 8:5 reaffirms, "Why then is this people of Jerusalem slidden back by a perpetual backsliding? they hold fast deceit, they refuse to return."

These scriptures provide enough evidence that Israel has deceit. Therefore, it is once again eliminated as the subject of Isaiah 53.

9. Isaiah 52:15: The Hebrew word yazeh

Isaiah 52:15 (KJV) states: "So shall he sprinkle [*yazeh*] many nations; the kings shall shut their mouths at him: for that which had not been told them shall they see; and that which they had not heard shall they consider."

In this verse the Hebrew word *yazeh,* a form of the verb *nazah,* is used. Throughout the entire Bible, this word is used a total of twenty-four times. In the King James Bible, it translates "sprinkle" on all twenty-four occasions. However, in the Jewish Publication Society Bible, this word translates "sprinkle" twenty-three times. The only exception is at Isaiah 52:15, where it translates "startle." As a result, the apparent mistranslation of Isaiah 52:15 in the Jewish Publication Society Bible reads, "So shall he startle many nations. . . ." Because of this, the true meaning of Isaiah 53 can become obscure and vague for those who depend on a Bible containing this inconsistency.

In addition to Isaiah 52:15, the word *yazeh* or *nazah* is used in Exodus 29:21; Leviticus 4:6; 4:17; 5:9; 6:27 (twice); 8:11; 8:30; 14:7; 14:16; 14:27; 14:51; 16:14 (twice); 16:15; 16:19; Numbers 8:7; 19:4; 19:18; 19:19; 19:21; 2 Kings 9:33; and Isaiah 63:3.

Based upon these illustrations, the question should be asked: Why would Isaiah use the word *yazeh* in a manner inconsistent with its previous uses in the Torah? The answer: he would not and should not! This word properly translates "sprinkle."

It is important to realize that Judaism's defenders fail to provide another verse in the Bible where *yazeh* or *nazah* translates "startle." For them, the incorrect translation of this word in Isaiah 52:15 is an exception. For believers in Jesus as the Messiah, the consistent translation of this word is the rule! Nonetheless, counter-missionaries will insist that *yazeh* translates "startle" in Isaiah 52:15 for obvious reasons: If it properly translates "sprinkle" in Isaiah 52:15, the question becomes, sprinkle with what? This is an issue they would rather avoid . . . Jesus of Nazareth's shed blood at the crucifixion. Therefore, Judaism obligates itself to remain firm that this word properly translates "startle," which is an exception rather than the rule!

10. Isaiah 53:10: "Yet it pleased the LORD to bruise him . . ."

Isaiah 53:10 states: "Yet it pleased the LORD to bruise him; he hath put him to grief: when thou shalt make his soul an offering for sin, he shall see his seed, he shall prolong his days, and the pleasure of the LORD shall prosper in his hand."

Throughout the centuries, millions upon millions of righteous Jews have been murdered. In World War II alone, approximately 6 million were killed. Since this verse states that "it pleased the LORD to bruise him," is God happy that His chosen people have been needlessly slaughtered? Could Israel logically be the subject of this verse? Ask the counter-missionaries. Deep down in their hearts, what do they really think?

Ezekiel 33:11 reveals that the LORD takes no pleasure in the death of the wicked. So why would He be pleased with deaths of righteous Jews? "Say unto them, As I live, saith the Lord GOD, I have no pleasure in the death of the wicked; but that the wicked turn from his way and live: turn ye, turn ye from your evil ways; for why will ye die, O house of Israel?"

Once again, the Scriptures eliminate Israel as the subject of Isaiah 53. Only the Messiah qualifies! The reason why God is pleased with the suffering death of the Messiah is that, through Him, mankind's sins are forgiven. The entire world can now be reconciled with its beloved Creator!

11. Isaiah 53:12: He [the servant] made intercession for the transgressors

Isaiah 53:12 states: "Therefore will I divide him a portion with the great, and he shall divide the spoil with the strong; because he hath poured out his soul unto death: and he was numbered with the transgressors; and he bare the sin of many, and made intercession for the transgressors."

According to this verse, the servant "made intercession for the transgressors." An intercessor is a priest. From the beginning Israel, as a nation, lost its priesthood when it was given only to the tribe of Levi. Hosea 4:1,6 reveals that Israel, as a nation, will no longer be priests:

> Hear the word of the LORD, ye children of Israel: for the LORD hath a controversy with the inhabitants of the land, because there is no truth, nor mercy, nor knowledge of God in the land. . . . My people are destroyed for lack of knowledge: because thou hast rejected knowledge, I will also reject thee, that thou shalt be no priest to me: seeing thou hast forgotten the law of thy God, I will also forget thy children.

Since Hosea 4:1,6 indicates that Israel would no longer be a nation of priests to God, how can it be the subject of Isaiah 53 since the servant will make intercession for transgressors?

12. Isaiah 53:12: He [the servant] made intercession for the transgressors

As in the previous example, there remains yet another credibility issue for those who believe that Israel makes intercession for transgressors. This is because the Siddur (Jewish prayer book) is void of any Jewish prayers on behalf of the wicked among the nations. Taken from this book, this is the Twelfth Benediction (actually a curse) of the Amida prayer, which is recited twice a day by religious Jews:

> Let there be no hope for informers, and may all the heretics and all the wicked instantly perish; may all the enemies of Your people be speedily extirpated; and may You swiftly uproot, break, crush and subdue the

reign of wickedness speedily in our days. Blessed are You Lord, who crushes enemies and subdues the wicked.

Another prayer against non-Jews taken from the Siddur, the Aleinu, is recited by the end of daily prayer services in synagogues:

> For they bow to vanity and emptiness and pray to a god which helps not. . . . Therefore we put our hope in You, Lord our God, that we may soon see in the splendor of Your might the removal of detestable idolatry from the earth, and false gods will be utterly cut off, to perfect the world through the Almighty's sovereignty.

Finally, the following provides another Jewish prayer against Gentiles taken from the Passover Haggadah, which is a quote from Psalm 79:6–7. Even though this is taken from an actual psalm, it is interesting to note that those following rabbinic traditions are required to pray to God to exact revenge on the enemies of Jews:

> . . . pour out Your wrath upon the nations that do not recognize You and upon the kingdoms that do not invoke Your Name. For they have devoured Jacob and destroyed his habitation. Pour Your anger upon them and let Your fiery wrath overtake them. Pursue them with wrath and annihilate them from beneath the heavens of the Lord.

These prayers and others like them demonstrate that those adhering to Judaism's traditions are not taught to pray for Israel's enemies. To the contrary, they are instructed to pray against Israel's enemies. This shows that Israel does not make intercession for transgressors and cannot be the subject of Isaiah 53:12. It provides the final evidence that they are not the subject of Isaiah 53.

II. Countering Judaism's Misrepresentations

There are generally three major misrepresentations made by Judaism's defenders in their attempt to justify Israel as the subject of Isaiah 53. They are as follows:

1. Isaiah 53:8: The Hebrew word lamo

... for he was cut off out of the land of the living: for the transgression of my people was he stricken.

The NASB renders it as follows:

... That He was cut off out of the land of the living, For the transgression of my people, to whom the stroke was due?

This rendering underscores the fact that His death was substitionary. In this verse the Hebrew word *lamo* is used and, with reference to "my people," is properly translated "to them," or in this case "to whom." But Judaism's defenders claim that it should read, "From the transgression of my people [the Gentile nations] the stroke to them [with reference to Israel]." This is how they assert that this verse foretells the Gentile kings speaking about Israel [in the future] and that they were the suffering servant.

However, the context of this verse describes a single individual, He, who was cut off out of the land of the living [killed] for the transgression of my people [Israel] . . . to them [*lamo*] the stroke was due. In other words someone—God's suffering servant—would vicariously take the punishment that should have befallen my people Israel . . . "to them" the stroke was due.

Judaism's position about this verse is also refuted by its own scholars. According to the 1917 JPS Bible, a single individual took the punishment for my people. The translation is in full agreement with the NASB Christian Bible as follows, ". . . For he was cut off out of the land of the living, For the transgression of my people to whom [*lamo*, to them] the stroke was due."

The Masoretic Text, upon which the KJV is based, does not include the words "to whom the stroke is due." We cite the NASB to show there is no evidence of a preconceived agenda on the part of non-rabbinic translations regarding Isaiah 53:8 and the Hebrew word *lamo*.

2. Isaiah 53:9: Death or deaths?

Isaiah 53:9 states: "And he made his grave with the wicked, and with the rich in his death; because he had done no violence, neither was any deceit in his mouth."

Judaism's defenders are quick to mention that the Hebrew word *b'motav*, translated death, is actually a plural word, not a singular word. Regarding this matter, they are absolutely correct! Because of this, they incorrectly conclude that Isaiah 53:9 could not refer to a single individual.

In response to their argument, it is important for us to remember that Isaiah 53:12 tells us that Jesus, God's righteous servant, "bare the sin of many." In other words, He died so that many would not perish! His foretold vicarious death counts for many deaths because He would atone for the sins of many people. All who believe in Him will have everlasting life. Regarding Jesus, 1 John 2:2 states: "And he is the propitiation for our sins: and not for ours only, but also for the sins of the whole world."

We also need to remember that Isaiah 53:9 should apply to a single individual because it prophesies he was to be buried in a single grave (His grave, not their graves).

Finally, it is important to realize that there are occasions when a Hebrew noun is used in its plural form to describe a state of being for a single individual. For example, the word "deaths" is used twice in Ezekiel 28:8,10 while describing the eventual death of the prince of Tyrus: "They shall bring thee down to the pit, and thou shalt die the deaths of them that are slain in the midst of the seas. . . . Thou shalt die the deaths of the uncircumcised by the hand of strangers: for I have spoken it, saith the Lord GOD."

In Ezekiel 28:8, the single death of a single person is likened to the deaths of those who are slain in the midst of the seas. Further, verse 10 continues to compare this single death to the deaths of the uncircumcised. Just as this passage likens the prince of Tyrus' death to deaths, Isaiah 53:9 describes the Messiah's death . . . in the plural . . . since He shed His blood for many people and, because of this, His death counts for many deaths.

Conclusion: In Isaiah 53:9, the Hebrew word *b'motav* (deaths) is plural.

But it still refers to a single person because he is buried in a single grave. Furthermore, Jesus' death is counted for the deaths of many sinners. This is why the plural word for deaths is used.

3. Isaiah 53:10: His seed

Isaiah 53:10 states: "Yet it pleased the LORD to bruise him; he hath put him to grief: when thou shalt make his soul an offering for sin, he shall see his seed, he shall prolong his days, and the pleasure of the LORD shall prosper in his hand."

Some of Judaism's defenders are quick to remind everyone that Jesus never had children. Therefore according to them, He cannot be the subject of this verse since it states that He "shall see his seed, etc."

First, it is important to keep in mind that, because the throne of David must be completely fulfilled in the Messiah, He must not have physical descendents. In this aspect, Jesus qualifies! Here is the explanation of Isaiah 53:10: The phrase "he shall see his seed" refers to Almighty God seeing His Son. Here, the Hebrew word *zera* (*Strong's*, #2233) is used and is translated seed. Although this word generally refers to a physical seed, it can also translate child or offspring. These examples can be found in Leviticus 22:13 and 1 Samuel 1:11:

- **Leviticus 22:13:** "But if the priest's daughter be a widow, or divorced, and have no child [*zera*], and is returned unto her father's house, as in her youth, she shall eat of her father's meat: but there shall no stranger eat thereof."
- **1 Samuel 1:11:** "And she vowed a vow, and said, O LORD of hosts, if thou wilt indeed look on the affliction of thine handmaid, and remember me, and not forget thine handmaid, but wilt give unto thine handmaid a man child [*zera*], then I will give him unto the LORD all the days of his life, and there shall no razor come upon his head."

Regarding Isaiah 53:10, the LORD seeing His seed and prolonging His days applies to the resurrection of Jesus Christ, God's begotten Son, since it states in Romans 10:9 and in Galatians 1:1 the following:

- **Romans 10:9:** "That if thou shalt confess with thy mouth the Lord Jesus, and shalt believe in thine heart that God hath raised him from the dead, thou shalt be saved."
- **Galatians 1:1:** "Paul, an apostle, (not of men, neither by man, but by Jesus Christ, and God the Father, who raised him from the dead)."

With all of these illustrations, there is only one logical conclusion that can be made: There is only one Servant who qualifies as the subject of Isaiah 53, and it is not Israel. Though they have suffered throughout the centuries, they fail to meet any of the requirements specified in Isaiah's fourth Servant Song. Only King Messiah, Jesus of Nazareth, meets all of the necessary provisions and qualifications.

Finally, these illustrations were not meant to fault Israel in any way. The intention was to demonstrate that it is not the subject of Isaiah 53.

Part Three

The Messiah's Deity

Chapter Eleven

Has Man Seen God?

Have men visually seen God? Does God have a form? The Hebrew scriptures not only teach that God has a form, but it also instructs that some of the patriarchs and prophets have seen Him with their eyes. In contrast, rabbinic Judaism teaches that no man has ever seen God and that He, being Spirit, could not be seen. If Judaism's defenders can use the Bible to show that no man has seen God, they could claim the entire basis for Christianity as false since it teaches that Jesus is God in the flesh. According to Judaism's line of reasoning he could not be God because God could not be seen and men have obviously seen Jesus. One of the primary challenges of our Messiah's Deity is the seeing God issue.

Interestingly, the Hebrew scriptures are clear that some men have seen God. In this respect, Moses is the perfect example. Numbers 12:6–8 testifies that he saw God's form and appearance. In this passage, the LORD reprimands Aaron and Miriam for challenging Moses' authority. He indicates to both of them that He held Moses in such a high esteem that He actually allowed Moses to see Him:

> And he said, Hear now my words: If there be a prophet among you, I the LORD will make myself known unto him in a vision, and will speak unto him in a dream. My servant Moses is not so, who is faithful in all mine house. With him will I speak mouth to mouth, even apparently,

and not in dark speeches; and the similitude of the LORD shall he behold: wherefore then were ye not afraid to speak against my servant Moses?

This passage provides the ultimate proof-text that Moses saw God. Here the LORD instructs Aaron and Miriam that if there were prophets among them, He would appear to them in a vision or dream. This was not the case with Moses! The conclusion is rather obvious: The LORD God appeared to Moses in a manner other than by vision or dream. Furthermore according to His own words in verse 8, He has an appearance that Moses actually saw. In this passage, the Hebrew word for similitude is *temunah*, (*Strong's*, #8544). This word refers to similitude, appearance, image, or likeness.

Moses Sees God

As we have seen, Numbers 12:6–8 teaches that Moses saw God in a manner other than by vision or dream. One instance where Moses saw Him is found in Exodus 34:29–35. In this passage, Moses came down from Mount Sinai with the two tablets of stone. Exodus 34:29–30 states:

> And it came to pass, when Moses came down from mount Sinai with the two tables of testimony in Moses' hand, when he came down from the mount, that Moses wist not that the skin of his face shone while he talked with him. And when Aaron and all the children of Israel saw Moses, behold, the skin of his face shone; and they were afraid to come nigh him.

When Moses returned, the children of Israel were so afraid to look upon his face which shone that he needed to cover it with a veil. Exodus 34:33 shows: "And till Moses had done speaking with them, he put a vail on his face."

After descending from Mount Sinai, though Moses wore a veil on his face when he spoke to the children of Israel, Exodus 34:34–35 states that he removed it when he returned to speak to the LORD:

> But when Moses went in before the LORD to speak with him, he took the vail off, until he came out. And he came out, and spake unto the children

of Israel that which he was commanded. And the children of Israel saw the face of Moses, that the skin of Moses' face shone: and Moses put the vail upon his face again, until he went in to speak with him.

This proves that Moses saw the LORD. The physical evidence that he saw Him is the fact that his face shone with God's glory. And according to Numbers 12:6–8, he did not see Him by vision or dream.

> And he said, I beseech thee, shew me thy glory. And he said, I will make all my goodness pass before thee, and I will proclaim the name of the LORD before thee; and will be gracious to whom I will be gracious, and will shew mercy on whom I will shew mercy. And he said, Thou canst not see my face: for there shall no man see me, and live. And the LORD said, Behold, there is a place by me, and thou shalt stand upon a rock: And it shall come to pass, while my glory passeth by, that I will put thee in a clift of the rock, and will cover thee with my hand while I pass by: And I will take away mine hand, and thou shalt see my back parts: but my face shall not be seen.
>
> —Exodus 33:18-23

Some people use this passage to support their claim that no man can see God and live. But this is not what this passage teaches. Exodus 33:18 indicates that Moses not only asked to see God, he asked to see His glory. And according to Exodus 33:20, the LORD told Moses that no man could see His face, for "there" shall no man see Him and live. The conclusion is rather obvious: God's glory is in His face! Though Moses actually saw God, he was forbidden to see His face. According to Exodus 33:23, he was only allowed to see God's back.

> And the LORD commanded me at that time to teach you statutes and judgments, that ye might do them in the land whither ye go over to possess it. Take ye therefore good heed unto yourselves; for ye saw no manner of similitude on the day that the LORD spake unto you in Horeb out of the midst of the fire: Lest ye corrupt yourselves, and make you a

graven image, the similitude of any figure, the likeness of male or female, The likeness of any beast that is on the earth, the likeness of any winged fowl that flieth in the air, The likeness of any thing that creepeth on the ground, the likeness of any fish that is in the waters beneath the earth: And lest thou lift up thine eyes unto heaven, and when thou seest the sun, and the moon, and the stars, even all the host of heaven, shouldest be driven to worship them, and serve them, which the LORD thy God hath divided unto all nations under the whole heaven.

—Deuteronomy 4:14-19

On occasion, Judaism's counter-missionaries cite this passage, specifically verse 15, in an attempt to support their claim that God does not have a similitude or appearance. Deuteronomy 4:15 states, ". . . for ye saw no manner of similitude on the day that the LORD spake unto you in Horeb out of the midst of the fire." They incorrectly conclude that this proves God does **not** have a similitude. This is a perfect example of isolating a verse in the Bible and coming to an incorrect conclusion because this is not what the entire passage is teaching.

Although Numbers 12:6–8 clearly tells us that God has a similitude and appearance, Deuteronomy 4:14–19 teaches that the LORD did not allow the children of Israel to see it. His reason for this is in verses 16–19: they would corrupt themselves and build a graven image. The LORD knew the hearts of the children of Israel because they had failed Him once before. When Moses went up to receive the tablets of the covenant, they built a golden calf. Exodus 32:35 states, "And the LORD plagued the people, because they made the calf, which Aaron made."

Other Passages Where Men Have Seen God

Although Numbers 12:6–8 and Exodus 34:29–35 provide the proof that Moses saw God, here are some additional Bible references testifying that others have seen Him as well:

+ **Genesis 17:1:** "And when Abram was ninety years old and nine, the LORD appeared to Abram, and said unto him, I am the Almighty God;

walk before me, and be thou perfect."

- **Genesis 18:1:** "And the Lᴏʀᴅ appeared unto him [Abraham] in the plains of Mamre: and he sat in the tent door in the heat of the day."

- **Exodus 6:3:** "And I appeared unto Abraham, unto Isaac, and unto Jacob, by the name of God Almighty, but by my name Jᴇʜᴏᴠᴀʜ was I not known to them."

- **Exodus 24:8–10:** "And Moses took the blood, and sprinkled it on the people, and said, Behold the blood of the covenant, which the Lᴏʀᴅ hath made with you concerning all these words. Then went up Moses, and Aaron, Nadab, and Abihu, and seventy of the elders of Israel: And they saw the God of Israel: and there was under his feet as it were a paved work of a sapphire stone, and as it were the body of heaven in his clearness."

- **Isaiah 6:5**—*regarding Isaiah:* "Then said I, Woe is me! for I am undone; because I am a man of unclean lips, and I dwell in the midst of a people of unclean lips: for mine eyes have seen the King, the Lᴏʀᴅ of hosts."

- **Amos 9:1**—*regarding Amos:* "I saw the Lord standing upon the altar: and he said, Smite the lintel of the door, that the posts may shake: and cut them in the head, all of them; and I will slay the last of them with the sword: he that fleeth of them shall not flee away, and he that escapeth of them shall not be delivered."

John 1:18: *"No man hath seen God at any time"*

Some counter-missionaries use John 1:18 against those who believe in our Messiah's deity in order to support their incorrect position that no man has seen God. They often misapply this verse for two reasons: they either misunderstand it or they are attempting to confuse those who disagree with them. Therefore it is imperative that believers in Jesus' deity fully understand John 1:18 which states: "No man hath seen God at any time; the only begotten Son, which is in the bosom of the Father, he hath declared him."

In order to fully understand this verse, it is important to recognize the difference between seeing God and seeing His similitude according to the Bible. Exodus 33:18,20 provides the distinction. "And he said, I beseech thee, shew me thy glory. . . . And he said, Thou canst not see my face: for there shall no man see me, and live."

As we can see, Moses asked to see God's glory . . . and he was forbidden to see God's face. Since no man can see God's face, Exodus 33:23 records that God only permitted Moses to see His back. This shows that God's definition of seeing Him is to see His face. God certainly has a form and Moses definitely saw it . . . when he saw God's back! This explanation provides the most logical response to those who challenge our Messiah's deity.

The New Testament writers support this explanation. According to John 5:37 and 6:46, Jesus Himself said that no man had seen the Father or has heard His voice at any time. Additionally, Colossians 1:15 calls Jesus "the image of the invisible God." The applicable scriptures follow:

+ **John 5:37:**—*Jesus said:* "And the Father himself, which hath sent me, hath borne witness of me. Ye have neither heard his voice at any time, nor seen his shape."
+ **John 6:46**—*Jesus said:* "Not that any man hath seen the Father, save he which is of God, he hath seen the Father."
+ **Colossians 1:15**—*regarding Jesus:* "Who is the image of the invisible God, the firstborn of every creature."

Since Moses and others have obviously seen God, John 1:18 could not be used to deny Jesus' deity. For those who truly understand, it can only be used to confirm His deity. After all, since Jesus is the image of the invisible God, and the Father has never been seen, it was not the Father who the patriarchs saw when they saw the LORD. It was His Son, the Messiah! And according to John 1:18, it was He [the Messiah] who declared Him [His Father].

Chapter Twelve

The Messiah's Deity

The Shema

Deuteronomy 6:4: "Hear, O Israel: The LORD our God is one LORD."

Perhaps the most widely known verse in the Bible stressing the unique nature of God is Deuteronomy 6:4, known as the Shema. This verse supports a fundamental principle of both rabbinic Judaism and mainstream Christianity. Rabbinic Judaism teaches that God is only one, while Christianity teaches that God is a "oneness in unity" or a compound unity.

In this verse, the Hebrew word for one is *echad*, (*Strong's*, #259). Though this word can refer to only one, there are a number of instances in the Bible where it refers to a compound unity. One example can be found in Genesis 1:5, the first time this Hebrew word is used in the Scriptures: "And God called the light Day, and the darkness he called Night. And the evening and the morning were the first [*echad*] day." In this verse, the evening and morning make up one (*echad*) day. This is a compound unity!

Another example where *echad* is used as a compound unity is found in Genesis 2:24, "Therefore shall a man leave his father and his mother, and shall cleave unto his wife: and they shall be one [*echad*] flesh." Here, a man is described as leaving his father and mother, cleaving to his wife, and becoming one (*echad*) flesh with his wife.

Another clear illustration where *echad* refers to a compound unity is found in Ezekiel 37:19. It states, "Thus saith the Lord GOD; Behold, I will take the stick of Joseph, which is in the hand of Ephraim, and the tribes of Israel his fellows, and will put them with him, even with the stick of Judah, and make them one [*echad*] stick, and they shall be one [*echad*] in mine hand." Here the Lord instructs Ezekiel that there will come a day when the House of Israel and the House of Judah will once again become one (*echad*) nation, demonstrated by the two sticks becoming one (*echad*) stick.

These examples show that although there are times when *echad* does not refer to a compound unity, there are some cases when it does. It should also be mentioned that, if God were only one, the Hebrew word *yachiyd* (*Strong's,* #3173), should have been used in the Shema. As a general Bible principle, *yachiyd* means only one while *echad* can, at times, refer to a compound unity. Since *echad* is used in the Shema with respect to the LORD our God being one (*echad*) LORD, it should therefore be considered inconclusive to claim that God is only one based on this verse alone.

Furthermore, in Genesis 1:26, God refers to Himself in the plural as follows, "And God said, Let us make man in our image, after our likeness."

In this verse, God could not have been talking to the angels since there is no indication in the Bible that angels were made in God's image. Additionally, there is no verse to indicate that men were made in the image of angels. However, the Scriptures are clear that men are made in God's image:

+ **Genesis 1:27:** "So God created man in his own image, in the image of God created he him; male and female created he them."
+ **Genesis 5:1:** "This is the book of the generations of Adam. In the day that God created man, in the likeness of God made he him;"

The logical conclusion regarding Genesis 1:26 is that God was speaking to someone with His image or likeness prior to mankind's creation because He said "our image." And the LORD could not have been talking to the angels because the Scriptures do not teach that the angels were created in His image. Since it is reasonable that a son has the same image as his father, was God talking to His begotten Son, the Messiah [see chapter 4]?

Remembering this, here are other examples where God refers to Himself in the plural:

- **Genesis 3:22:** "And the Lord God said, Behold, the man is become as one of us, to know good and evil: and now, lest he put forth his hand, and take also of the tree of life, and eat, and live for ever."
- **Genesis 11:7:** "Go to, let us go down, and there confound their language, that they may not understand one another's speech."
- **Isaiah 6:8:** "Also I heard the voice of the Lord, saying, Whom shall I send, and who will go for us? Then said I, Here am I; send me."

The Messiah: Almighty God in the Flesh

The following are seven clear illustrations provided in the Hebrew scriptures demonstrating that the Messiah is the Lord, Almighty God in the flesh. Though this fact is firmly established and developed in the Hebrew scriptures and fulfilled in the New Testament, this position is contrary to the beliefs held by those embracing rabbinic Judaism.

1. One Eternal King

One of the strongest arguments in support of the Messiah's deity is the fact that when God sets up His everlasting kingdom, the Scriptures indicate that there will be one King who will reign over all the earth. Zechariah 14:9 and Ezekiel 37:22 confirm:

- **Zechariah 14:9:** "And the Lord shall be king over all the earth: in that day shall there be one Lord, and his name one."
- **Ezekiel 37:22:** "And I will make them [the House of Judah and the House of Israel] one nation in the land upon the mountains of Israel; and one king shall be king to them all: and they shall be no more two nations, neither shall they be divided into two kingdoms any more at all."

Since there will be one King over all the earth, the following evidence establishes the indisputable fact that the Messiah must be the Lord. According to the Bible, when God establishes His kingdom, it is He Himself who will reign in Zion as King over all the earth. Psalm 132:13–14, Zephaniah 3:15–17, Zechariah 14:16–17, and Ezekiel 43:7 tell us:

- **Psalm 132:13–14:** "For the LORD hath chosen Zion; he hath desired it for his habitation. This is my rest for ever: here will I dwell; for I have desired it."

- **Zephaniah 3:15–17:** "The LORD hath taken away thy judgments, he hath cast out thine enemy: the king of Israel, even the LORD, is in the midst of thee: thou shalt not see evil any more. In that day it shall be said to Jerusalem, Fear thou not: and to Zion, Let not thine hands be slack. The LORD thy God in the midst of thee is mighty; he will save, he will rejoice over thee with joy; he will rest in his love, he will joy over thee with singing."

- **Zechariah 14:16–17:** "And it shall come to pass, that every one that is left of all the nations which came against Jerusalem shall even go up from year to year to worship the King, the LORD of hosts, and to keep the feast of tabernacles. And it shall be, that whoso will not come up of all the families of the earth unto Jerusalem to worship the King, the LORD of hosts, even upon them shall be no rain."

- **Ezekiel 43:7**—*God told Ezekiel:* ". . . Son of man, the place of my throne, and the place of the soles of my feet, where I will dwell in the midst of the children of Israel for ever, and my holy name, shall the house of Israel no more defile, neither they, nor their kings, by their whoredom, nor by the carcases of their kings in their high places."

The Scriptures are quite clear that the LORD God fully intends to dwell in the midst of the children of Israel forever as King over all the earth. For those who deny the Messiah's deity, this is where a major reconciliation dilemma begins. According to the Scriptures, it is the Messiah who will reign forever as King over all the earth. Isaiah 9:6–7, Ezekiel 37:22,24–25, and Daniel 7:13–14 indicate:

- **Isaiah 9:6–7:** "For unto us a child is born, unto us a son is given: and the government shall be upon his shoulder: and his name shall be called

Wonderful, Counsellor, The mighty God, The everlasting Father, The Prince of Peace. Of the increase of his government and peace there shall be no end, upon the throne of David, and upon his kingdom, to order it, and to establish it with judgment and with justice from henceforth even for ever. The zeal of the LORD of hosts will perform this."

- **Ezekiel 37:22,24–25:** "And I will make them one nation in the land upon the mountains of Israel; and one king shall be king to them all: and they shall be no more two nations, neither shall they be divided into two kingdoms any more at all: . . . And David my servant shall be king over them; and they all shall have one shepherd: they shall also walk in my judgments, and observe my statutes, and do them. And they shall dwell in the land that I have given unto Jacob my servant, wherein your fathers have dwelt; and they shall dwell therein, even they, and their children, and their children's children for ever: and my servant David shall be their prince for ever."

- **Daniel 7:13–14:** "I saw in the night visions, and, behold, one like the Son of man came with the clouds of heaven, and came to the Ancient of days, and they brought him near before him. And there was given him dominion, and glory, and a kingdom, that all people, nations, and languages, should serve him: his dominion is an everlasting dominion, which shall not pass away, and his kingdom that which shall not be destroyed."

The Ezekiel passage was written approximately four hundred years after King David died. As previously mentioned, most Jewish and Christian scholars agree that its fulfillment will be realized in King Messiah, who is sometimes called David in the Scriptures.[30]

All three of these passages inform us that the Messiah will be King and that His kingdom will last forever. But Psalm 132:13–14, Zephaniah 3:15–17, Zechariah 14:16–17, and Ezekiel 43:7 tell us that the LORD will be King and that His kingdom will last forever. Therefore, since the Bible teaches us that there will be only one King over all the earth, and that King is called the Messiah and that King is called the LORD, logic tells us that the Messiah must be the LORD.

2. One Shepherd

As we have already seen in example #1, there are occasions in the Scriptures when the Messiah is called David. Ezekiel 37:24 is one of those instances. In this verse, the prophet is referring to the Messiah when God Himself said, "And David my servant shall be king over them; and they all shall have one shepherd: they shall also walk in my judgments, and observe my statutes, and do them."

According to this verse, there will come a day when the children of Israel will have one shepherd. He is called David, with reference to the Messiah. However, the Scriptures also teach the following:

+ **Psalm 23:1:** [A Psalm of David.] "The LORD is my shepherd; I shall not want."
+ **Psalm 80:1:** "Give ear, O Shepherd of Israel, thou that leadest Joseph like a flock; thou that dwellest between the cherubims, shine forth."

These scriptures clearly reveal that the LORD, Almighty God Himself, is Israel's Shepherd. Since Ezekiel 37:24 refers to the Messiah as Israel's one Shepherd and the psalmist refers to the LORD as Israel's Shepherd, logic dictates that the Messiah must be the LORD.

3. Isaiah 9:6: One mighty God

The most obvious single verse in the entire Bible pointing to the Messiah's deity is found in Isaiah 9:6. It states, "For unto us a child is born, unto us a son is given: and the government shall be upon his shoulder: and his name shall be called Wonderful, Counsellor, The mighty God, The everlasting Father, The Prince of Peace."

As we have already seen, it seems quite apparent that this is a messianic verse because, regarding this child, Isaiah 9:7 states, "Of the increase of his government and peace there shall be no end, upon the throne of David, and upon his kingdom, to order it, and to establish it with judgment and with justice from henceforth even for ever. The zeal of the LORD of hosts will perform this."

Isaiah 9:6–7 describes the Messiah, the eternal King and Prince of

Peace, who will sit on the throne of David. He will establish judgment and justice upon the earth, and have an everlasting kingdom of peace. In the past, no earthly king of Judah was able to accomplish this . . . but He will!

One of the titles given to Him is "The mighty God" (in Hebrew, *el gibbor*). This is a name reserved for God alone because in Isaiah 10:20–21, one chapter later, the LORD Himself is referred to in exactly the same manner as the mighty God, (*el gibbor*) as follows:

> And it shall come to pass in that day, that the remnant of Israel, and such as are escaped of the house of Jacob, shall no more again stay upon him that smote them; but shall stay upon the LORD, the Holy One of Israel, in truth. The remnant shall return, even the remnant of Jacob, unto the mighty God [*el gibbor*].

Deuteronomy 6:4 teaches that there is one LORD, not two. Because of this, should anyone claim that the subject of Isaiah 9:6–7 is not the LORD, they would be claiming that there are two separate and distinct mighty Gods. To acknowledge more than one God is considered polytheism and is a violation of the Shema.

There can only be one logical conclusion regarding this matter: According to Isaiah 9:6, the prophet refers to the prophesied child as *el gibbor*. In Isaiah 10:20–21, he calls the LORD *el gibbor*. The Shema teaches that there is only one God. Therefore, the prophesied child of Isaiah 9:6, the Messiah, must be the LORD.

4. *Malachi 3:1:* **ha'adon**

Malachi 3:1 states: "Behold, I will send my messenger, and he shall prepare the way before me: and the Lord, whom ye seek, shall suddenly come to his temple, even the messenger of the covenant, whom ye delight in: behold, he shall come, saith the LORD of hosts."

In this verse, the LORD of hosts states that there will come a day when the Lord shall suddenly come to His temple. Malachi 3:2–3 continues to explain what will happen on that day: He will purify and purge the sons of Levi like a refiner's fire and like fullers' soap:

> But who may abide the day of his coming? and who shall stand when
> he appeareth? for he is like a refiner's fire, and like fullers' soap: And he
> shall sit as a refiner and purifier of silver: and he shall purify the sons of
> Levi, and purge them as gold and silver, that they may offer unto the
> LORD an offering in righteousness.

An interesting connection is made between this passage and Zechariah
3:8–9 which portrays the Messiah, sometimes called the BRANCH, as the
stone laid before Joshua the high priest. According to this prophecy, it is
He who will remove all iniquity:

> Hear now, O Joshua the high priest, thou, and thy fellows that sit be-
> fore thee: for they are men wondered at: for, behold, I will bring forth
> my servant the BRANCH. For behold the stone that I have laid before
> Joshua; upon one stone shall be seven eyes: behold, I will engrave the
> graving thereof, saith the LORD of hosts, and I will remove the iniquity
> of that land in one day.

Throughout the Hebrew scriptures, the Hebrew *adon* is always used with
reference to deity when the definite article is present, i.e. *ha'adon*.[40] In
Malachi 3:1, the prophet uses this exact word, *ha'adon*, to show that it
will be the LORD [God] who comes to His temple to purify and purge the
priesthood, the sons on Levi (vss. 2–3). And according to the prophecy
in Zechariah 3:8–9 it would be the BRANCH, the Messiah, who will come
before Joshua the high priest (representing the Levitical priesthood), and
remove all iniquity. Therefore, since Malachi 3:1–3 foretells that *ha'adon*
will come to the temple and purge the sons of Levi, and Zechariah 3:8–9
teaches that the Messiah will do the same, the Messiah must be *ha'adon*.
The Messiah is the LORD!

5. Daniel 7:13–14 & Daniel 7:22: The Ancient of days
Daniel 7 records the dream and vision of the prophet as he is taken into

Heaven to witness what would take place in the last days. In Daniel 7:9, he describes the LORD God in the following manner: "I beheld till the thrones were cast down, and the Ancient of days did sit, whose garment was white as snow, and the hair of his head like the pure wool: his throne was like the fiery flame, and his wheels as burning fire."

It is important to realize that, in Daniel 7, the prophet refers to the LORD as the Ancient of days. In verses 13 and 14, he continues to describe what he saw. He observed one like the Son of man (the Messiah) being brought before the Ancient of days immediately after coming with the clouds of Heaven:

> I saw in the night visions, and, behold, one like the Son of man came with the clouds of heaven, and came to the Ancient of days, and they brought him near before him. And there was given him dominion, and glory, and a kingdom, that all people, nations, and languages, should serve him: his dominion is an everlasting dominion, which shall not pass away, and his kingdom that which shall not be destroyed.

Though Daniel foretells that the Son of man came with the clouds of Heaven in verse 13, it is important to note that he calls the One who came "the Ancient of days" (the LORD) in Daniel 7:21–22: "I beheld, and the same horn made war with the saints, and prevailed against them; Until the Ancient of days came, and judgment was given to the saints of the most High; and the time came that the saints possessed the kingdom."

After reading Daniel 7:9,22, the conclusion is rather obvious: The Son of man who came—the Messiah (Dan. 7:13)—is the Ancient of days who came—the LORD (Dan. 7:22).

6. Isaiah 9:6: One everlasting Father

Isaiah 9:6 states: "For unto us a child is born, unto us a son is given: and the government shall be upon his shoulder: and his name shall be called Wonderful, Counsellor, The mighty God, The everlasting Father, The Prince of Peace."

When the Messiah establishes His everlasting kingdom, He will be called "The everlasting Father," in Hebrew *'abi 'ad*. This title further verifies His deity. According to Exodus 4:22, God calls Israel His firstborn son as follows: "And thou shalt say unto Pharaoh, Thus saith the LORD, Israel is my son, even my firstborn."

Exodus 4:22 emphasizes God's Father-son relationship with the children of Israel. And regarding Israel, Malachi 2:10 tells us: "Have we not all one father? hath not one God created us?"

This verse teaches that the descendents of Jacob have one father, not two! Therefore, since Isaiah 9:6 indicates that the Messiah will be called "The everlasting Father," and the LORD Himself is Israel's one Father according to Exodus 4:22 and Malachi 2:10, logic dictates that the Messiah must be the LORD.

Author's note: Isaiah 9:6 does *not* teach that the Messiah is God the Father. The reason why the foretold son of Isaiah 9:6 is called "The everlasting Father" is because He, being the incarnate Word of His Father, is the source or origin of all creation. In other words, He is the Creator! See John 1:1,14; Colossians 1:15–17; and Revelation 3:14.

7. Psalm 82:8

Psalm 82:8 states: "Arise, O God, judge the earth: for thou shalt inherit all nations."

While keeping this verse in mind, Psalm 24:1 tells us that the earth and everything in it belongs to the LORD. It states, "The earth is the LORD's, and the fulness thereof; the world, and they that dwell therein."

Although Psalm 24:1 teaches that all things belong to God, Psalm 82:8 shows that God, in Hebrew *Elohim*, will inherit all nations. The Hebrew word *nachal* (*Strong's*, #5157), is used in Psalm 82:8 and is defined as "taking possession by inheritance." In the Scriptures, it was first used in Exodus 23:30 describing Israel, God's firstborn son according to Exodus 4:22, inheriting the land.

- **Exodus 4:22:** "And thou shalt say unto Pharaoh, Thus saith the LORD, Israel is my son, even my firstborn."

- **Exodus 23:30**—*regarding Israel:* "By little and little I will drive them out from before thee, until thou be increased, and inherit [*nachal*] the land."

In Psalm 82:8, why would the psalmist use the Hebrew word *nachal* to describe God inheriting anything? Unless of course, God is a firstborn Son!

Another interesting fact about Psalm 82:8 is that it not only teaches that God will inherit all nations, but that He will also judge the earth. Meanwhile, the Bible is clear that the Messiah will do both. Psalm 2:6–8 and Jeremiah 23:5 provide the evidence:

- **Psalm 2:6–8**—*regarding the Messiah, the begotten Son of God:* "Yet have I set my king upon my holy hill of Zion. I will declare the decree: the LORD hath said unto me, Thou art my Son; this day have I begotten thee. Ask of me, and I shall give thee the heathen for thine inheritance, and the uttermost parts of the earth for thy possession."
- **Jeremiah 23:5**—*regarding the Messiah:* "Behold, the days come, saith the LORD, that I will raise unto David a righteous Branch, and a King shall reign and prosper, and shall execute judgment and justice in the earth."

Since Psalm 82:8 teaches that God will judge the earth and inherit all nations, and Psalm 2:6–8 and Jeremiah 23:5 reveal that the Messiah will do the same, the conclusion is rather obvious: The Messiah is God!

Chapter Thirteen

The LORD at the Right Hand of the LORD

As we have seen, there are a number of ways to demonstrate the Messiah's deity in the Bible. However, the illustration of the LORD at the right hand of the LORD provides irrefutable evidence. The Hebrew scriptures teach that the Messiah would not only be the son of David and the Son of God, but would also be highly exalted at the right hand of His Father.

According to the Bible, when an individual is said to be "at the right hand" of another, he is both the provider and source of support, strength, power, and authority. Here are a few examples:

- **Psalm 109:30–31:** "I will greatly praise the LORD with my mouth; yea, I will praise him among the multitude. For he shall stand at the right hand of the poor, to save him from those that condemn his soul."
- **Psalm 16:8:**—*David said*: "I have set the LORD always before me: because he is at my right hand, I shall not be moved."

After Jesus' baptism, the Bible teaches that He began His ministry immediately after being taken up and tempted by the devil. The Scriptures also show that up until the time of His death on the cross, it was His Father who was His source of support, strength, power, and authority.

Philippians 2:5–8 teaches that God became a man. Since Jesus took on human flesh, He experienced all the weaknesses of a mere mortal man. For example, there were times when He hungered, thirsted, and became fatigued, etc. Hebrews 4:15 states that He was "in all points tempted like as we are, yet without sin." As a result, during his lifetime, all of His power and strength came directly from His Father. Accordingly, His Father was "at His right hand."

> Let this mind be in you, which was also in Christ Jesus: Who, being in the form of God, thought it not robbery to be equal with God: But made himself of no reputation, and took upon him the form of a servant, and was made in the likeness of men: And being found in fashion as a man, he humbled himself, and became obedient unto death, even the death of the cross.
>
> —Philippians 2:5–8

The Hebrew scriptures foretell that the LORD would assist the Messiah, i.e. hold His hand, help Him, and preserve Him, etc. Isaiah's first three Servant Songs provide the proof as follows:

- **Isaiah 42:6:** "I the LORD have called thee in righteousness, and will hold thine hand, and will keep thee, and give thee for a covenant of the people, for a light of the Gentiles."
- **Isaiah 49:8:** "Thus saith the LORD, In an acceptable time have I heard thee, and in a day of salvation have I helped thee: and I will preserve thee, and give thee for a covenant of the people, to establish the earth, to cause to inherit the desolate heritages."
- **Isaiah 50:7:** "For the Lord GOD will help me; therefore shall I not be confounded: therefore have I set my face like a flint, and I know that I shall not be ashamed."

In support of these three verses, Acts 2:25 quotes Psalm 16:8 indicating that it would be the LORD at the right hand of David's son the Messiah helping Him and providing His source of strength up until the time of His crucifixion:

- **Acts 2:25:** "For David speaketh concerning him, I foresaw the Lord always before my face, for he is on my right hand, that I should not be moved."
- **Psalm 16:8:** "I have set the LORD always before me: because he is at my right hand, I shall not be moved."

After His death on the cross, Philippians 2:8–11 testifies that Jesus is now highly exalted. Though His Father was at His right hand, Hebrews 1:3 indicates that both the Father's and Son's roles have been changed. It states that the Son now sits "on the right hand of the Majesty on high." In order to confirm this, before he was stoned to death, Stephen saw Jesus standing "on the right hand" of God. At the time Stephen was stoned, Jesus had already ascended into Heaven. The applicable passages and verses follow:

- **Philippians 2:8–11:** "And being found in fashion as a man, he humbled himself, and became obedient unto death, even the death of the cross. Wherefore God also hath highly exalted him, and given him a name which is above every name: That at the name of Jesus every knee should bow, of things in heaven, and things in earth, and things under the earth; And that every tongue should confess that Jesus Christ is Lord, to the glory of God the Father."
- **Hebrews 1:3:** "Who being the brightness of his glory, and the express image of his person, and upholding all things by the word of his power, when he had by himself purged our sins, sat down on the right hand of the Majesty on high."
- **Acts 7:56**—*Stephen said:* ". . . Behold, I see the heavens opened, and the Son of man standing on the right hand of God."

Acts 2:34–35 cites Psalm 110:1 indicating that Jesus is now on the Father's right hand and that the Father is no longer on His Son's right hand:

- **Acts 2:34–35**—*regarding Jesus:* "For David is not ascended into the heavens: but he saith himself, The LORD said unto my Lord, Sit thou on my right hand, Until I make thy foes thy footstool."

- **Psalm 110:1:** [A Psalm of David.] "The Lord said unto my Lord, Sit thou at my right hand, until I make thine enemies thy footstool."

Though the Bible teaches that the Messiah is now on the right hand of His Father, the following passages will prove beyond doubt that He is the Lord. In Psalm 110:5–6, David foretells the day when the Messiah will execute judgment on the nations. In verse 5, the Bible uses the Hebrew word *Adonai* (*Strong's*, #136). This is a title used for God alone! As a result, Psalm 110:1,5–6 teaches that the Messiah, who is Adonai, will come on the right hand of the Lord and execute judgment on His enemies:

- **Psalm 110:1:** [A Psalm of David.] "The Lord said unto my Lord, Sit thou at my right hand, until I make thine enemies thy footstool."
- **Psalm 110:5–6:** "The Lord [*Adonai*] at thy right hand shall strike through kings in the day of his wrath. He shall judge among the heathen, he shall fill the places with the dead bodies; he shall wound the heads over many countries."

Psalm 110:1 portrays David's Lord, the Messiah, at the right hand of the Lord. According to Psalm 110:5, the individual at the right hand is called Adonai, the title used for God. In other words, Psalm 110:1,5 portrays the Lord at the right hand of the Lord.

Furthermore Isaiah 11:4, Jeremiah 23:5, and Revelation 19:15 all confirm that it is the Messiah, Jesus Himself, who will come and smite the kingdoms of the earth and destroy His enemies. According to the Bible, He is the Adonai of Psalm 110:5:

- **Psalm 110:5:** "The Lord [*Adonai*] at thy right hand shall strike through kings in the day of his wrath."
- **Isaiah 11:4:** "But with righteousness shall he judge the poor, and reprove with equity for the meek of the earth: and he shall smite the earth with the rod of his mouth, and with the breath of his lips shall he slay the wicked."
- **Jeremiah 23:5:** "Behold, the days come, saith the Lord, that I will raise

unto David a righteous Branch, and a King shall reign and prosper, and shall execute judgment and justice in the earth."

- **Revelation 19:15:** "And out of his mouth goeth a sharp sword, that with it he should smite the nations: and he shall rule them with a rod of iron: and he treadeth the winepress of the fierceness and wrath of Almighty God."

As further confirmation of the Messiah's deity, Psalm 110:1,5 shows us that "the Lord [*Adonai*] at thy right hand shall strike through kings in the day of his wrath." Psalm 2:12 informs us that it is the Son's wrath that is kindled. This further supports the fact that the Lord's Son is the Lord:

- **Psalm 110:1:** [A Psalm of David.] The Lord said unto my Lord, Sit thou at my right hand, until I make thine enemies thy footstool."
- **Psalm 110:5:** "The Lord at thy right hand shall strike through kings in the day of his wrath."
- **Psalm 2:12:**—*Isaac Leeser's 1844 Hebrew to English translation:* "Do homage to the son, lest he be angry, and ye be lost on the way; for his wrath is speedily kindled. Happy are all they that put their trust in him."

According to Matthew 26:63–64, when the high priest asked Jesus who He claimed to be, He cited Daniel 7:13 testifying that He was the Son of man. Jesus added that "ye shall see the Son of man sitting *on the right hand* of power, and coming in the clouds of heaven." The applicable scriptures follow:

- **Matthew 26:63–64:** ". . . And the high priest answered and said unto him, I adjure thee by the living God, that thou tell us whether thou be the Christ, the Son of God. Jesus saith unto him, Thou hast said: nevertheless I say unto you, Hereafter shall ye see the Son of man sitting on the right hand of power, and coming in the clouds of heaven."
- **Daniel 7:13:** "I saw in the night visions, and, behold, one like the Son of man came with the clouds of heaven, and came to the Ancient of days, and they brought him near before him."

How did the high priest react? As we have already seen, the Bible teaches us that when an individual is at the right hand of another, he provides the source of support, strength, power, and authority. The high priest made the connection between Daniel 7:13 and Psalm 110:5, and accused Jesus of blasphemy. Why? The reason is clear: Jesus claimed to not only be the Son of man, but also the source of support, strength, power, and authority for the LORD Himself. Who would dare make such a claim? Unless of course, He was the LORD Himself! Matthew 26:65–66 records the high priest's reaction: "Then the high priest rent his clothes, saying, He hath spoken blasphemy; what further need have we of witnesses? behold, now ye have heard his blasphemy. What think ye? They answered and said, He is guilty of death."

The high priest understood Jesus' claim to be God. This is why he called it blasphemy, punishable by death.

Psalm 110:1 and Psalm 110:5 provide another clear illustration of Jesus' deity. They are ironclad proof-texts because the Hebrew scriptures fully support the events in the New Testament.

The Blindness of the Pharisees

Throughout Jesus' ministry, He constantly demonstrated to the Pharisees and to the crowds that they did not have a clear understanding of who the Messiah would be. They had a partial understanding of him as follows: they believed that he would be a descendent of David who would come to eliminate their enemies. However, Jesus repeatedly showed them that they did not have the complete understanding as revealed in the Scriptures.

One example of this can be found in Matthew 22:41–42 which states, "While the Pharisees were gathered together, Jesus asked them, Saying, What think ye of Christ? whose son is he? They say unto him, The Son of David."

Though the Pharisees correctly answered His question, Matthew 22:43–45 records Jesus' second set of questions: "He saith unto them, How then doth David in spirit call him Lord, saying, The LORD said unto my Lord, Sit thou on my right hand, till I make thine enemies thy footstool? If David then call him Lord, how is he his son?"

According to the following verse, in Matthew 22:46, these questions baffled Jesus' audience, "And no man was able to answer him a word, neither durst any man from that day forth ask him any more questions."

In Matthew 22:44, Jesus quotes Psalm 110:1, a psalm of David, "The LORD said unto my Lord, Sit thou at my right hand, until I make thine enemies thy footstool." Since David is the writer of this psalm, Jesus asks the Pharisees another question in Matthew 22:45, " If David then calls him Lord, how is he his son?" Though people who deny the Messiah's deity may believe that he is the son of David, they fail to make the important connection that David refers to Him two ways in Psalm 110 . . . as his Lord in Psalm 110:1, and as Adonai in Psalm 110:5.

The Pharisees could not answer Jesus' question but the lesson is clear: they did not place the Messiah in His proper position of deity. According to the prophets, the Messiah is not only David's son, but also Adonai, the Son of God. He is David's Lord who is exalted at the right hand of His Father. He is the LORD at the right hand of the LORD!

Chapter Fourteen

The Deity of Jesus—
Answering the Objections

In spite of all of the evidence supporting the Messiah's deity, some will remain in denial simply because they have been indoctrinated to believe otherwise. In order to refute what the Bible teaches, they are taught to incorrectly isolate specific verses in the Scriptures, quote only half verses, or take certain verses within a passage out of context so that they could justify their beliefs. In this respect, counter-missionaries, Jehovah's Witnesses, Mormons, and Muslims all make the same rhetorical arguments against the Messiah's deity.

For believers, it is important to remain confident that there are scriptural answers to every argument made against Jesus' deity. With apostasy and false teachings on the rise, it is necessary now more than ever before to be prepared to respond with the applicable verses and passages so that we can stand firmly in the truth and defend our faith.

The assumption that Jesus is anyone less than the LORD Himself limits and challenges God's plan of salvation and His saving grace for mankind. After all, how could anyone honestly believe that the death of a mere mortal man can bring atonement and salvation for everyone? But if Jesus were God in the flesh, no one can deny that the blood He shed in His death would have unlimited redemptive qualities with respect to mankind's spiritual salvation and the forgiveness of sins. Therefore, the beauty of the Gospel of Jesus Christ cannot be fully realized until we understand that it was our beloved Creator, the LORD Himself, who was crucified approximately two thousand years ago.

There is one other matter to consider: Since the Messiah was sent by God to redeem mankind, He must be the perfect offering made without blemish. If the Messiah was born of a human father, He would have inherited Adam's sin nature and would have been an imperfect and blemished offering. Romans 5:12 and Romans 5:19 explain:

+ **Romans 5:12:** "Wherefore, as by one man sin entered into the world, and death by sin; and so death passed upon all men, for that all have sinned."
+ **Romans 5:19:** "For as by one man's disobedience many were made sinners, so by the obedience of one shall many be made righteous."

For these reasons it became necessary for the Messiah, the Savior of the world, to be deity. He could not have had a human father and, as a result, must have been born of a virgin. Since some may attempt to illustrate their position by isolating certain scriptures and taking various verses and passages out of context, believers in Jesus' deity should always harmonize the Scriptures and allow scripture to interpret scripture and verse to interpret verse. By doing this, they can always rely on the Word of God, the Bible, to provide the answers.

Those who deny our Messiah's deity repeatedly misuse or misapply the following twelve scriptures and passages. The opposition's argument is followed by the appropriate response:

1. John 17:3: Jesus said, "And this is life eternal, that they might know thee the only true God, and Jesus Christ, whom thou hast sent."

The Opposition's Argument: Here, Jesus calls the Father "the only true God." Therefore, Jesus could not be the true God.

Response: In this verse Jesus did not say that the Father alone is the only true God. Regarding the only true God, the Father and Son are mutually inclusive. In other words the Father, along with the Son, is the true God. When Jesus said in John 10:30, "I and my Father are one," He meant it, literally! And here's the explanation:

First John 5:20 reveals that the true God is both the Father and Son. It also provides the following equation that the true God = eternal life. It states, "And we know that the Son of God is come, and hath given us an understanding, that we may know him that is true, and we are in him that is true, even in his Son Jesus Christ. This is the true God, and eternal life."

Since 1 John 5:20 tells us that the true God is eternal life, 1 John 1:2–3 reveals that eternal life was with the Father and manifested unto us in the person of His Son Jesus Christ:

(For the life was manifested, and we have seen it, and bear witness, and shew unto you that eternal life, which was with the Father, and was manifested unto us;) That which we have seen and heard declare we unto you, that ye also may have fellowship with us: and truly our fellowship is with the Father, and with his Son Jesus Christ.

The conclusion: According to 1 John 1:2, Jesus Christ, who was with the Father, is eternal life. And since eternal life is the true God according to 1 John 5:20, Jesus must be the true God.

2. Numbers 23:19: "God is not a man . . ."

The Opposition's Argument: Here, the Scriptures teach that God is not a man. Therefore Jesus Christ, who was a man, could not be God.

Response: This verse needs to be read to its completion. Numbers 23:19 states as follows: "God is not a man, that he should lie; neither the son of man, that he should repent: hath he said, and shall he not do it? or hath he spoken, and shall he not make it good?"

When reading the Bible, context is always critical. Numbers 23:19 reveals that God is not a man . . . "that he should lie." It is telling us that God does not lie like men lie. He always tells the truth! Whatever He says He means, and whatever He means He says! Using the opposition's same argument, Exodus 15:3 states: "The LORD is a man of war: the LORD is his name." Does this verse actually teach us that the LORD is a man? Of course not, because it is a metaphor! Though the Scriptures indicate that God in His natural state is not a man, Philippians 2:5–8 reveals that God became a man by taking on the form of man:

> Let this mind be in you, which was also in Christ Jesus: Who, being in the form of God, thought it not robbery to be equal with God: But made himself of no reputation, and took upon him the form of a servant, and was made in the likeness of men: And being found in fashion as a man, he humbled himself, and became obedient unto death, even the death of the cross.

3. John 5:19: "Then answered Jesus and said unto them, Verily, verily, I say unto you, The Son can do nothing of himself. . . ." Note: Sometimes John 5:30 is used where Jesus said, "I can of mine own self do nothing. . . ."

The Opposition's Argument: These verses teach that the Son can do nothing of Himself. Therefore, how can he be God? This is impossible!

Response: Finish John 5:19 and read the entire passage in its context! In John 5:19, Jesus said the following: "Verily, verily, I say unto you, The Son can do nothing of himself, but what he seeth the Father do: for what things soever he doeth, these also doeth the Son likewise."

This is a perfect example of how someone can arrive at an incorrect conclusion by using only a portion of a verse. People who challenge Jesus' deity often misapply verses like this because this is the way they were taught. After reading John 5:19 in its completion and context, it begs the question: What individual can claim to do everything that God can do except for God Himself? In John 5:19, Jesus claims to have the ability to do everything that the Father does. Not even the angels in Heaven would dare make such a claim. John 5:19 does not disprove Jesus' deity; it proves His deity!

4. John 14:28: "Ye have heard how I said unto you, I go away, and

*come again unto you. If ye loved me, ye would rejoice, because I said,
I go unto the Father: for my Father is greater than I."*

The Opposition's Argument: Since Jesus said, "my Father is greater
than I," he could not be Almighty God. After all, his Father is greater
than him.

Response: Not necessarily! Jesus' statement in John 14:28 can easily
be understood as a claim of submission. Jesus always taught that He was
submissive to His Father. When a person is in submission to someone,
does it mean that he or she is less "in essence" than the other?

For example, according to the Bible, the woman is in submission to
the man, and the man is the head of the woman. However in the eyes of
God, they are equal because He made both in His image (Gen. 1:26–27).
Jesus' submission to the Father is likened to a woman's submission to a
man. First Corinthians 11:3 provides the explanation as follows: "But I
would have you know, that the head of every man is Christ; and the head
of the woman is the man; and the head of Christ is God."

First Corinthians 11:3 tells us that though men and women are equal in
essence, the woman is in submission to the man. In like manner, although
Jesus and His Father are equal in essence, the Son is in submission.

For Christians, there is another logical explanation provided for John
14:28. Philippians 2:5–8 states that Jesus, being in the form of God, took
upon Him the form of a servant:

> Let this mind be in you, which was also in Christ Jesus: Who, being
> in the form of God, thought it not robbery to be equal with God: But
> made himself of no reputation, and took upon him the form of a servant,
> and was made in the likeness of men: And being found in fashion as a
> man, he humbled himself, and became obedient unto death, even the
> death of the cross.

At the time Jesus said, "the Father is greater than I," He had taken upon
Himself the form of a servant. He experienced all of the attributes and
qualities of humanity. Therefore during His life on earth, the Father was
greater.

5. John 20:17: *"Jesus saith unto her, Touch me not; for I am not yet ascended to my Father: but go to my brethren, and say unto them, I ascend unto my Father, and your Father; and to my God, and your God"* (see Mic. 5:4).

The Opposition's Argument: In this verse Jesus said that he has a God. Therefore, he could not be Almighty God.

Response: Not necessarily! In this verse Jesus did not say, "I go to our Father and to our God." He said "my Father, and your Father, and to my God, and your God." By stating these words in this way, Jesus reveals that His relationship with the Father is separate and distinct from the relationship that we have with our heavenly Father. For example, Jesus was born of a virgin and is the only-begotten Son of God (Matt. 1:18–23; John 3:16; Luke 1:26–35; Isa. 7:14). In other words, Almighty God is Jesus' literal Father! For the rest of us, Romans 8:14–15 says that we are sons of God, but only by the Spirit of adoption: "For as many as are led by the Spirit of God, they are the sons of God. For ye have not received the spirit of bondage again to fear; but ye have received the Spirit of adoption, whereby we cry, Abba, Father."

Though God is Jesus' Father in a very different way than He is our Father, the same principle is applied to God being Jesus' God. God is our God for many reasons. He is our Creator, etc. Jesus calls His Father "my God" because He is in submission to God, just like Sarah was in submission to Abraham and referred to him as "my lord" in Genesis 18:12 as follows: "Therefore Sarah laughed within herself, saying, After I am waxed old shall I have pleasure, my lord being old also?"

Just as Sarah called Abraham "my lord," Jesus referred to God as "my God." As we have seen in the previous example, Jesus is in submission to the Father just like the woman is in submission to the man. Because of this, it is important to realize that Jesus is no less Almighty God because He is in submission to His Father, just as Sarah was no less human because she was in submission to Abraham.

6. Revelation 3:14: *"And unto the angel of the church of the Laodiceans write; These things saith the Amen, the faithful and true*

witness, the beginning of the creation of God."

The Opposition's Argument: In this verse, Jesus is referred to as the faithful and true witness, the beginning of the creation of God. Therefore, Jesus was God's first creation and could not be Almighty God since only God has no beginning.

Response: That is absolutely incorrect! When God created, He spoke creation into existence. He said, "Let there be light, and there was light," etc. Isaiah 44:24 also teaches that God created all things by Himself. It reads, "Thus saith the LORD, thy redeemer, and he that formed thee from the womb, I am the LORD that maketh all things; that stretcheth forth the heavens alone; that spreadeth abroad the earth by myself."

God made all things with His Word. John 1:14 states: "And the Word was made flesh, and dwelt among us, (and we beheld his glory, the glory as of the only begotten of the Father,) full of grace and truth."

Revelation 3:14 teaches that Jesus, the Word of God, *is* the beginning and source of all creation since God made all things with His Word. By God's Word who is Christ, all things exist. He is our Creator!

7. Colossians 1:15: "Who is the image of the invisible God, the firstborn of every creature."

The Opposition's Argument: This verse teaches that Jesus is the firstborn of every creature. Therefore, he is part of God's creation. He could not be God since only God has no beginning.

Response: The term firstborn does not necessarily mean "first in sequence." The Bible provides the explanation why Jesus is called the firstborn of every creature in Colossians 1:16–17 which states: "For by him were all things created, that are in heaven, and that are in earth, visible and invisible, whether they be thrones, or dominions, or principalities, or powers: all things were created by him, and for him: And he is before all things, and by him all things consist."

God's Word, who is Jesus Christ, is the source or origin of all creation. He is our Creator! As a result, He is placed at the head of all creation. Additionally, one who has firstborn status owns the rights to his father's patriarchal position. This can certainly apply to Jesus who, according to

Hebrews 1:2 and Psalm 2:8, is the heir of all things.

As further explanation, this birthright can be lost or transferred from one individual to another. It does not always apply to the oldest son or the son who is first in sequence. As an example, Psalm 89:27 applies to David, though 1 Chronicles 2:13–15 indicates that he was the youngest of all of his brothers. The applicable scriptures follow:

- **Psalm 89:27**—*regarding David:* "Also I will make him my firstborn, higher than the kings of the earth."
- **1 Chronicles 2:13–15:** "And Jesse begat his firstborn Eliab, and Abinadab the second, and Shimma the third, Nethaneel the fourth, Raddai the fifth, Ozem the sixth, David the seventh."

Another example of a son's firstborn status being lost or transferred to another son can be found in 1 Chronicles 5:1. It shows that Jacob's son Reuben lost it because he defiled his father's bed. It states, "Now the sons of Reuben the firstborn of Israel, (for he was the firstborn; but, forasmuch as he defiled his father's bed, his birthright was given unto the sons of Joseph the son of Israel: and the genealogy is not to be reckoned after the birthright."

Isaac's sons Esau and Jacob provide another example how a son's firstborn status or birthright can be lost or transferred to another. In this case, though Esau and Jacob were twins, Esau was the elder and was Isaac's firstborn. However according to Genesis 27, Esau sold his birthright and traded it to Jacob for some stew.

Joseph's two sons Ephraim and Manasseh are another example. Though Ephraim was the younger, Genesis 48:8–20 records that Jacob blessed him instead of the elder Manasseh. As a result, Ephraim received the firstborn's blessing.

God refers to others as His firstborn, not only His Son Jesus Christ. He calls Israel His firstborn, as well as Ephraim. Exodus 4:22 and Jeremiah 31:9 provide the illustrations:

- **Exodus 4:22:** "And thou shalt say unto Pharaoh, Thus saith the LORD,

Israel is my son, even my firstborn."

✦ **Jeremiah 31:9:** "They shall come with weeping, and with supplications will I lead them: I will cause them to walk by the rivers of waters in a straight way, wherein they shall not stumble: for I am a father to Israel, and Ephraim is my firstborn."

Israel was not the first nation, and Ephraim was not Joseph's elder son. These illustrations teach that, although Jesus is called firstborn in Colossians 1:15, it does not necessarily mean that He was first in sequence. Based on these illustrations, to make the assertion that Jesus is created because He is referred to as firstborn can result in a serious mistake.

8. Mark 14:36: "And he said, Abba, Father, all things are possible unto thee; take away this cup from me: nevertheless not what I will, but what thou wilt."

The Opposition's Argument: This verse indicates that Jesus and the Father have different wills. Therefore, He could not be God since He has a different will than God.

Response: Not at all! The Bible clearly teaches that Jesus never acted on behalf of Himself, but only did the Father's will. In John 6:38, Jesus said: "For I came down from heaven, not to do mine own will, but the will of him that sent me."

It was not in Jesus' nature to act independently from the Father. John 5:19 confirms: "Then answered Jesus and said unto them, Verily, verily, I say unto you, The Son can do nothing of himself, but what he seeth the Father do: for what things soever he doeth, these also doeth the Son likewise." Since Jesus explained that by His very nature He could not act independently from God, He must have the same will as God. Mark 14:36 does not disprove Jesus' deity, it confirms His deity!

9. Mark 13:32: Jesus said, "But of that day and that hour knoweth no man, no, not the angels which are in heaven, neither the Son, but the Father."

The Opposition's Argument: In this verse, Jesus stated that He does not know the day or hour of His return. He said that only the Father knows. As a result, since only God knows all things, how could Jesus possibly be God? This is impossible!

Response: Not at all! Jesus was a Jew and subject to the traditions and culture of the Jewish people. In Matthew 22:1–3 and Matthew 25:1–13, He referred to Himself as the bridegroom and to the church as His bride. And according to Jewish tradition, when a man is betrothed to his bride, he goes to prepare a place for her prior to their marriage. In John 14:2–3, Jesus said: "In my Father's house are many mansions: if it were not so, I would have told you. I go to prepare a place for you. And if I go and prepare a place for you, I will come again, and receive you unto myself; that where I am, there ye may be also."

In the New Testament, Jesus likens His relationship with His church as a future marriage between a bridegroom and a bride. According to Ephesians 5:25–27 and Ephesians 5:31–32, the apostle Paul verifies the connection:

* **Ephesians 5:25–27:** "Husbands, love your wives, even as Christ also loved the church, and gave himself for it; That he might sanctify and cleanse it with the washing of water by the word, That he might present it to himself a glorious church, not having spot, or wrinkle, or any such thing; but that it should be holy and without blemish."
* **Ephesians 5:31–33:** "For this cause shall a man leave his father and mother, and shall be joined unto his wife, and they two shall be one flesh. This is a great mystery: but I speak concerning Christ and the church. Nevertheless let every one of you in particular so love his wife even as himself; and the wife see that she reverence her husband."

In John 14:2–3, Jesus tells us that He would leave and prepare a place for His bride, His church. In Jewish custom, before a marriage, it is the father who informs his son when it is time to return for his bride.[41] Therefore, in conformity with Jewish tradition, it is Jesus' Father who will advise Him when to return for His bride. Revelation 19:7–9 describes this great moment when the church will be called to the marriage supper of the Lamb:

Let us be glad and rejoice, and give honour to him: for the marriage of the Lamb is come, and his wife hath made herself ready. And to her was granted that she should be arrayed in fine linen, clean and white: for the fine linen is the righteousness of saints. And he saith unto me, Write, Blessed are they which are called unto the marriage supper of the Lamb. And he saith unto me, These are the true sayings of God.

10. First Corinthians 8:6: "But to us there is but one God, the Father, of whom are all things, and we in him; and one Lord Jesus Christ, by whom are all things, and we by him."

The Opposition's Argument: This verse specifically states that there is one God, the Father. Therefore, Jesus Christ could not be God.

Response: This is an incorrect conclusion! In Matthew 11:25, Jesus referred to His Father as "Lord of heaven and earth." Matthew 11:25 states: "At that time Jesus answered and said, I thank thee, O Father, Lord of heaven and earth, because thou hast hid these things from the wise and prudent, and hast revealed them unto babes."

By presuming that Jesus cannot be God based on 1 Corinthians 8:6, a similar incorrect conclusion can be made that the Father cannot be the Lord. And based on Jesus' words in Matthew 11:25, this cannot be the case since He calls His Father "Lord of heaven and earth."

First Corinthians 8:6 should not be used to deny Jesus' deity. It is intended to establish that the Father and Son are distinct from one another. The Father is not the Son and the Son is not the Father. Actually, this is a good verse to illustrate the LORD as a compound unity, i.e. *echad.*

11. Malachi 3:6: "For I am the LORD, I change not; therefore ye sons of Jacob are not consumed."

The Opposition's Argument: This verse clearly teaches that the LORD does not change. Therefore, Jesus could not be God since fundamental Christianity holds to the position that God became a man in the person of Jesus Christ (Phil. 2:5–8).

Response: This is not the context of Malachi 3:6. In this verse, God indicates that He will honor the everlasting covenant He made with

Abraham, Isaac, and Jacob. Because of this, Jacob will not be consumed! Therefore regarding His covenant relationship with Abraham, Isaac, and Jacob, God does **not** change! Malachi 3:7, the following verse, justifies this position when it says: "Even from the days of your fathers ye are gone away from mine ordinances, and have not kept them. Return unto me, and I will return unto you, saith the LORD of hosts. . . ."

Regarding Jesus' deity, He never changed. Hebrews 13:8 states that when He came into the world, "Jesus Christ the same yesterday, and to day, and for ever." In other words, Jesus was always deity. When Jesus was born in Bethlehem, Colossians 2:9 teaches: "For in him dwelleth all the fulness of the Godhead bodily."

12. Psalm 90:2 teaches that the LORD is "from everlasting to everlasting."

The Opposition's Argument: God is eternal and cannot die. Since Jesus died at the crucifixion, he could not be Almighty God.

Response: Jesus' flesh died, not His deity. Regarding Him, Philippians 2:8 states, "And being found in fashion as a man, he humbled himself, and became obedient unto death, even the death of the cross.

Though Jesus' humanity perished at the cross, Colossians 2:9 teaches that though He was fully man, He was also fully God, "For in him dwelleth all the fulness of the Godhead bodily." Though He was crucified, His deity continued and did not die!

These are twelve of the most common arguments made against Jesus' deity. Though there are lesser objections, believers in His deity should be convinced that there is an appropriate response to every challenge that is given. But we should always remember that when defending our faith, God requires that we explain our position in a clear and loving manner. There is no reason to argue. Remember, only He can change minds.

Chapter Fifteen

Understanding the Trinity

Introduction

According to the Bible, God is described as one triune Being: Father, Son, and Holy Ghost. The Holy Ghost is sometimes called the Holy Spirit. All three are not separate Gods, but one God *in unity*. The Father, Son, and Holy Spirit are called *God* individually as well as collectively. All three are co-equal *in essence* as well as co-eternal. Christians use the term *Trinity* or *Godhead* when describing this unique nature of God.

I. Step 1—One God, the Father

There are six easy steps to follow in order to explain the Trinity. The first is to draw a diagram portraying God as one. As we have seen in chapter twelve, Deuteronomy 6:4 explains that there is one God, and in the New Testament, 1 Corinthians 8:6 tells us, "But to us there is but one God, the Father, of whom are all things, and we in him. . . ."

So let us begin by portraying God the Father using one circle. This is because the Bible tells us that there is one God, not three Gods:

Illustration 1:
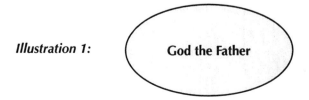

God the Father

II. Step 2—The Creation Account

The next step is to recall what Jesus said in John 8:42, John 16:27, and John 17:8 . . . that He *proceeded forth* and *came out from* God. The applicable verses follow:

- **John 8:42:** "Jesus said unto them, If God were your Father, ye would love me: for I proceeded forth and came from God; neither came I of myself, but he sent me."
- **John 16:27**—*Jesus said:* "For the Father himself loveth you, because ye have loved me, and have believed that I came out from God."
- **John 17:8**—*Jesus said:* "For I have given unto them the words which thou gavest me; and they have received them, and have known surely that I came out from thee, and they have believed that thou didst send me."

In these three verses, the Greek word *exerchomai* is used (*Strong's,* #1831) and is translated as either *proceeded forth* or *came out from.* This Greek word is defined as follows:

1. With mention of the place out of which one goes, or the point from which he departs,
2. To come forth from physically, arise from, to be born of,
3. To come forth, i.e. emitted as from the heart or the mouth, to flow forth from the body, to emanate, issue.

Keeping this in mind for a moment, we should next refer to John 1:1–3 and John 1:14 which teach that God made all things with His Word . . . and the Word became flesh in the person of Jesus Christ:

- **John 1:1–3:** "In the beginning was the Word, and the Word was with God, and the Word was God. The same was in the beginning with God. All things were made by him; and without him was not any thing made that was made."
- **John 1:14:** "And the Word was made flesh, and dwelt among us, (and we beheld his glory, the glory as of the only begotten of the Father,) full of grace and truth."

Since Jesus came out from God and the Bible teaches that all things were made by God with His Word (which is Christ) we can now depict the creation account by the following illustration:

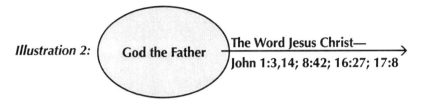

Illustration 2: God the Father | The Word Jesus Christ— John 1:3,14; 8:42; 16:27; 17:8 →

Note: This diagram shows Jesus Christ, the Word of God, having the same divine nature as His Father because He came out from God.

III. Step 3—Jesus' Promise to His Disciples

Keeping the last illustration in mind for a moment, the third step is simple. We need to recall Jesus' promise to His disciples when He told them in John 16:7 the following: "Nevertheless I tell you the truth; It is expedient for you that I go away: for if I go not away, the Comforter will not come unto you; but if I depart, I will send him unto you."

And in John 14:26, Jesus told them that the Comforter was the Holy Ghost: "But the Comforter, which is the Holy Ghost, whom the Father will send in my name, he shall teach you all things, and bring all things to your remembrance, whatsoever I have said unto you."

This is important: Jesus instructed His disciples that when the time came when He left, He would send them the Holy Ghost.

IV. Step 4—Jesus Ascends into Heaven

Where did Jesus tell His disciples He would go when He left? The answer is provided in John 16:28 when He said: "I came forth from the Father, and am come into the world: again, I leave the world, and go to the Father."

Remembering this, the books of John and Acts were written after Jesus left His disciples and ascended into Heaven. John 1:18 and Acts 13:33 describe Him *in the bosom of* and *begotten of* the Father as follows:

- **John 1:18**—*Jesus is described as*: ". . . the only begotten Son, which is in the bosom of the Father. . . ."

- **Acts 13:33:** "God hath fulfilled the same unto us their children, in that he hath raised up Jesus again; as it is also written in the second psalm, Thou art my Son, this day have I begotten thee."

Keeping all of this in mind, the fourth step is to draw an illustration of Jesus *in the bosom of* His Father and *begotten of* His Father after He ascended into Heaven:

Illustration 3: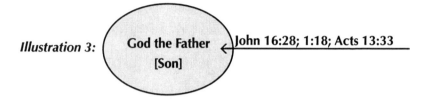

Note: But remember, before Jesus left His disciples in Acts 1:8–11, He reminded them of His promise in John 16:7. He told them that He would send them the Holy Ghost. In Acts 1:5 He said: "For John truly baptized with water; but ye shall be baptized with the Holy Ghost not many days hence."

V. Step 5—The Holy Ghost Arrives

Just as Jesus promised, shortly after He left His disciples and ascended into Heaven in Acts 1, the Holy Ghost arrived. Acts 2:1–4 tells us that He descended upon the disciples when they were gathered together on the day of Pentecost:

> And when the day of Pentecost was fully come, they were all with one accord in one place. And suddenly there came a sound from heaven as of a rushing mighty wind, and it filled all the house where they were sitting. And there appeared unto them cloven tongues like as of fire, and it sat upon each of them. And they were all filled with the Holy Ghost, and began to speak with other tongues, as the Spirit gave them utterance.

But where did the Holy Ghost come from? The answer: Jesus had already told His disciples in John 15:26. Just like Him, the Holy Ghost proceeded from the Father: "But when the Comforter is come, whom I will send unto you from the Father, even the Spirit of truth, which proceedeth from the Father, he shall testify of me."

Remembering this, here is a final illustration of the Trinity or Godhead, portraying three co-equal and co-eternal persons in one God: Father, Son, and Holy Ghost:

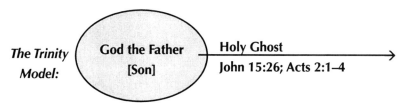

The Trinity Model: **God the Father** [Son]   **Holy Ghost** John 15:26; Acts 2:1–4

Note: In John 14:26 and John 15:26, Jesus told His disciples:

+ **John 14:26:** "But the Comforter, which is the Holy Ghost, whom the Father will send in my name, he shall teach you all things. . . ."
+ **John 15:26:** "But when the Comforter is come, whom I will send unto you from the Father. . . ."

Notice that in John 15:26 and in John 16:7, Jesus told His disciples that He would send the Holy Ghost. Meanwhile back in John 14:26 He instructed them that His Father would send the Holy Ghost. The explanation for this is as follows: According to this diagram, when the Holy Ghost descended upon the disciples, Jesus was in the bosom of His Father. So both Father and Son sent the Holy Ghost.

VI. Step 6—The Deity of the Holy Ghost

The sixth and final step in showing the Trinity or Godhead is the easiest. Since the Bible teaches the deity and person of Jesus Christ, we need to show the deity and person of the Holy Ghost. His deity is proven in Acts 5:1–4 which reads:

> But a certain man named Ananias, with Sapphira his wife, sold a possession, And kept back part of the price, his wife also being privy to it,

and brought a certain part, and laid it at the apostles' feet. But Peter said, Ananias, why hath Satan filled thine heart to lie to the Holy Ghost, and to keep back part of the price of the land? Whiles it remained, was it not thine own? and after it was sold, was it not in thine own power? why hast thou conceived this thing in thine heart? thou hast not lied unto men, but unto God.

Here, Ananias and his wife sold their land. The entire proceeds were to be given to Peter and used for the kingdom of God. But when they received the money, they selfishly held back a portion for themselves. In Acts 5:3, when Peter became aware of this he told Ananias that by committing this act of deception, he lied to the Holy Ghost. And according to Acts 5:4, Peter added that he had "not lied unto men, but unto God."

This passage clearly confirms the Holy Ghost's deity since verse 3 tells us that Ananias lied to the Holy Ghost while verse 4 tells us that he lied to God. Quite obviously, a person can only lie to someone who knows they are being lied to . . . another person!

VII. Confirming the Person of the Holy Ghost

As we have just seen, when Ananias lied to the Holy Ghost, Peter told him that he lied to God. As confirmation that the Holy Ghost is a person within the Godhead or Trinity, we need to refer to some of the passages where Jesus Himself taught that this is the case. John 16:13–15 is one of those instances. In this passage, Jesus described the Spirit in the following manner:

Jesus said: Howbeit when **he,** the Spirit of truth, is come, **he** will guide you into all truth: for **he** shall not speak of **himself;** but whatsoever **he** shall hear, that shall **he** speak: and **he** will shew you things to come. **He** shall glorify me: for **he** shall receive of mine, and shall shew it unto you. All things that the Father hath are mine: therefore said I, that **he** shall take of mine, and shall shew it unto you.

Notice that in this short passage alone, Jesus describes the Spirit in the masculine gender a total of ten times. This confirms once and for all that, just like Jesus, the Holy Spirit is a *person* within the Godhead or Trinity.

VIII. Summary

Should Christians be given the opportunity to explain the Trinity to those embracing Judaism, it is important to remember that they do not accept the New Testament as Scripture. But Jesus said "my sheep shall know my voice," and many people become believers in Jesus as our Messiah every day. The Holy Spirit eventually shows them to rely on both the Hebrew scriptures and the New Testament to find the truth.

We never know who God will place in our path and many people who honestly seek the truth have a difficult time understanding complicated issues such as the Trinity. For Christians, it is important to be firmly grounded and educated in their faith. The more we study and learn, the more we can be used effectively by God to educate others. But remember, though the message is important, the love, understanding, and patience we convey to our audience is of greater significance. Remember, we are only there to plant seeds, but only God can change minds.

Part Four

A Warning to the Nations

Chapter Sixteen

The Second Coming of Jesus Christ

The people that walked in darkness have seen a great light: they that dwell
in the land of the shadow of death, upon them hath the light shined.

—Isaiah 9:2

Throughout the centuries and up until this present time, the children of
Israel have endured overwhelming torment, anguish, and affliction as a
result of the many nations that have set siege against them. Though this
has been the case, the Bible teaches that there will come a day when all
nations will join together in a unified effort to crush them once and for all.
In spite of the warnings in the Scriptures, Israel's adversaries will openly
ignore and challenge God's everlasting covenant with Abraham, Isaac,
and Jacob. As a result, they will incite the LORD to anger. This will be the
biggest mistake they will ever make!

For the descendents of Jacob, there will be no hope for escape. They
will be outnumbered and overpowered as the greatest army ever assembled
in history will shake their fists and mock God's chosen people:

> Blow ye the trumpet in Zion, and sound an alarm in my holy moun-
> tain: let all the inhabitants of the land tremble: for the day of the LORD
> cometh, for it is nigh at hand; A day of darkness and of gloominess, a
> day of clouds and of thick darkness, as the morning spread upon the
> mountains: a great people and a strong; there hath not been ever the like,

neither shall be any more after it, even to the years of many generations. A fire devoureth before them; and behind them a flame burneth: the land is as the garden of Eden before them, and behind them a desolate wilderness; yea, and nothing shall escape them.

—Joel 2:1–3

Fear will consume the inhabitants of Jerusalem as the Bible bears witness to this army's great and awesome power. Joel 2:6–10 reveals that nothing on this earth can stop them. Absolutely nothing! They are invincible!

Before their face the people shall be much pained: all faces shall gather blackness. They shall run like mighty men; they shall climb the wall like men of war; and they shall march every one on his ways, and they shall not break their ranks: Neither shall one thrust another; they shall walk every one in his path: and when they fall upon the sword, they shall not be wounded. They shall run to and fro in the city; they shall run upon the wall, they shall climb up upon the houses; they shall enter in at the windows like a thief. The earth shall quake before them; the heavens shall tremble: the sun and the moon shall be dark, and the stars shall withdraw their shining.

Throughout the Scriptures, the prophets record Israel's continual sufferings. As a people, up until this very moment, the Jews have turned away from God. The Bible also stresses that, though this has been the case, God has never turned His back on them. Romans 11:25–26 states that there would come a day when ". . . the fulness of the Gentiles be come in," and the church is complete; then God will turn to His people and all Israel shall be saved. That day has arrived! On this day, the LORD will plead with His people, ". . . turn ye even to me with all your heart, and with fasting, and with weeping, and with mourning: And rend your heart, and not your garments, and turn unto the LORD your God: for he is gracious and merciful, slow to anger, and of great kindness, and repenteth him of the evil" (Joel 2:12–13).

The descendents of Jacob will cry out with prayers and supplications as they urgently plead to the LORD for help. In response, God will not ask for an outward expression. He will ask for their hearts! Joel 2:17 states, "Let the priests, the ministers of the LORD, weep between the porch and the altar, and let them say, Spare thy people, O LORD, and give not thine heritage to reproach, that the heathen should rule over them: wherefore should they say among the people, Where is their God?"

The pleadings and outcries of the children of Israel will be understandable as many will suffer and die. It will be a terrible day as they are on the brink of total defeat and annihilation resulting from the awesome power that has come against them. Zechariah 13:8 reveals that, on that day, two-thirds of them will be killed, "And it shall come to pass, that in all the land, saith the LORD, two parts therein shall be cut off and die; but the third shall be left therein."

Though they petition HaShem; there will be no answer. When they cry out to Adonai; there will be no response. When they shout to YHWH; they will find no relief. On this day, those who remain will wonder why God has ignored their cries for help. The Bible shows that, at this moment in time, the LORD will completely remove Israel's blindness. Then they will see why their tears and sorrows are ignored and why this is happening. When they finally come to understand as the veil is lifted, they will cry out once again—this time to Yeshua, the One whom they had forsaken. Joel 2:16 states, ". . . let the bridegroom go forth of his chamber, and the bride out of her closet." According to Joel 2:18, "Then will the LORD be jealous for his land, and pity his people."

In Matthew 23:39 Jesus told the Jews the following, "For I say unto you, Ye shall not see me henceforth, till ye shall say, Blessed is he that cometh in the name of the Lord." That day has arrived! At the moment they cry out for Yeshua, the sky will open and the LORD will respond. Redemption for the children of Israel is at hand!

To the nations of the earth: you are warned! Brace yourselves! Your destruction awaits you! Jesus Christ, the children of Israel's Deliverer, Redeemer, and Messiah, is coming!

Jesus Returns
When the people who lived in darkness (Israel) see the great Light, there

will be complete repentance in the land. Zechariah 12:10–14 reveals that on that day all those who remain will mourn for the One who was pierced, ". . . as one mourneth for his only son." The following verse, Zechariah 13:1, states as follows: "In that day there shall be a fountain opened to the house of David and to the inhabitants of Jerusalem for sin and for uncleanness."

When His people repent, Jesus' shed blood will save them from spiritual death. Zechariah 3:9 tells us that in one day He will remove iniquity in the land. Micah 4:7 states, "And I will make her that halted a remnant, and her that was cast far off a strong nation: and the LORD shall reign over them in mount Zion from henceforth, even for ever." Before the Messiah establishes His kingdom and rules in Zion, it will first become necessary to punish His enemies for what they had done.

When Jesus came into Jerusalem in fulfillment of the sixty-ninth week of Daniel, He was lowly, riding on a donkey. According to Matthew 21:6–9, this was in fulfillment of Zechariah 9:9. On the day that He returns and the seventieth week of Daniel is completed, He will come with awesome power and glory as He utterly defeats and destroys His enemies and those who have come against His people. Zechariah 14:3–4 prophesies that He will appear on the Mount of Olives:

> Then shall the LORD go forth, and fight against those nations, as when he
> fought in the day of battle. And his feet shall stand in that day upon the
> mount of Olives, which is before Jerusalem on the east, and the mount
> of Olives shall cleave in the midst thereof toward the east and toward
> the west, and there shall be a very great valley; and half of the mountain
> shall remove toward the north, and half of it toward the south.

The Messiah will judge the nations of the earth with fire. Joel 3:13 speaks to those who dared cross the line to come against Israel, "Put ye in the sickle, for the harvest is ripe: come, get you down; for the press is full, the fats overflow; for their wickedness is great." Regarding the Messiah, Psalm 97:3–5, Isaiah 9:5 (KJV), and Zechariah 14:12 all prophesy of a great battle won by fire:

- **Psalm 97:3–5:** "A fire goeth before him, and burneth up his enemies round about. His lightnings enlightened the world: the earth saw, and trembled. The hills melted like wax at the presence of the LORD, at the presence of the Lord of the whole earth."
- **Isaiah 9:5** *refers to a battle won with burning and fuel of fire as follows:* "For every battle of the warrior is with confused noise, and garments rolled in blood; but this shall be with burning and fuel of fire."
- **Zechariah 14:12:** "And this shall be the plague wherewith the LORD will smite all the people that have fought against Jerusalem; Their flesh shall consume away while they stand upon their feet, and their eyes shall consume away in their holes, and their tongue shall consume away in their mouth."

These passages testify that the Messiah's war will not end until the enemy is utterly consumed. Fire destroys and fire refines! According to the Bible, the one-third who remain, called "the remnant," will be refined by the same fire that destroyed their enemies: "And I will bring the third part through the fire, and will refine them as silver is refined, and will try them as gold is tried: they shall call on my name, and I will hear them: I will say, It is my people: and they shall say, The LORD is my God" (Zech. 13:9).

The enemy will be destroyed. Sin will be removed. Zechariah 14:14 teaches that Judah will gather their spoils in victory, "And Judah also shall fight at Jerusalem; and the wealth of all the heathen round about shall be gathered together, gold, and silver, and apparel, in great abundance."

The New Covenant is now established with God's chosen people. In fulfillment of Jeremiah 33:15–16, Jesus Christ executes judgment and righteousness in the land. The Messiah's reign will begin!

Nebuchadnezzar's Fiery Furnace

As we see in chapter one, the book of Daniel provides the prophetic calendar pointing directly to Jesus of Nazareth as the Messiah. God used Daniel mightily, as his writings provide further information about the Son of God.

A primary illustration can be found in Daniel 3. In this chapter

Nebuchadnezzar, the king of Babylon, made an idol, an image of gold. He commanded that all the people in the land bow down to worship it. According to Daniel 3:6 he said: "And whoso falleth not down and worshippeth shall the same hour be cast into the midst of a burning fiery furnace."

Shortly after the king's decree, there were certain Chaldeans who took it upon themselves to make sure that the people obeyed his order. They noticed that there were several men among the Jews who were not heeding the king's command to bow down and worship the image. After witnessing this, they approached the king and reminded him of his decree. According to Daniel 3:12, they told him the following: "There are certain Jews whom thou hast set over the affairs of the province of Babylon, Shadrach, Meshach, and Abednego; these men, O king, have not regarded thee: they serve not thy gods, nor worship the golden image which thou hast set up."

According to the next verse, Nebuchadnezzar became infuriated with this news. Daniel 3:13 states, "Then Nebuchadnezzar in his rage and fury commanded to bring Shadrach, Meshach, and Abednego. Then they brought these men before the king." The following passage shows that he questioned them about their loyalty and gave them an ultimatum to obey his command:

> Nebuchadnezzar spake and said unto them, Is it true, O Shadrach, Meshach, and Abednego, do not ye serve my gods, nor worship the golden image which I have set up? Now if ye be ready that at what time ye hear the sound of the cornet, flute, harp, sackbut, psaltery, and dulcimer, and all kinds of musick, ye fall down and worship the image which I have made; well: but if ye worship not, ye shall be cast the same hour into the midst of a burning fiery furnace; and who is that God that shall deliver you out of my hands?
>
> —Daniel 3:14–15

The king of Babylon's words end with sheer arrogance and defiance against the God of Israel as he asked, ". . . who is that God that shall deliver you out of my hands?" In the same way, when the nations of the earth come against Jerusalem in the future, their arrogance will be similar as they defiantly ask: ". . . wherefore should they say among the people, Where is their God?" (Joel 2:17).

Daniel 3:17 records the resistance of Shadrach, Meshach, and Abednego as they refused to bow down to Nebuchadnezzar's pagan idol. They declared their sole loyalty and confidence in the true God, the God of Abraham, Isaac, and Jacob when they told the king the following, "If it be so, our God whom we serve is able to deliver us from the burning fiery furnace, and he will deliver us out of thine hand, O king."

They remained steadfast, asserting that God was perfectly capable of rescuing them from the furnace of death. In like manner, God will be fully capable to rescue Israel from the fire and destruction of the nations of the earth. Regarding these nations of the future, Joel 2:3 declares, "A fire devoureth before them; and behind them a flame burneth: the land is as the garden of Eden before them, and behind them a desolate wilderness; yea, and nothing shall escape them."

Nebuchadnezzar became enraged at the continued defiance and disobedience of these three men. According to Daniel 3:19–21, he directed his soldiers to increase the heat of the furnace by seven times, tie them up, and cast them into the furnace:

> Then was Nebuchadnezzar full of fury, and the form of his visage was changed against Shadrach, Meshach, and Abednego: therefore he spake, and commanded that they should heat the furnace one seven times more than it was wont to be heated. And he commanded the most mighty men that were in his army to bind Shadrach, Meshach, and Abednego, and to cast them into the burning fiery furnace. Then these men were bound in their coats, their hosen, and their hats, and their other garments, and were cast into the midst of the burning fiery furnace.

When the king saw these men thrown into the fire, he was confident that he succeeded in setting an example to the rest of the kingdom should anyone else decide to disobey him. Unfortunately for him, a sudden change in events took place! Daniel 3:22 records the immediate demise of the soldiers as they came too close to the fire, "Therefore because the king's commandment was urgent, and the furnace exceeding hot, the flame of the fire slew those men that took up Shadrach, Meshach, and Abednego." The Bible portrays an interesting connection that just as Nebuchadnezzar's soldiers were consumed and killed by fire, the nations of the earth that come against Jerusalem in the future will also be destroyed by fire.

The Scriptures depict another amazing parallel between the incident at the fiery furnace and what will happen on the Day of the LORD when all nations come against Jerusalem. According to the next passage, a miraculous event took place! When the king looked into the furnace to witness the destruction of these three saints of God, they were unharmed:

> Then Nebuchadnezzar the king was astonied, and rose up in haste, and spake, and said unto his counsellors, Did not we cast three men bound into the midst of the fire? They answered and said unto the king, True, O king. He answered and said, Lo, I see four men loose, walking in the midst of the fire, and they have no hurt; and the form of the fourth is like the Son of God.
>
> —Daniel 3:24–25

The king witnessed a fourth man walking in the fire with the others. During this time, the fire had no affect on the saints and they were not burned. The fourth man's appearance was "like the Son of God." In like manner, Zechariah 13:9 teaches that the remnant of God's people, the saints, will be brought through the fire and not burned when the Son of God appears on the Mount of Olives in flaming fire to destroy His enemies: "And I will bring the third part through the fire, and will refine them as silver is refined, and will try them as gold is tried: they shall call on my name, and I will hear them: I will say, It is my people: and they shall say, The LORD is my God."

Nebuchadnezzar was astounded at the events that had taken place to a point that he made a decree exalting the God of Abraham, Isaac, and Jacob. Daniel 3:29 records the king's command, ". . . every people, nation, and language, which speak any thing amiss against the God of Shadrach, Meshach, and Abednego, shall be cut in pieces, and their houses shall be made a dunghill: because there is no other God that can deliver after this sort."

As Nebuchadnezzar decreed that any nation that comes against the God of Israel will be "cut in pieces," Psalm 2:6–7,9 and Psalm 72:4 state that it will be the Messiah, the Son of God, who will cut the nations of the earth that come against His people into pieces! Daniel 2:44–45 confirms this position. The applicable passages follow:

- **Psalm 2:6–7,9:** "Yet have I set my king upon my holy hill of Zion. I will declare the decree: the LORD hath said unto me, Thou art my Son; this day have I begotten thee. . . . Thou shalt break them with a rod of iron; thou shalt dash them in pieces like a potter's vessel."
- **Psalm 72:4:** "He shall judge the poor of the people, he shall save the children of the needy, and shall break in pieces the oppressor."
- **Daniel 2:44–45**—*Daniel's interpretation of Nebuchadnezzar's dream:* "And in the days of these kings shall the God of heaven set up a kingdom, which shall never be destroyed: and the kingdom shall not be left to other people, but it shall break in pieces and consume all these kingdoms, and it shall stand for ever. Forasmuch as thou sawest that the stone was cut out of the mountain without hands, and that it brake in pieces the iron, the brass, the clay, the silver, and the gold; the great God hath made known to the king what shall come to pass hereafter: and the dream is certain, and the interpretation thereof sure."

In the Daniel passage, the prophet told the king of Babylon that the interpretation of his dream was certain. In other words, it would definitely happen in the future! On the Day of the LORD it will be the Messiah, the Son of God described as a "stone" in Nebuchadnezzar's dream, who breaks in pieces the nations of the earth before He sets up His kingdom that will never be destroyed.

Though the nations of the earth have been warned, many will not heed what is written in the Scriptures.

Israel's Blindness

By the sovereign will of God, everything written in the Scriptures will be fulfilled. In order to accomplish this, the Bible teaches that there are times when the LORD Himself will intervene regarding those in power and authority by affecting their decisions.

As an example, the Word of God records the time when God told Moses that He would intercede on behalf of His people and harden Pharaoh's heart. As a result of the king of Egypt's eventual stubbornness, the LORD's mighty arm was lifted against Egypt, and His awesome power was revealed. Egypt, along with her armies, was destroyed!

Exodus 7:2–5 is written as a witness to all nations that dare come between God and His special relationship with His people. In this passage, the LORD told Moses the following:

> Thou shalt speak all that I command thee: and Aaron thy brother shall speak unto Pharaoh, that he send the children of Israel out of his land. And I will harden Pharaoh's heart, and multiply my signs and my wonders in the land of Egypt. But Pharaoh shall not hearken unto you, that I may lay my hand upon Egypt, and bring forth mine armies, and my people the children of Israel, out of the land of Egypt by great judgments. And the Egyptians shall know that I am the LORD, when I stretch forth mine hand upon Egypt, and bring out the children of Israel from among them.

As we have seen, God will always remain faithful to Israel and He fully intends to honor His covenant with Abraham, Isaac, and Jacob. In the meantime, Isaiah 29:13–14 states that, as a punishment for Israel's hardness of heart, the LORD took away their understanding:

> Wherefore the Lord said, Forasmuch as this people draw near me with their mouth, and with their lips do honour me, but have removed their heart far from me, and their fear toward me is taught by the precept of men: Therefore, behold, I will proceed to do a marvellous work among this people, even a marvellous work and a wonder: for the wisdom of

their wise men shall perish, and the understanding of their prudent men shall be hid.

Because of their inability to fully realize their situation, the children of Israel will make a number of critical political mistakes in the future, especially regarding matters pertaining to their everlasting covenant with the LORD. Nonetheless, God remains faithful to His Word! He will use Israel's mistakes as well as the arrogance and pride of the nations of the earth to fulfill and accomplish His written Word and magnify His Holy name. When this day comes, everyone in the world will know that He is the LORD!

Nebuchadnezzar's Dream: The "Stone"

Daniel 2 records the time when the king of Babylon had dreams that greatly disturbed him, "And in the second year of the reign of Nebuchadnezzar Nebuchadnezzar dreamed dreams, wherewith his spirit was troubled, and his sleep brake from him" (Dan. 2:1).

Even though Nebuchadnezzar demanded an interpretation of these troublesome dreams from his wise men, they were unable to comply with the king's order. Since none of the Chaldeans were able to interpret his dreams, the king became infuriated. Daniel 2:12–13 reveals that he ordered all of the wise men in his land to be killed, including Daniel and his friends: "For this cause the king was angry and very furious, and commanded to destroy all the wise men of Babylon. And the decree went forth that the wise men should be slain; and they sought Daniel and his fellows to be slain."

Regarding Daniel, Daniel 1:17 describes him as follows, ". . . Daniel had understanding in all visions and dreams." When the captain of the guard advised Daniel of the reason for the king's decree, Daniel 2:16 states that he went in to the king and asked him for some time, assuring him that he would provide the interpretation: "Then Daniel went in, and desired of the king that he would give him time, and that he would shew the king the interpretation."

The king granted Daniel's request, and he permitted Daniel to go to his house. When he arrived, he explained the situation to his three friends. They prayed to the God of their fathers for mercy and asked Him to provide the interpretation. According to Daniel 2:17–19, the LORD answered their prayers and gave Daniel a vision to interpret the king's dream:

> Then Daniel went to his house, and made the thing known to Hananiah, Mishael, and Azariah, his companions: That they would desire mercies of the God of heaven concerning this secret; that Daniel and his fellows should not perish with the rest of the wise men of Babylon. Then was the secret revealed unto Daniel in a night vision. Then Daniel blessed the God of heaven.

Daniel advised Arioch, the king's guard, that he was ready to give the king the interpretation. So Daniel went before the king. However, before Daniel gave the king the interpretation, he explained that it was his God who revealed to him what he was about to say. He told Nebuchadnezzar the following:

> Thou, O king, sawest, and behold a great image. This great image, whose brightness was excellent, stood before thee; and the form thereof was terrible. This image's head was of fine gold, his breast and his arms of silver, his belly and his thighs of brass, His legs of iron, his feet part of iron and part of clay.
> —Daniel 2:31–33

In Daniel 2:34, the next verse, the prophet told the king what transpired next in his dream as follows, "Thou sawest till that a stone was cut out without hands, which smote the image upon his feet that were of iron and clay, and brake them to pieces."

Daniel indicated that this awful image represents the great kingdoms of the earth from that present day into the future. According to the interpretation he gave, the head of gold of this image represented the Babylonian Empire, Nebuchadnezzar's kingdom. There will be four great kingdoms to follow (Dan. 2:38–43). As the scripture shows, the "stone" cut out of the mountain without hands will crush the image into pieces. According to Daniel, the destruction of the image representing the nations of the earth is the great God of Heaven setting up His kingdom that will never end. Daniel 7:13–14 illustrates that the "stone" represents the Son of man, the Messiah. It is He who will be given a kingdom that will last forever:

> I saw in the night visions, and, behold, one like the Son of man came with the clouds of heaven, and came to the Ancient of days, and they brought him near before him. And there was given him dominion, and glory, and a kingdom, that all people, nations, and languages, should serve him: his dominion is an everlasting dominion, which shall not pass away, and his kingdom that which shall not be destroyed.

The "Stone" Ends the Seventieth Week of Daniel

Isaiah 28 reveals some troubling news for God's chosen people. Before the Messiah establishes His kingdom and His people are exalted, many will be led astray due to the absence of understanding of their leaders. Regarding Israel's spiritual leaders, Isaiah 28:7 states, "But they also have erred through wine, and through strong drink are out of the way; the priest and the prophet have erred through strong drink, they are swallowed up of wine, they are out of the way through strong drink; they err in vision, they stumble in judgment."

As we see from the first chapter, Daniel 9:27 teaches that there will come a day when Israel will make a one-"week" covenant with death and with hell. This seven-year period will culminate with Israel's enemies being defeated. According to the Scriptures, the victory for the children of Israel will be achieved through the Stone, Israel's King Messiah, who is Jesus of Nazareth. Isaiah 28:16–18 teaches that it is through this precious cornerstone that Israel's seven-year covenant with death ends:

> Therefore thus saith the Lord God, Behold, I lay in Zion for a foundation a stone, a tried stone, a precious corner stone, a sure foundation: he that believeth shall not make haste. Judgment also will I lay to the

line, and righteousness to the plummet: and the hail shall sweep away the refuge of lies, and the waters shall overflow the hiding place. And your covenant with death shall be disannulled, and your agreement with hell shall not stand; when the overflowing scourge shall pass through, then ye shall be trodden down by it.

Because all that is written in the Scriptures will be fulfilled, every person in the world has a decision to make. When Isaac gave Jacob God's blessing, Genesis 27:29 tells us His words: ". . . cursed be every one that curseth thee, and blessed be he that blesseth thee." Do we curse Israel, or do we bless her? Do we stand with Israel or do we stand against her and side with the nations of the earth? Do we reap the wrath of Almighty God and dare come against the covenant that He made with His people? Again, we have been warned!

When Jesus the Messiah came into Jerusalem riding on a donkey, His reward was with Him (Zech. 9:9; Matt. 21:6–9). His reward was salvation as He took the punishment for our sins so that we could have everlasting life. The next time He comes, Matthew 16:27 shows that "he shall reward every man according to his works."

Do we side with the nations of the earth and seek our own destruction? Or, do we stay on the side of God's people and live forever? First Corinthians 2:9 states, "Eye hath not seen, nor ear heard, neither have entered into the heart of man, the things which God hath prepared for them that love him." This is the Messiah's reward!

And I saw heaven opened, and behold a white horse; and he that sat upon him was called Faithful and True, and in righteousness he doth judge and make war. His eyes were as a flame of fire, and on his head were many crowns; and he had a name written, that no man knew, but he himself. And he was clothed with a vesture dipped in blood: and his name is called The Word of God. And the armies which were in heaven followed him upon white horses, clothed in fine linen, white and clean. And out of his mouth goeth a sharp sword, that with it he should smite the nations: and he shall rule them with a rod of iron: and he treadeth the winepress of the fierceness and wrath of Almighty God. And he hath on his vesture and on his thigh a name written, KING OF KINGS, AND LORD OF LORDS.

—Revelation 19:11–16

We can never say we were never warned! Revelation 22:20–21 concludes:

He which testifieth these things saith, Surely I come quickly. Amen. Even so, come, Lord Jesus. The grace of our Lord Jesus Christ be with you all. Amen.

Appendix A

Notes

1. This date is taken from the timeline in *The Encyclopaedia Judaica* (New York, N.Y.: Macmillan, 1971), Vol. 8, Col. 769/770. This date is further referenced in Bruce M. Metzger and Roland E. Murphy, editors of *The New Oxford Annotated Bible* (New York, NY: Oxford University Press, 1994), p. 1126.

2. Alexander the Great takes Erez Israel in 332 B.C. in *The Encyclopaedia Judaica* timeline source listed in note 1. This date is confirmed in a number of sources including N. G. L. Hammond's *The Genius of Alexander the Great* (London: Duckworth, 1997), p. 47.

3. Cyrus the Great's reign and events that impact Israel can be found in the timeline listed in note 1, but also a very clear and detailed description can be found in *The Jewish Encyclopedia: A Descriptive Record of the History, Religion, Literature, and Customs of the Jewish People from the Earliest Times* (Further referenced in the notes simply as *The Jewish Encyclopedia*) (New York, N.Y.: KTAV Publishing, 1964), Vol. 4, pp. 402–405, as well as a number of Jewish and secular history sources.

4. Cambyses II/Ahasuerus appears in the timeline in note 1 with his victory over Egypt in 525 B.C. Cambyses' dates of his reign can be found in *Herodotus*, with an English translation by A. D. Godley (Cambridge, MA: Harvard University Press, 1920), *Histories: Vol. III*, pp. 62–66 and *Laws, by Plato in Twelve Volumes*, Vol. 3, translated by R. G. Bury, (Cambridge, MA: Harvard, Univeristy Press), 1968, Vol. 3, 694c–695b.

5. Evidence of Smerdis' seven-month reign is recorded in *Herodotus* (see note 4), *Histories: Vol. III*, pp. 61–88.

6. Darius the Great's dates appear in recorded history in *Herodotus* (see note 4), *Histories: Vol. III*, pp. 61–88. Much is written about his reign in *Plato's Laws* (see note 4) Vol. 3, 695c.

7. Xerxes/Ahasuerus' dates are confirmed in *The Jewish Encyclopedia*, Vol. 12, p. 575. Additionally, information of his reign can be found in *The Encyclopaedia Judaica*, Vol. 14, Col. 728, and also appears in *Herodotus* (see note 4), *Histories: Vol. VII*, pp. 1–4.

8. The dates for the reign of Artaxerxes I, Longimanus may be found in *The Jewish Encyclopedia*, Vol. 2, pp. 145–146. They are also confirmed in *The Encyclopaedia Judaica*, Vol. 3, Col. 646–647, as well as a number of Jewish and secular sources.

9. Darius II appears on the timeline in note 1. His reign can also be found in *Herodotus* (note 4) *Histories: Vol. II*, p. 1106.

10. Artaxerxes II and his reign can be found in *The Encyclopaedia Judaica*, Vol. 3, Col. 647, as well as in *The Jewish Encyclopedia*, Vol. 2, p. 146. Additionally, he is cited in the timeline in note 1.

11. Artaxerxes III and his dates appear in *The Encyclopaedia Judaica*, Vol. 3, Col. 647. *The Jewish Encyclopedia*, Vol. 2, pp. 146–147 also concurs with this date. This king also appears in the timeline in note 1.

12. Darius III as well as his defeat by Alexander the Great can be found in A. B. Bosworth's *Conquest and Empire: The Reign of Alexander the Great* (Cambridge: Cambridge University Press, 1993) and N. Sekunda's "The Persians," in J. Hackett [ed.], *Warfare in the Ancient World* (New York: Oxford University Press, 1989).

13. *The Annals of Nabonid* refer to the inscriptions of Nabonid, the king of Babylon's stone inscriptions, *The Jewish Encyclopedia* (see note 3), Vol. 2, pp. 402–405, from *Die Entstehung des Judenthums*, 1896.

14. Cyrus conquered Lydia in 546 B.C. This is recorded in *Herodotus* (see note 4) *Histories: Vol. I*, pp. 6–94.

15. Cyrus takes Asia Minor in *Herodotus* (note 4) *Histories: Vol. I*, pp. 90–94.

16. Cyrus' decree is mentioned in many sources, both Jewish and secular. This date appears in the timeline in note 1, in *The Jewish Encyclopedia*, Vol. 4, pp.

402–405, and *The Encyclopaedia Judaica*, Vol. 5, Col. 1184–1186.

17. Cambyses' victory over Egypt appears in the timeline in note 1. He is made Pharaoh in Egypt in *Herodotus* (see note 4) *Histories: Vol. III*, pp. 62–66.

18. *Herodotus* (note 4) *Histories: Vol. III*, pp. 65–66.

19. *Herodotus* (note 4) *Histories: Vol. I*, pp. 142–146.

20. *Herodotus* (note 4) *Histories: Vol. VI*, pp. 102–120.

21. The date for the completion of the second temple at 516/515 B.C. can be found in the timeline in note 1. A biblical reference for this date can also be found in Ezra 6:15 as completed in Darius' sixth year.

22. Xerxes defeated at Thermopylae, *Herodotus* (note 4) *Histories: Vol. VII*, pp. 1–4.

23. *Herodotus* (note 4) *Histories: Vol. VI*, pp 59–100.

24. *Herodotus* (note 4) *Histories: Vol. IX*, pp. 25–85.

25. Artaxerxes I, Longimanus, and the end of the Persian wars can be found in *The Jewish Encyclopedia*, Vol. 2, pp. 145–146. This is also cited in *The Encyclopaedia Judaica*, Vol. 3, Col. 646–647, and confirmed in Harry T. Peck's *Harper's Dictionary of Classical Antiquities* (New York, NY: Harper and Bros.), 1898.

26. Peck's *Harper's Dictionary of Classical Antiquities* (note 25) and in *The Jewish Encyclopedia*, Vol. 2, pp. 145–146.

27. C. Caragounis' "History and Supra-History: Daniel and the Four Empires." in A. S. Van der Woude [ed.] *The Book of Daniel in the Light of New Findings* (Leuven: Leuven University Press, 1993), pp. 386f; and J. J. Collins: *Daniel: A Commentary* (Minneapolis: Fortress Press, 1993), pp. 104f. Additionally, E. Badian's "The Struggle for the Succession to Alexander the Great" in *Gnomon*, 34, 1962, 381–387 initially shows the four kingdoms to include Cassander's Macedonia and Grecian empire; Lysimachus' Thrace and West Anatolia; Ptolemy's Israel, Cyprus, and Egyptian kingdom; and Seleucus' territories of Babylon and South Anatolia, possessions that claimed lands deep into India.

28. The arithmetic regarding the fulfillment of the first advent of the Messiah is fully documented in Lord Robert Anderson's *The Coming Prince*, 1895.

29. The destruction of the temple in A.D. 70 can be found in the timeline in note 1. Also the Jewish historian, Flavius Josephus in W. Whiston's translation of

The Complete Works of Josephus, "Wars of the Jews" (Grand Rapids: Kregel Publications, 1960) pp. 580–581 writes a detailed account of the event.

30. According to Dr. Michael L. Brown's book, *Answering Jewish Objections to Jesus* (Grand Rapids, MI: Baker Books, 2000) Vol. 1, p. 226, note 36, he states the following: "This is universally recognized by traditional Jewish and Christian scholars; for key biblical references in which the Messianic king is actually called 'David,' cf. Jer. 30:8–9; Ezek 34:20–24; 37:24–28; Hos. 3:5."

31. J. McClintock and J. Strong's *Cyclopaedia of Biblical, Theological, and Ecclesiastical Literature* (New York, NY: Arno Press, 1969) Vol. 3,4 pp. 771–775: "Mary is called by the Jews batHeli, 'daughter of Heli.'" The divinity and rabbinical scholar, John Lightfoot in his *Harmony of the Four Evangelists*, details Mary's genealogy. J. R. Dummelow in his *Commentary on the Holy Bible* (New York, NY: Macmillan Co., 1937) on p. 739 further expounds that it is significant that Elizabeth was a relative, a cousin of Mary (Luke 1:36), but this does not mean that Mary also belonged to the tribe of Levi, for "Male descent alone determined the tribe, and Mary may have been related to Elizabeth on her mother's side."

32. Mikra'ot Gedolot—Rashi on Judges 17:7.

33. Mikra'ot Gedolot – Rashi on Song of Songs 1:3.

34. John McTernan & Louis Ruggiero, *Jesus of Nazareth: King Messiah*, chapter 3, pp. 40–56 (Oklahoma City, OK: Hearthstone Publishing, 2002).

35. Ibid., chapter 4, pp. 59–70.

36. Ibid., chapter 5, pp. 71–77.

37. Ibid., chapter 6, pp. 78–89.

38. Ibid., chapter 7, pp. 90–116.

39. Ibid., chapter 8, pp. 117–132.

40. According to Dr. Michael L. Brown's book, *Answering Jewish Objections to Jesus* (Grand Rapids, MI: Baker Books, 2000) Vol. 1, p. 77, he states the following: "We see from the passage that the Lord (in Hebrew *ha'adon*, is always used with reference to God in the Hebrew Bible when it has the definite article)." And on p. 223 of this book, note 14, he indicates other verses where *ha'adon* is used with reference to the Lord God. They are Exodus 23:17, Exodus 34:23, Deuteronomy 10:17, Isaiah 1:24, Isaiah 3:1, Isaiah 10:16, Isaiah 10:33, and Isaiah 19:4.

41. Isaac Landman [ed.], *The Universal Jewish Encyclopedia* (New York, NY: Universal Jewish Encyclopedia Co. Inc, 1948), p. 7 and 372 list this ancient wedding custom. Isidore Singer's *The Jewish Encyclopedia* (New York, NY: Funk and Wagnals Co., 1907) in Vol. III, 126, also cites this custom.

Appendix B

Index

Hebrew Scriptures

Selected Words